The Impact of the WTO

The Environment, Public Health and Sovereignty

Trish Kelly

Senior Lecturer, Department of Leadership, Policy and Organizations, Peabody College, Vanderbilt University, USA

Edward Elgar
Cheltenham, UK • Northampton, MA, USA

Published by
Edward Elgar Publishing Limited
Glensanda House
Montpellier Parade
Cheltenham
Glos GL50 1UA
UK

1005728746

Edward Elgar Publishing, Inc.
William Pratt House
9 Dewey Court
Northampton
Massachusetts 01060
USA

A catalogue record for this book
is available from the British Library

Library of Congress Cataloguing in Publication Data

Kelly, Trish, 1958–
    The impact of the WTO : the environment, public health and sovereignty /
    Trish Kelly.
        p. cm.
    Includes bibliographical references and index.
    1. International trade—Environmental aspects. 2. International
    trade—Health aspects. 3. World Trade Organization. I. Title.
    HF1385.K46 2007
    382'.92—dc22   2007017592

ISBN 978 1 84720 081 5 (cased)

Typeset by Cambrian Typesetters, Camberley, Surrey
Printed and bound in Great Britain by MPG Books Ltd, Bodmin, Cornwall

Contents

Abbreviations

ACWL	Advisory Centre on WTO Law
ADI	Acceptable daily intake
AFL–CIO	American Federation of Labor – Congress of Industrial Organizations
API	American Petroleum Institute
CBD	Convention on Biological Diversity
CIEL	Center for International Environmental Law
CIT	US Court of International Trade
CITES	Convention on International Trade in Endangered Species in Wild Fauna and Flora
CMC	Center for Marine Conservation
CMS	Convention on the Conservation of Migratory Species of Wild Animals
CTE	WTO Committee on Trade and Environment
DOE	US Department of Energy
EC	European Commission
EPA	US Environmental Protection Agency
EU	European Union
FAO	Food and Agriculture Organization
FDC	Fish Disease Commission
GATS	General Agreement on Trade in Services
GATT	General Agreement on Tariffs and Trade
GM	Genetically modified
GMOs	Genetically Modified Organisms
HT	Herbicide tolerant
IAC	Inter-American Convention for the Protection and Conservation of Sea Turtles
IARC	International Agency for Research on Cancer
ILO	International Labor Organization
INSERM	Institut National de la Science et de la Recherche Médicale
IOSEA	Indian Ocean–South-East Asian Marine Turtle Secretariat

IPCS	International Program on Chemical Safety
IPPC	International Plant Protection Convention
ISO	International Organization for Standards
JECFA	Joint Expert Committee on Food Additives
LMOs	Living modified organisms
LOS	Convention on the Law of the Sea
MEA	Multilateral Environmental Agreement
MOU	Memorandum of Understanding
MRL	Maximum residue limit
NAFTA	North American Free Trade Agreement
NGO	Non-Governmental Organization
NMFS	US National Marine Fishery Service
OIE	Office International des Epizootics
PDVSA	Petroleos de Venezuela Sur America
PPMs	Process and production methods
SCP	EU Scientific Committee on Plants
SIGMA	Society of Independent Gas Marketers of America
SPS	Sanitary and Phytosanitary Agreement
TBT	Agreement on Technical Barriers to Trade
TEDs	Turtle excluder devices
TRIPS	Agreement on Trade-Related Aspects of Intellectual Property Rights
USTR	United States Trade Representative
VOC	Volatile organic compound
WHO	World Health Organization
WTO	World Trade Organization

1. Introduction

A product of the General Agreement on Tariffs and Trade (GATT), the World Trade Organization (WTO), was established in 1995 to create a stronger set of institutions to administer the various trade agreements negotiated under the GATT framework. Since its inception, the WTO has been dogged by controversy. With a wider mandate and greater enforcement powers than its predecessor GATT institutions, the WTO is widely perceived to pose a greater threat to national sovereignty. While corporations and traditionalists oppose extending the organization's reach beyond trade, consumer groups and environmental organizations complain that the WTO favors trade at the expense of environmental and health objectives. They fear that new provisions negotiated during the Uruguay Round (1986–1994) threaten industrialized nations' high environmental and health standards by promoting the adoption of international standards (leveling down) and requiring governments that choose higher standards to provide scientific justification. On the other hand, critics in the developing world charge that the provisions allow wealthy nations to impose their standards on their trade partners (leveling up) and to engage in a new form of protection in which measures that favor domestic producers masquerade as environmental or health regulations.

Since 1995, the WTO has made rulings in nine disputes involving environmental and public health measures affecting gasoline, shrimp–turtles, hormones, asbestos, salmon, apples, other agricultural products, generic drugs and genetically modified organisms (GMOs). Based on these nine disputes, which collectively address nearly all of the environmental and health controversies surrounding the WTO, the book investigates the WTO's impact on the environment, public health and sovereignty.

Although the rulings in these nine disputes affirm national sovereignty over environmental and health policy, they have not been seen as doing so because most have gone against the governments imposing the regulations in dispute owing to discriminatory implementation or lack of scientific support. Couched in trade terminology, the rulings tend to be dense and lengthy. Drafted by trade experts, they often hinge on quite subtle and narrow sets of issues. They are not a quick or easy read, especially for those unschooled in trade law. Many of the environment and health provisions are new, virtually all are complex. In some cases, the rulings explore multiple provisions containing different requirements before determining which provisions take precedence. In other instances, the provisions are defined in broad terms and, arguably, are open to varying interpretations. Because governments tend to present self-serving arguments to defend their regulations and to challenge those of their trade partners, their arguments tend to cloud rather than clarify the issues in dispute. Finally, as the controversies suggest, the pursuit of trade, the environment and public health is inherently divisive. Most nations will pursue goals in all three areas. However, they are likely to do so in ways that differ from other nations thanks to varying preferences, resources and other factors. Hence, disputes are likely to arise between nations pursuing different strategies. The outcomes of these disputes are likely to leave some constituencies confused and unhappy especially in the early going when new rules and procedures are being developed and implemented.

The book is the first to provide a comprehensive analysis of the environmental and health disputes that have been adjudicated by the WTO. Its exploration of the regulations, agreements and rulings that factor in these disputes promotes a better understanding of the WTO's dispute resolution process and its implications for national environmental and health policy and the controversies surrounding the WTO on these matters.

1.1   CONTROVERSIES: THE WTO, THE ENVIRONMENT, PUBLIC HEALTH AND SOVEREIGNTY

The considerable controversy that marked the creation of the WTO in 1995 has not abated in the ensuing years. Instead, the organization has become the embodiment of globalization in a period when globalization has come under fire from all directions. Anti-globalization forces include such diverse groups as environmentalists, consumer advocates, union members, protectionists, anarchists, academics, policymakers and others both in developing and developed nations. While these groups oppose globalization and the WTO, they do so for different reasons

(Hornblower, 1999; Luttwak, 1999; Mitra, 1999). These differences are quite striking in the debate over the WTO's impact on the environment and public health. This debate frequently pits policymakers and activists in developed and developing nations against one another. While groups in both regions oppose many of the environmental and health provisions negotiated during the Uruguay Round, they cite different and, at times, conflicting grounds.

On the one hand, activists and some policymakers in developed nations fear that the WTO poses several threats to the environment and public health. They claim that harmonization provisions affecting food and product safety will encourage nations to adopt international standards that will level down the generally higher ones in their nations (French, 2002). They also argue that the scientific justification requirements affecting food safety standards might stop nations from taking preventative measures against health risks in the absence of scientific certainty. They favor the precautionary principle, which holds that governments may take action against potential as well as proven health threats (McDonald, 1998).

On a more fundamental level, environmentalists, consumer advocates and others in the developed world object to the WTO's priorities. These critics hold that the organization advances trade at the expense of the environment, public health and other social objectives (*Ecologist*, 2000; Stiglitz, 2002). Some object to requirements that nations pursue environmental and health goals in ways that are least disruptive to trade. They fear that these requirements jeopardize multilateral environmental agreements (MEAs) that use trade restrictions to conserve wildlife, prevent climate change and pursue other environmental goals (Wallach and Woodall, 2004). Others question whether it is legitimate for the WTO to address non-trade goals. With a relatively low budget and small staff of primarily trade experts, some wonder whether the organization has the resources, expertise or will to grapple with environmental, health and other non-trade issues (Cottier, 2001; Robertson, 2001; Rollo and Winters, 2001).

On the other hand, critics in developing nations believe that linking trade to the environment, labor and other social issues jeopardizes economic growth in the South. They assert that non-trade issues are beyond the purview of the WTO and should be addressed by other institutions (Lloyd-Smith, 2001; Srinivasan, 2002). These critics charge that expanding the WTO's mandate beyond trade will allow wealthy nations to impose their environmental and health agendas on their trade partners

(Durbin, 1995; *New Strait Times Press*, 2001). As a result, developing nations will be forced to adopt higher and more costly standards. Meeting these standards will strain already thin technical and financial resources and become especially burdensome should countries choose different standards (Athukorala, 2002; Finger and Schuler, 2001). Consequently, officials in some developing nations favor strengthening the WTO's harmonization provisions in order to improve access to markets in developed nations (Sareen, 2004).

In addition, the adoption of higher environmental and health standards might have far-reaching and potentially adverse consequences for the structure of developing economies. Since small producers are likely to have the greatest difficulty meeting higher standards, domestic production might become more concentrated among large producers. The consequences include higher unemployment and higher prices for domestic consumers. As a result, compliance with a trade partner's higher standards could provide fewer and more narrowly distributed benefits than anticipated (Abila, 2003; Calvin, Flores and Foster, 2003; Norton et al., 2003; Unnevehr, 2003).

Of course, non-compliance entails the complete loss of export earnings in affected markets. Such losses can be severe, as Otsuki, Wilson and Sewadeh (2001) found in the case of nine African nations whose nut, cereal and dried fruit exports to the EU declined by $400 million when the EU implemented a new regulation to address alfatoxin, a mold which can cause liver cancer and immune deficiency disorders. However, the new standard was estimated to save merely 1.4 lives per billion residents annually in a region that experiences some 33 000 liver cancer deaths during the course of a year (Otsuki, Wilson and Sewadeh, 2001).

With these tradeoffs in mind, critics in the developing world question the value of such standards and suggest that they amount to a new form of protection (Durbin, 1995; Athukorala, 2002). In this view, as tariff and other barriers to trade are dismantled in agriculture and other markets, developed countries seek to use environmental and health standards as a backdoor way to protect their markets from lower-cost producers in developing nations. The use of quarantines and other unnecessarily restrictive measures are a major concern (Anderson, 2001; Sareen, 2003). For example, health officials in the US have detained processed food exports from developing nations at higher rates than comparable exports from other nations (Athukorala, 2002). And policy-makers from developing nations cite safety requirements as the most significant obstacle affecting food and agricultural exports to the EU (Spencer and Loader, 2001). No doubt these experiences reflect in part the capacity limitations addressed above as well as the tendency of importing nations to resort to new forms of protection as older forms are being restricted.

While increasing assistance to developing nations can enhance capacity building, an effective dispute resolution process is needed to address protectionist environmental and health measures. However, critics charge that the high cost of challenging a trade partner's regulation in the WTO's dispute resolution process reduces the opportunity for developing nations to seek redress against such measures (Srinivasan, 2002). Further, these costs might be particularly difficult to justify given the relatively low economic and political clout that developing countries bring to the proceedings. A developing country might win a favorable WTO ruling only to find that a wealthier trade partner chooses to maintain an offending regulation since the resulting trade penalties are likely to be commensurate with the small size of the developing nation's market (Hoekman and Mavroidis, 2001).

Environmental and consumer advocates in developed and developing nations find common ground on some issues. Both groups have grave concerns about the commitments made with respect to intellectual property. These commitments are seen as promoting biotechnology despite uncertainty about its short- and long-run impacts on the environment and public health (Greenpeace, 2002; Bernauer, 2003). In addition, environmentalists object that biotechnology might pose a risk to biodiversity through various mechanisms including cross-pollination between genetically modified organisms (GMOs) and traditional plant life (Brendel, 2002; Egziabher, 2003).

Environmentalists also emphasize that new intellectual property rules favor corporations at the expense of indigenous communities because the new rules facilitate the former's ability to secure property rights over the latter's traditional knowledge (Dutfield, 2001). For some, these changes amount to legalizing biopiracy and creating a new form of colonialism. These critics view traditional knowledge as cultural heritage that is nurtured and managed by the community rather than property that is sold to the highest bidder (Indigenous Peoples' Caucus, 1999; GRAIN 2003, 2004a, 2004b).

Others emphasize the need to prevent the misappropriation of genetic resources and to promote an equitable distribution of their benefits along the lines laid out in the Convention on Biological Diversity (IUCN,

2004b). Those who share this perspective believe that it is essential to clarify the relationship between the WTO and multilateral environmental agreements (MEAs) like the Convention on Biological Diversity (CBD) and to do so in ways that do not advance trade at the expense of the environment (IUCN, 2004a). Further, assuring that nations can impose environmental measures that restrict trade is likely to require strengthening the governance and enforcement mechanisms of the CBD and other MEAs in order to counterbalance those of the more powerful WTO (French, 2002).

Similarly, organizations in the developing and developed worlds dispute the requirement that governments in developing nations honor patents on medicine. Non-governmental organizations like Oxfam (2001, 2002) and Médecins Sans Frontières (Boulet, Garrison and 't Hoen, 2003) protest that the requirement threatens developing nations' access to the low-cost, generic drugs used to combat AIDS, tuberculosis, malaria and other life-threatening diseases. The same concern led developing nations to launch a campaign within the WTO to waive certain requirements affecting access to generic drugs (WTO, 2001b, 2003d).

There is near universal agreement among activists that the WTO and especially the revamped dispute resolution process pose a threat to national sovereignty (Durbin, 1995; *Ecologist*, 2000; Harrington, 1999; Wallach and Woodall, 2004). As under the GATT, the WTO's dispute resolution process begins with mandatory consultations between the disputants. And when consultations are not able to resolve the matter, a panel is formed to investigate the dispute. But to address concerns that the GATT process was lengthy and ineffective, several changes were instituted. First, timetables apply to each phase of the process. Second, the Appellate Body was created to hear appeals of panel rulings. And third, dispute rulings are now binding as they go into effect unless there is a consensus *against* adoption (WTO, 1994). This 'reverse consensus' approach ensures that the adoption of dispute resolution rulings is virtually automatic because 'winners' are unlikely to oppose decisions that favor them. By contrast, the GATT process required a consensus *supporting* adoption. Consequently, 'losers' were able to block the adoption of panel reports (Pauwelyn, 2000). WTO panel and appellate reports urge governments to remove offending regulations but do not mandate specific implementation steps. However, the dispute resolution rules oblige governments to comply within a reasonable period of time (no more than 15 months); those that do not must pay compensation to or face trade penalties from the other parties to the dispute (WTO, 1994).

The WTO's decision making is characterized as undemocratic and unaccountable by a broad group of critics that includes academics, policy-makers and activists (French, 2002; Stiglitz, 2002; Wallach and Woodall, 2004). Similarly, there is broad consensus that WTO proceedings should be more transparent (Bacchus, 2004; Barfield, 2001; Kelly, 2003; Khor, 2002; Ragosta, 2000; Wolfe, 2001). However, while activists, scholars and policymakers in developed nations call for more public participation in the WTO, their counterparts in the developing world are wary about taking steps to enhance participation by non-governmental organizations (NGOs) (Bacchus, 2004; French, 2002; Kanth, 2000; Raghavan, 2002; Ragosta, 2000; Wolfe, 2001). A key concern is that greater NGO participation might accentuate the existing disadvantages facing developing countries since NGOs from the developed world are more numerous, active and wealthier (Bates, 1999).

1.2 ENVIRONMENTAL AND PUBLIC HEALTH DISPUTES AT THE WTO

As of January 2007, WTO members had lodged 352 complaints against their trade partners. Forty-two complaints involved challenges to environmental or health measures. These 42 complaints represented 33 disputes because multiple complaints were filed in several cases. Twenty-six of the disputes concerned restrictions on imports of food and agricultural products (including bottled water, live animals, wine and pet food). The other seven disputes involved various products including matches, retreaded tires and pharmaceuticals. The WTO has issued rulings in nine of these disputes: gasoline, shrimp–turtle, hormones, asbestos, salmon, apples, agricultural products, generic drugs and genetically modified organisms (GMOs). The parties reached mutually agreed solutions in seven disputes.[1] The dispute resolution process was suspended for unspecified reasons in 14 disputes.[2] Panel action was pending in three disputes (WTO, 2007).[3] Most of these disputes, including four of the nine for which there were rulings, involved protectionist measures that were imposed under the guise of promoting the environment or public health (Kelly, 2003).

The book uses these nine disputes to explore the WTO's impact on the environment, public health and sovereignty. What the rulings lack in number, they make up in breadth. The nine disputes address virtually all of the environmental and health controversies surrounding the WTO.

While the WTO is widely perceived to advance trade at the expense of the environment and public health and to undermine national sovereignty over these matters, the nine rulings suggest that the organization is able to balance all three sets of goals and that nations retain sovereignty over environmental and health policy. These conclusions are by no means definitive given the small number of disputes upon which they are based. And, because the disputes tell us only about the jurisprudence to date, we can do no more than speculate about their implications for future disputes.

1.3 PLAN OF THE BOOK

The book is divided into several chapters. Chapters 2 and 3 explore the WTO's rulings in the two major environmental disputes to come before the organization. Chapter 2 discusses Brazil's and Venezuela's complaint against US reformulated gas standards. Chapter 3 examines the Indian, Malaysian, Pakistani and Thai challenge to a US ban on shrimp imports from countries that did not employ turtle excluder devices (TEDs). The gasoline and shrimp–turtle disputes were widely perceived to support the leveling down hypothesis because developing nations challenged US environmental regulations and won. But this conclusion does not withstand more careful analysis. In both disputes, the Appellate Body held that the environmental regulations imposed by the US were permissible under GATT provisions that allowed nations to preserve exhaustible natural resources (Article XX(g)) but rejected the discriminatory programs, which were developed to implement them (WTO, 1996 and 1998b). Chapters 2 and 3 discuss varying reactions to the environmental rulings within developed and developing nations and their implications for the WTO and the debates surrounding it. Chapter 3 addresses the controversy sparked by environmental organizations seeking to submit amicus (friend of the court briefs) in the shrimp–turtle dispute. Chapter 3 also explores the interaction of the WTO, multilateral environmental agreements (MEAs), non-governmental organizations (NGOs) and the courts in the shrimp-turtle dispute, which concerned an MEA protecting sea turtles and resulted in a court challenge by environmental organizations to US compliance measures.

Chapter 4 examines the dispute between the US and the EU regarding the latter's ban on imports of beef treated with growth hormones. The WTO ruled against the import ban, leading to protests that the rulings jeopardized public health and food safety. However, critics tended to overlook the careful and narrow nature of the Appellate Body's rulings. For example, the Appellate Body rejected the US and Canadian claims that the ban was a protectionist measure. The Appellate Body also relaxed the panel's more restrictive interpretation of the Sanitary and Phytosanitary Agreement's (SPS) risk assessment and scientific justification requirements explaining that governments were not required to support their regulations with a preponderance of evidence but merely with enough evidence to offer reasonable support (WTO, 1998a). The chapter investigates the Appellate Body's unsuccessful attempt to sidestep ruling on the precautionary principle, the role of scientific experts in the panel process, the EU's options at the implementation phase and steps taken to enhance the transparency of the dispute resolution proceedings during the compliance phase of the dispute.

Chapter 5 discusses Canada's challenge to France's ban on asbestos imports. Arguably, this case featured the most serious health risks to figure in a WTO dispute, yet it has received the least attention, possibly because the WTO upheld the asbestos import ban. The dispute is noteworthy for several reasons. First, Canada's challenge to France's asbestos ban demonstrates that domestic political pressures exert a substantial influence on governments and can press them to challenge regulations that protect the public from serious health risks. Second, in rejecting Canada's claim that controlled use of asbestos reduced these health risks to an acceptable level, the WTO affirmed that nations have a right to determine their own acceptable risk levels. Third, the amicus controversy ignited in the shrimp–turtle dispute reached a stalemate as the Appellate Body's attempt to widen the scope for NGO submissions in the asbestos dispute elicited strong opposition from WTO members (WTO, 2001a). Fourth, the decision boosted international efforts to ban asbestos. Shortly after the rulings were issued, several nations instituted complete or partial asbestos bans (Kazan-Allen, 2005).

Chapter 6 explores WTO dispute resolution rulings on three food safety measures: an Australian ban on certain salmon imports and Japanese import restrictions on apples and other agricultural products (WTO, 1998c, 1999, 2003e). Like the hormones dispute, the salmon, apples and agricultural products disputes hinged on the SPS Agreement's risk assessment (Article 5.1) and scientific justification (Article 2.2) requirements. But the regulations at issue in the salmon, apples and agricultural products disputes appeared to be designed primarily to promote domestic producers rather than public health. Because most of the environmental and health complaints lodged at the WTO involve similar efforts to disguise protectionist measures as food safety regulations, the three disputes illustrated the important role that the risk assessment and scientific justification requirements play in distinguishing between protectionist and legitimate health measures. The precautionary principle figured in all three disputes. Although it was not deployed with success, the apples and agricultural products rulings provided helpful guidance for governments seeking to invoke it in the future. The chapter also examines the efficacy of panel consultations with scientific experts and the implications of Australia's and Japan's poor compliance records for the credibility of the dispute resolution system.

Chapter 7 analyzes the dispute between Canada and the EU over regulations that promoted the development of generic drugs. At the time, Canadian law permitted generic drug manufacturers to perform investigative work related to regulatory approval requirements (regulatory review or early working exemption) and to stockpile production (stockpiling exemption) prior to a patent's expiration. In its defense, Canada invoked exceptions provided in the Agreement on Trade-Related Aspects of Intellectual Property Rights (TRIPS, Article 30). The rulings in the case affirmed the early working exemption but struck the stockpiling exemption (WTO, 2000). The decision was an important victory for Canadian policymakers, generic manufacturers and consumers because the ability 'to work' patents expedites the introduction of generic drugs to a far greater extent than stockpiling. But developing nations feared that the panel's narrow reasoning constrained their ability to invoke other provisions in the TRIPS Agreement affecting access to generic drugs necessary to fight AIDS, TB, malaria and other diseases. The chapter concludes by exploring developing nations' response: the TRIPS and Public Health initiative, the most significant development at the WTO with respect to patent protection and public health (WTO, 2001b, 2003d).

Chapter 8 examines the biotech dispute between the EU and Argentina, Canada and the US (WTO, 2003a, 2003b, 2003c). This complex case involved delays in the processing of 27 applications to market products containing genetically modified organisms (GMOs), a general moratorium on new product approvals and six state-level bans on biotech products approved prior to the moratorium (European Commission, 2004). The lengthy and long-awaited dispute left much unresolved, apparently by design. The US, Argentina and Canada filed their complaints in 2003, several months before the entry into force of stringent, new labeling and traceability standards for GMOs in the EU. Once the new rules went into effect, the EU resumed consideration of GMO marketing applications but five of the six state-level bans remained in effect. Although the moratorium and the product-specific approvals delays were found to be incompatible with WTO rules prohibiting undue delay in the completion of approval procedures, the panel's conclusion that the six states had not produced evidence justifying their bans on a precautionary basis was most significant. The panel ignored testimony supporting the bans from the scientific experts advising the panel. Since the rulings were not appealed, they stand unless action during the compliance phase brings the Appellate Body into the dispute. The chapter concludes by examining the likely impact of developments in the biotech industry and the regulatory arena on future disputes.

Chapter 9 summarizes the key findings from the analysis of the dispute resolution rulings in the nine disputes. The chapter emphasizes the issues that figure in the controversies surrounding the WTO, including the extent to which the WTO favors trade at the expense of the environment and public health, infringes upon sovereignty by imposing universal standards on its members, allows importing nations (especially in the North) to use environmental and health measures to protect domestic producers and provides developing nations with an effective set of mechanisms to resolve trade disputes. The chapter proposes improvements in the dispute resolution process, identifies unresolved issues, and anticipates future developments at the WTO.

NOTES

1. Korea – Measures Concerning the Shelf-Life of Products (WT/DS5); Korea – Measures Concerning Bottled Water (WT/DS20); Chile – Measures Affecting the Transit and Importing of Swordfish (WT/DS193); Mexico – Measures Affecting the Import of Matches (WT/DS232); Turkey – Certain Import Procedures for Fresh Fruit (WT/DS237); Romania – Import Prohibition on Wheat and Wheat Flour (WT/DS240); and Mexico – Certain Measures Preventing the Import of Black Beans from Nicaragua (WT/DS284).
2. Korea – Measures Concerning the Testing and Inspection of Agricultural Products (WT/DS3); Korea – Measures Concerning Inspection of Agricultural Products (WT/DS41); Japan – Measures Affecting Imports of Pork (WT/DS66); US – Measures Affecting Imports of Poultry Products (WT/DS100); Slovak Republic – Measures Concerning the Importation of Dairy Products and the Transit of Cattle

(WT/DS133); EC – Measures Affecting Imports of Wood Conifers from Canada (WT/DS137); US – Certain Measures Affecting the Import of Cattle, Swine and Grain from Canada (WT/DS144); Mexico – Measures Affecting Trade in Live Swine (WT/DS203); Egypt – Import Prohibition on Canned Tuna with Soybean Oil (WT/DS205); Argentina – Measures Affecting the Import of Pharmaceutical Products (WT/DS233); Turkey – Import Ban on Pet Food from Hungary (WT/DS256); EC – Measures Affecting Imports of Wine (WT/DS263); India – Import Restrictions Maintained under the Export and Import Policy 2002–2007 (WT/DS279); and Croatia – Measures Affecting Imports of Live Animals and Meat Products (WT/DS279).
3. Australia – Certain Measures Affecting the Importation of Fresh Fruit and Vegetables (WT/DS270); Australia – Quarantine Regime for Imports (WT/DS287); and Brazil – Measures Affecting Imports of Retreaded Tires (WT/DS332).

REFERENCES

Abila, R. (2003), 'Case study: Kenyan fish exports', in Laurian Unnevehr (ed.), *Food Safety in Food Security and Food Trade*, Washington, DC: IFPRI, 2020 Vision Paper, Focus 10, Brief 8, September.

Anderson, K. (2001), 'Bringing discipline to agricultural policy via the WTO', in Bernard Hoekman and Will Martin (eds), *Developing Countries and the WTO: A Pro-Active Agenda*, Oxford: Blackwell Publishers.

Athukorala, P. (2002), 'Asian developing countries and the global trading system for agriculture, textiles and clothing', in Ramesh Adhikari and Prema-chandra Athukorala (eds), *Developing Countries in the World Trading System*, Cheltenham, UK and Northampton, MA, USA: Edward Elgar, pp. 68–94.

Bacchus, J. (2004), 'The WTO must open up its trade dispute proceedings', *European Affairs*, 5(2), 88–92.

Barfield, C. (2001), 'Free trade, sovereignty, democracy: the future of the World Trade Organization', *Chicago Journal of International Law*, 2(2), 403–15.

Bates, J. (1999), 'Civil society and the World Trade Organization', Progressive Policy Institute, *Backgrounder*, 1 November.

Bernauer, Thomas (2003), *Genes, Trade and Regulation, The Seeds of Conflict in Food Biotechnology*, Princeton: Princeton University Press.

Boulet, P., E. Garrison and E. 't Hoen (2003). 'Drug patents under the spotlight', Médecins Sans Frontières, Campaign for Access to Essential Medicines, Geneva, May.

Brendel, U. (2002), 'The dangers of genetically engineered plants', Greenpeace, European Unit, *Reports and Briefing Papers* (website accessed during July 2004).

Calvin, L., L. Flores and W. Foster (2003), 'Case study: Guatemalan raspberries and cyclospora', in Laurian Unnevehr (ed.), *Food Safety in Food Security and Food Trade*, Washington, DC: IFPRI, 2020 Vision Paper, Focus 10, Brief 7, September.

Cottier, Thomas (2001), 'Risk management experience in WTO dispute settlement', in David Robertson and Aynsley Kellow (eds), *Globalization and the Environment, Risk Assessment and the WTO*, Cheltenham, UK and Northampton, MA, USA: Edward Elgar, pp. 41–62.

Durbin, A. (1995), 'Trade and the environment: the North–South divide', *Environment*, **37**(7), 16–25.

Dutfield, G. (2001), 'TRIPS-related aspects of traditional knowledge', *Case Western Reserve Journal of International Law*, **33**(2), 233–75.

Ecologist (The) (2000), 'WTO-shrink or sink!' **30**(6), R52.

Egziabher, T. (2003), 'When elephants fight over gmos', *Seedling*, October.

European Commission (2004), 'Questions and answers on the regulation of gmos in the EU', *Press Release*, Memo/04/102, 30 April.

Finger, J. and P. Schuler (2001), 'Implementation of Uruguay Round commitments: the development challenge', in Bernard Hoekman and Will Martin (eds), *Developing Countries and the WTO: A Pro-Active Agenda*, Oxford: Blackwell Publishers, pp. 115–30.

French, H. (2002), 'Reshaping global governance', in Christopher Flavin, Hillary French and Gary Gardner (eds), *State of the World Report*, Washington, DC: Worldwatch Institute, pp. 174–254.

GRAIN (2003), 'Global patents for world domination?' *Seedling*, October.

GRAIN (2004a), 'The great protection racket: imposing IPRs on traditional knowledge', *Seedling*, January.

GRAIN (2004b), 'Biodiversity Convention to develop "regime" on benefit sharing', *Seedling*, April.

Greenpeace (2002), 'Summary of considerations regarding the co-existence of gmo, non-gmo and organic farming', European Unit, *Reports and Briefing Papers* (website accessed during July 2004).

Harrington, P. (1999), 'Nature groups see WTO pact as threat', *The Seattle Times*, 29 June, F1.

Hoekman, B. and P. Mavroidis (2001), 'WTO dispute settlement, transparency and surveillance', in Bernard Hoekman and Will Martin (eds), *Developing Countries and the WTO: A Pro-Active Agenda*, Oxford: Blackwell Publishers, pp. 131–46.

Hornblower, M. (1999), 'The battle in Seattle', *Time*, 29 November, 40.

Indigenous Peoples' Caucus (1999), 'Indigenous peoples' Seattle declaration', WTO Ministerial Conference, Seattle, 30 November–3 December.

IUCN (The World Conservation Union) (2004a), 'Ensuring that WTO and MEA rules are mutually supportive', *Policy Briefs, Trade and Biodiversity*, January.

IUCN (The World Conservation Union) (2004b), 'Intellectual property rights (iprs) and regimes on access to genetic resources and benefit sharing', *Policy Briefs, Trade and Biodiversity*, January.

Kanth, R. (2000), 'Storm brewing over WTO move', *Business Times*, 22 November, World News, 29.

Kazan-Allen, L. (2005), 'National asbestos bans', London: International Ban Asbestos Secretariat, Revised 4 January (website accessed during January).

Kelly, T. (2003), 'The WTO, the environment and health and safety standards', *The World Economy*, **26**(2), 131–51.

Khor, M. (2002). 'The WTO, the post-Doha agenda and the future of the trade system: a development perspective', Penang, Malaysia: Third World Network, prepared for the WTO seminar at the Asian Development Bank Annual Meeting, May.

Lloyd-Smith, J. (2001), 'Mahathir turns up heat on trade body', *South China Morning Post*, 11 September, Business Post, 9.

Luttwak, E. (1999), 'Commentary: perspective on WTO: globalizers are the Bolsheviks of their day . . .' *Los Angeles Times*, 10 December.

McDonald, J. (1998), 'Big beef or consumer health threat: the WTO food safety agreement, bovine growth hormone and the precautionary principle', *Environmental and Planning Law Journal*, **15**(2), 115–26.

Mitra, B. (1999), 'WTO protesters vs. the poor', *The Wall Street Journal*, 9 December.

New Strait Times Press (2001), 'Turning turtle the environment', 25 October, Trends, 6.

Norton, G., G. Sanchez, D. Clarke-Harris and H. Kone Traore (2003), 'Case study: reducing pesticide residues on horticultural crops', in Laurian Unnevehr (ed.), *Food Safety in Food Security and Food Trade*, Washington, DC: IFPRI, 2020 Vision Paper, Focus 10, Brief 10, September.

Otsuki, T., J. Wilson and M. Sewadeh (2001). 'A race to the top? A case study of food safety standards and African exports', World Bank, Development Research Group, Policy Research Working Paper 2563, Washington, DC, March.

Oxfam. (2001), 'Patent injustice: how world trade rules threaten the health of poor people', Oxfam, Oxford.

Oxfam (2002), *Rigged Rules and Double Standards, Trade, Globalization and the Fight Against Poverty*, Oxford: Oxfam.

Pauwelyn, J. (2000), 'Enforcement and countermeasures in the WTO: rules are rules – toward a more collective approach', *The American Journal of International Law*, **94**(2), 335–47.

Raghavan, C. (2002), 'AB and DSU functioning getting curiouser and curi-ouser', *South–North Development Monitor* (SUNS), 11 October.

Ragosta, J. (2000), 'Unmasking the WTO – access to the DSB system: can the WTO DSB live up to its moniker "World Trade Court"?', *Law & Policy in International Business*, **3**(3), 739–68.

Robertson, D. (2001), 'GM foods and global trade', in David Robertson and Aynsley Kellow (eds), *Globalization and the Environment, Risk Assessment and the WTO*, Cheltenham, UK and Northampton, MA, USA: Edward Elgar, pp. 206–26.

Rollo, J. and L. Winters (2000), 'Subsidiarity and governance: challenges for the WTO: environment and labour standards', in Bernard Hoekman and Will Martin (eds), *Developing Countries and the WTO: A Pro-Active Agenda*, Oxford: Blackwell Publishers, pp. 185–200.

Sareen, S. (2003), 'Case study: India responds to international food safety', in Laurian Unnevehr (ed.), *Food Safety in Food Security and Food Trade*, Washington, DC: IFPRI, 2020 Vision Paper, Focus 10, Brief 11, September.

Sareen, S. (2004), 'Environmental requirements & market access – India's ex-perience and views', Presentation at WTO Public Symposium, Environmental Requirements and Market Access Session, Geneva, 26 May.

Spencer, H. and R. Loader (2001), 'Barriers to agricultural exports from devel-oping countries: the role of sanitary and phytosanitary requirements', *World Development*, **29**(1), 85–102.

Srinivasan, T. (2002), 'Emerging issues in the world trading system', in Ramesh Adhikari and Prema-chandra Athukorala (eds), *Developing Countries in the World Trading System*, Cheltenham, UK and Northampton, MA, USA: Edward Elgar, pp. 24–39.

Stiglitz, J. (2002), *Globalization and Its Discontents*, London: Penguin Books.

Unnevehr, L. (2003), 'Overview', in Laurian Unnevehr (ed.), *Food Safety in Food Security and Food Trade*, Washington, DC: IFPRI, 2020 Vision Paper, Focus 10, Brief 1, September.

Wallach, Lori and Patrick Woodall (2004), *Whose Trade Organization? A Comprehensive Guide to the WTO*, New York: The New Press for Public Citizen.

Wolfe, A. (2001), 'Problems with WTO dispute settlement', *Chicago Journal of International Law*, **2**(2), 417–26.

WTO (1994), *Understanding on Rules and Procedures Governing the Settlement of Disputes* (DSU), Geneva: WTO.

WTO (1996), *US – Standards for Reformulated and Unconventional Gasoline, Report of the Appellate Body* (WT/DS2/AB/R), Geneva: WTO, 29 April.

WTO (1998a), *EC – Measures Concerning Meat and Meat Products (Hormones), Report of the Appellate Body* (WT/DS26/AB/R and WT/DS48/AB/R), Geneva: WTO, 26 January.

WTO (1998b), *US – Import Prohibition of Certain Shrimp and Shrimp Products, Report of the Appellate Body* (WT/DS58/AB/R), Geneva: WTO, 12 October.

WTO (1998c), *Australia – Measures Affecting Importation of Salmon, Report of the Appellate Body* (WT/DS18/AB/R), Geneva: WTO, 20 October.

WTO (1999), *Japan – Measures Affecting Agricultural Products, Report of the Appellate Body* (WT/DS76/AB/R), Geneva: WTO, 22 February.

WTO (2000), *Canada – Patent Protection of Pharmaceutical Products, Report of the Panel* (WT/DS114/R), Geneva: WTO, 17 March.

WTO (2001a), *EC – Measures Affecting Asbestos and Products Containing Asbestos, Report of the Appellate Body* (WT/DS135/AB/R), Geneva: WTO, 12 March.

WTO (2001b), *Declaration on the TRIPS Agreement and Public Health* (WT/MIN(01/DEC/2))   , Geneva: WTO, 20 November.

WTO (2003a), *EC – Measures Affecting the Approval and Marketing of Biotech Products, Request for the Establishment of a Panel by the United States* (WT/DS291/23), Geneva: WTO, 8 August.

WTO (2003b), *EC – Measures Affecting the Approval and Marketing of Biotech Products, Request for the Establishment of a Panel by Canada* (WT/DS292/17), Geneva: WTO, 8 August.

WTO (2003c), *EC – Measures Affecting the Approval and Marketing of Biotech Products, Request for the Establishment of a Panel by Argentina* (WT/DS293/17), Geneva: WTO, 8 August.

WTO (2003d), *Implementation of Paragraph 6 of the Doha Declaration on the TRIPS Agreement and Public Health* (WT/L/540), Geneva: WTO, 1 September.

WTO (2003e), *Japan – Measures Affecting the Importation of Apples, Report of the Appellate Body* (WT/DS245/AB/R), Geneva: WTO, 26 November.

WTO (2007), *The Disputes*, Geneva: WTO (website accessed during January).

2. Gasoline

Soon after the World Trade Organization was established in January of 1995, Venezuela and Brazil lodged complaints against US reformulated gas standards that were designed to improve air quality under 1990 amendments to the Clean Air Act. Venezuela and Brazil charged that the standards discriminated against foreign refiners by imposing more stringent regulations on them than on US refiners. The dispute was controversial within the environmental community from the outset. The controversy grew as WTO rulings in the dispute were perceived by many to compromise US sovereignty over environmental regulations rather than to reject the discriminatory aspects of the program. The dispute made its way into the 1996 presidential campaign and showed that politics does indeed make strange bedfellows. Environmentalists were joined in opposition to the rulings by Republican presidential candidates Pat Buchanan and Bob Dole. Sun, Mobil and other oil companies with domestic refineries favored imposing more stringent standards on foreign refiners and had strong support in Congress. The gasoline rulings had become embroiled in domestic politics. That was fitting because it was the politics of protection that was responsible for the differential baseline rule in the first place.

2.1 IMPLEMENTING THE 1990 AMENDMENTS TO THE CLEAN AIR ACT

The Clean Air Act of 1990 mandated the sale of reformulated gasoline in areas with the most severe air pollution in the United States while permitting the sale of conventional gasoline in other areas. Nine metropolitan areas with high smog levels were required to shift to reformulated gasoline (Baltimore, Chicago, Hartford, Houston, Los Angeles, Milwaukee, New York, Philadelphia, and San Diego). During Phase I (1995–99), emissions of volatile organic compounds (VOCs) and toxics were required to decline by 15 percent compared to 1990 levels. VOCs created ozone, the major determinant of smog. Toxics were linked to cancer and other health risks arising from air pollution. Emissions of nitrogen oxide and various other substances were to be no greater than 1990 levels. During Phase II (2000–), VOC and toxic emissions were required to decrease by 25 percent relative to 1990 levels. The law also mandated that conventional gasoline emissions be at least as clean as those in 1990 to insure that air quality did not deteriorate in other regions of the country (US House of Representative (US House hereafter), 1995).

In a process that included extensive negotiations with representatives from other federal agencies, the oil industry, consumer groups, and environmental organizations, the Environmental Protection Agency (EPA) developed what became known as 'the gasoline rule' to implement the emissions program. Spanning the latter part of the Bush (George H.W.) Administration and the first year of the Clinton Administration, the process was protracted and contentious. As it lengthened, Congressman Henry Waxman (D-California) and environmentalists accused the EPA of dragging its feet. After suing the EPA, they reached a court-supervised settlement in which the EPA agreed to issue the final version of the gasoline rule by 15 September 1993. Despite the deadline, the EPA sought more time. After securing an extension of three months, the agency issued the gasoline rule on 15 December 1993 (US House, 1995).

2.2 THE GASOLINE RULE

The gasoline rule established the baselines necessary to implement the emission targets set in the 1990 Clean Air Act. During 1995–97, the EPA permitted domestic refiners to establish individual baselines for reformulated gasoline. During this thee-year interim period, domestic oil refiners' emissions were benchmarked against their emissions in 1990. Effective 1 January 1998, domestic refiners were subject to a more stringent statutory baseline based on average emission levels from all domestically produced gasoline in 1990. Domestic refiners were required to use one of three methods to establish individual baselines. Under Method 1, refiners were to use volume and quality data based on actual gasoline production in 1990. In the absence of these data, Methods 2 and 3 permitted refiners to use less exacting 1990 and post-1990 production data, respectively (EPA, 1997).

Importers of foreign gasoline were permitted to establish individual baselines provided that they were able to do so under the more demanding Method 1. They were not permitted to use Methods 2 and 3 even though the EPA acknowledged that most lacked the data necessary to employ Method 1. An exception was made for importers with foreign refineries that exported 75 percent or more of their production to the US. Other importers were assigned the more stringent statutory baseline. Similar arrangements applied to conventional gasoline. Importers were held to a statutory baseline based on average conventional gasoline emissions in 1990, while domestic refiners established individual baselines (US House, 1995).

2.3 DOMESTIC POLITICS: REFINERS & ENVIRONMENTALISTS VS. INDEPENDENT GAS DEALERS & CITIZEN ACTION

The American Petroleum Institute (API), led by Mobil, Sun and other oil refiners, favored imposing the statutory baseline on foreign refiners. According to the industry, US environmental policy created competitive disadvantages for US refiners because foreign refiners were held to less rigorous standards. Imposing the statutory baseline on foreign refiners would level the 'environmental' playing field. Refiners mobilized environmental groups and state governments with the argument that the statutory baseline would prevent 'dirty' foreign gasoline from compromising US air quality (US House, 1995).

It was a strange coalition. The industry had opposed the reformulated gas program (as well other changes mandated by the 1990 clean air amendments) and continued to attempt to delay its implementation, citing a variety of record-keeping, storage and other obstacles (Choinski, 2002; US House, 1995). In addition, oil refiners stood to benefit through greater market share and higher prices should US gasoline imports decline as anticipated with the imposition of the statutory baseline on foreign refiners. But the industry's claims that individual baselines would permit dirty foreign gasoline to degrade US air quality seemed plausible in light of the more stringent environmental standards in the US. As a result, a clear, definitive answer from regulators was needed to resolve the matter. It was not forthcoming. As discussed below, at one point, the EPA appeared to accept the industry's claims. Later, it concluded that foreign gasoline, in particular Venezuelan gasoline, posed no threat to air quality in the US. But, by then, the damage was done. Conventional wisdom within the environmental community held that, unless foreign refiners were held to the statutory baseline, US air quality would decline.

A smaller coalition supported individual baselines for foreign refiners. Its two principal members were the consumer group, Citizen Action, and the Society of Independent Gas Marketers of America (SIGMA). Independent gas dealers did not refine the gas that they sold and competed with the major oil companies. Both Citizen Action and SIGMA emphasized that permitting foreign refiners to establish their own baselines would increase gasoline supply, promote competition and reduce prices (US House, 1995).

The oil refiner and environmentalist coalition had considerable support in Congress. Eighteen US senators and 31 members of the House of Representatives sent letters opposing individual baselines for foreign refiners to the EPA during the gasoline rule development process. SIGMA and Citizen Action enjoyed less Congressional support. Just five members of the House wrote letters to the EPA supporting foreign refiner individual baselines (US House, 1995).[1]

2.4 VENEZUELA PROTESTS

As a major exporter of gasoline to the northeastern US, Venezuela's national oil company, Petroleos de Venezuela Sur America (PDVSA), was subject to the gasoline rule's baseline requirements. PDVSA sold gasoline under the CITGO brand primarily in New England and the Mid-Atlantic states and accounted for about 2 percent of the gasoline sold in those regions. Venezuelan officials charged that different baseline requirements for domestic and foreign producers violated the General Agreement on Tariffs and Trade's (GATT or General Agreement hereafter) national treatment provisions prohibiting discrimination against foreign products (US House, 1995). PDVSA estimated that its exports would decline by $150 million annually if it were held to the statutory baseline during 1995–97 (Bahree, 1995). To avert those losses, Venezuela was prepared to launch a GATT challenge to the gasoline rule.

In July 1991, the EPA's initial draft rule proposed individual baselines for both domestic and foreign producers. By August 1992, the EPA's position had shifted to an individual baseline for domestic refiners and a statutory baseline for foreign refiners. Citing jurisdictional limitations, the EPA's legal staff questioned whether the agency had the authority to obtain the data necessary to verify and enforce individual baselines for foreign refiners. The agency also raised two air quality concerns. First, EPA data indicated that Venezuelan gasoline contained greater amounts of olefin, sulfur and T-90 than US gasoline. These substances were linked to nitrogen oxide emissions, a major determinant of smog in the Northeast. Second, the EPA feared that foreign refiners had incentives to manipulate the system. The principal concern was that foreign refiners with cleaner than average gasoline would choose to forgo individual baselines and, instead, opt for the statutory baseline, which would allow them to produce dirtier gasoline. Under that scenario, overall air quality would decline because foreign refiners producing dirtier than average gasoline were certain to choose individual baselines, which would permit them to continue to produce 'dirty' gasoline during the three-year interim period (US House, 1995).

Venezuelan officials acknowledged that PDVSA's gas contained higher levels of olefin, sulfur and T-90 than US gasoline of average quality. However, they suggested that the comparison was misleading because Venezuelan gas outperformed US gasoline in other respects. Notably, toxic emissions from Venezuelan gas were anticipated to decline by 18 percent more than those from reformulated US gasoline of average quality. Venezuelan officials dismissed the EPA's other concerns. Having made substantial investments in new equipment, 'clean' refiners had no incentives to degrade their gasoline. Even 'dirty' refiners were likely to improve their performance because they would be expected to meet the statutory baseline by January 1998 (US House, 1995). Venezuelan officials agreed to work with the EPA and went so far as to 'guarantee' that PDVSA would address the verification, enforcement and air quality concerns in a manner satisfactory to the EPA (US House, 1995, p. 698).

By August 1993, the EPA reverted toward its initial position. PDVSA would be able to establish an individual baseline. However, to address concerns that 'dirtier' Venezuelan gas might degrade US air quality, the amount of PDVSA gasoline subject to an individual baseline would be capped at the company's 1990 export volume. The statutory baseline would apply to exports of reformulated gasoline in excess of the 1990 level. Under these conditions, air quality would be maintained at least at 1990 levels (US House, 1995). However, later that year, the EPA changed its position again. As discussed previously, the December 1993 gasoline rule subjected most foreign refiners including PDVSA to the statutory baseline while most domestic refiners were required to use individual baselines. Soon after, Venezuela proceeded with its GATT challenge.

2.5 THE MAY PROPOSAL AND CONGRESSIONAL BACKLASH

The GATT dispute was vexing for the Clinton Administration. The office of the United States Trade Representative (USTR) and the State Department maintained that differential treatment of domestic and foreign refiners would not survive a GATT challenge. Venezuela's complaint was particularly unwelcome in the context of the Uruguay Round negotiations. The United States, the leading proponent of free trade, appeared to be sacrificing this principle to favor domestic producers at a time when it sought to garner international support for the Uruguay Round agreements. And, by doing so under the guise of promoting clean air, the US might undermine its efforts to promote stronger environment provisions within the agreements under negotiation. The dispute might also complicate Senate approval of the agreements by underscoring environmentalists' and isolationists' objections to free trade and the WTO (US House, 1995; US Senate, 1994).

In March 1994, the matter came before the National Economic Council (NEC), the body that coordinated economy policy within the Clinton Administration. The NEC recommended that the EPA permit foreign refiners to establish individual baselines for reformulated gasoline subject to 1990 volume caps along the lines discussed with Venezuela in August 1993 (US House, 1995). NEC meeting notes revealed that these terms were to be made contingent on the willingness of Venezuela to drop its GATT challenge and remain silent until 'the politics of this (Hill, oil and others) can be worked in US' (US House, 1995, p. 16). At first, Venezuela balked. It sought individual baselines for both conventional and reformulated gasoline but the offer applied only to reformulated gasoline. When informed that the offer was firm, Venezuela accepted on the condition that the US promulgate a new rule within five months. Failing that, Venezuela would request that a GATT panel take up its complaint (US House, 1995).

When news of the Administration's agreement with Venezuela reached Congress, members reacted with dismay and outrage. The NEC's meeting notes proved to be especially inflammatory. Some members of Congress believed that Congressional prerogatives were at stake. Others were troubled by the failure of the Administration to take the minimal step of keeping Congress informed of the status of its policy toward Venezuela. Another camp felt that the EPA had been forced to subordinate environmental policy to trade objectives. A smaller contingent was bothered that the EPA had issued a rule that other federal agencies thought would not survive a GATT challenge (US House, 1995; US Senate, 1994).

As the EPA prepared a new rule (known as the May Proposal) permitting individual baselines for foreign refiners, both houses of Congress called hearings to investigate the matter. The Senate Committee on Environment and Public Works held its hearing in April 1994. At the Senate hearing, Mary Nichols, the EPA's Assistant Administrator for Air and Radiation, was asked to account for the EPA's erratic position on the appropriate baseline for foreign refiners. She explained that the EPA initially proposed individual baselines for both domestic and foreign refiners because the agency anticipated no difficulties. Later, the agency moved away from foreign refiner individual baselines owing to concerns about data availability, enforcement and air quality. After further study, the agency concluded that those concerns were misplaced at least in the case of PDVSA. PDVSA had the data necessary to establish individual baselines. The EPA had developed an effective enforcement program that included labeling, independent audits and unannounced EPA inspections. Finally, the EPA was persuaded that individual baselines would not permit foreign refiners to degrade air quality (US Senate, 1994).

Senator Max Baucus (D-Montana) was dissatisfied with Ms Nichols' responses and continued to press her for an explanation as to why the EPA had imposed the statutory baseline on foreign refiners as recently as the previous December. Under his persistent questioning, she provided what should have been the definitive explanation. According to Ms Nichols, the EPA's technical staff opposed imposing the statutory baseline on foreign refiners because they believed that the data, enforcement and air quality issues could be addressed. But there was some uncertainty and ultimately the decision was hers. Concerned that the program and others burdened domestic refiners, she thought that it would be desirable, 'if we had a choice, to lean in the direction of doing something that would favor their competitive position vis-à-vis the Venezuelans' (US Senate, 1994, p. 30).

At the same Senate hearing, the Committee asked the Department of Energy's (DOE) John Riggs why the DOE's representative at the NEC meeting had favored the statutory baseline for foreign refiners. His remarks were not quite as blunt as Ms Nichols' but they conveyed the same intent: 'I have been told by the DOE representative at that meeting that his statement was, other things being equal, if we are in compliance with the Clean Air Act and the GATT, we should try to help US industry' (US Senate, 1994, p. 40). Mr Riggs' written testimony explained why the DOE had subsequently withdrawn its objections to individual baselines for foreign refiners:

> It is not always popular to accord a foreign competitor the same opportunities that we provide domestic producers. This is especially true for foreign refiners. They do not face the same tough environmental controls as do US refiners . . . However, the Clean Air Act has a single, clear purpose: to reduce US air pollution. *No matter how much those interested in the health of the domestic refining industry might like to use it to redress other inequities* (emphasis added), the Act provides no legal authority to treat foreign refiners more stringently than US refiners. (US Senate, 1994, pp. 76–7)

Although Ms Nichols' and Mr Riggs' remarks made it clear that the case for differential baselines was based on a protectionist rather than an environmental agenda, their testimony had little impact on the debate surrounding the EPA's May Proposal. Congressional opponents, oil refiners and environmentalists continued to maintain that Venezuelan gasoline should be held to the statutory baseline to prevent its higher olefin, sulfur and T-90 content from raising nitrogen oxide emissions in the Northeast.

Ms Nichols and Mr Riggs testified on that matter as well. According to Ms Nichols, using the statutory baseline as the basis of comparison, nitrogen oxide levels would rise in the Northeast. However, the anticipated increase was quite small (0.2 percent and possibly as little as 0.08 percent above the statutory level) and more than offset by the superior performance of Venezuelan gasoline in other respects. Venezuelan gasoline emitted smaller quantities of volatile organic compounds and toxics, the substances targeted for the largest reductions under the 1990 clean air legislation. She noted that the clean air amendments were designed to insure that air quality did not deteriorate below 1990 levels. Benchmarking against 1990 Venezuelan gas, there would be no increase in nitrogen oxide emissions since the olefin, sulfur and T-90 content of Venezuelan gas was at or below 1990 levels. Mr Riggs added that, if Venezuelan gas sales were to decline as anticipated under the statutory baseline, the impact on air quality in the Northeast was uncertain. Since not all US refiners met the statutory baseline, the effect on air quality depended on whether 'clean' or 'dirty' domestic refiners picked up market share (US Senate, 1994).

The Committee Chairman, Senator Baucus, was unmoved. He concluded the hearing with a warning: if the EPA proceeded with the May Proposal, he would introduce legislation denying funding for foreign refiner individual baselines (US Senate, 1994). Evidently, he found the testimony of the proposal's critics more persuasive. According to the American Petroleum Institute (API), 'The PDVSA approach would compromise air quality and would put domestic refiners at a significant competitive disadvantage' (US Senate, 1994, p. 78). Similarly, the National Petroleum Refiners Association argued that the proposal 'would have anticompetitive impacts on US refiners' (US Senate, 1994, p. 91). A coalition that included environmentalists and independent refiners described the proposal as 'flawed trade policy, unsound environmental policy and nonsensical economic policy' (US Senate, 1994, p. 80).

Opponents reiterated these arguments in June at the House Reformulated Gasoline Hearings (US House, 1995). In September, language was added to an appropriations bill prohibiting the EPA from allocating funds to implement foreign refiner individual baselines. Without funding, the EPA could not proceed. The May Proposal was dropped and the agency reverted to the baseline program promulgated in the December 1993 rule. PDVSA and most other foreign refiners would face the statutory baseline (Choinski, 2002).

2.6   THE WTO DISPUTE

When Congress cut off funding to implement the May Proposal, the agreement with Venezuela lapsed. In January 1995, Venezuela filed a complaint against the gasoline rule at the newly established WTO (WTO, 1995a). Brazil filed a separate complaint in April alleging that its exports of conventional gasoline were affected adversely (WTO, 1995b). With the imposition of the gasoline rule, its conventional gasoline was designated as blendstock rather than finished gasoline. Blendstock sold at a lower price than finished gasoline because importers and blenders were required to blend it with gasoline of higher quality to achieve the emission targets set by the clean air legislation. To avoid duplication, the parties agreed that the panel established at

Venezuela's request would investigate both disputes jointly. The EU and Norway participated as third parties in the proceedings and submitted testimony supporting Venezuela and Brazil in both the panel and appellate proceedings. Australia and Canada reserved their rights to participate as third parties but did not submit arguments (WTO, 1996a).

Venezuela and Brazil charged that the gasoline rule violated the General Agreement on Tariffs and Trade's (GATT or agreement) national treatment (Article III) and most-favored nation provisions (Article I). Article III prohibited discrimination against imports but the gasoline rule imposed the statutory baseline on most foreign refiners while allowing most domestic refiners to set individual baselines for a three-year transitional period. Article I banned discrimination among trade partners but the 75 percent rule permitted certain importers to establish individual baselines while holding most to the statutory requirement. Venezuela and Brazil maintained that the US was obliged to avoid both types of discrimination because the differential baseline rules did not qualify for an exception under Article XX. The differential baselines were also incompatible with the Agreement on Technical Barriers to Trade (TBT). The TBT required members to provide scientific or technical support for environmental measures and to adopt measures that restricted trade no more than necessary (WTO, 1996a).

As it was to do frequently in the dispute, the panel made a case for judicial economy explaining that its rulings under Articles III and XX made it unnecessary to rule on Article I and the Agreement on Technical Barriers to Trade (TBT). The panel concluded that the differential baselines violated Article III's national treatment provisions. According to the EPA's compliance data, most domestic refiners were permitted to market gasoline that did not meet the statutory baseline but nearly all foreign refiners were prohibited from doing so. The US was obliged to treat imported gasoline as favorably as domestic gasoline of identical quality but had failed to do so (WTO, 1996a).

Since the differential baselines were incompatible with Article III's national treatment obligations, US hopes for a successful defense of the gasoline rule shifted to Article XX. Article XX provided exceptions to GATT obligations. The US argued that three exceptions applied to the gasoline rule: (1) the Article XX(b) exception for regulations that were 'necessary to protect animal, human or plant life or health;' (2) the Article XX(g) exception for measures 'relating to the conservation of exhaustible natural resources;' and (3) the Article XX(d) exception for measures that were 'necessary to secure compliance with laws or regulations which are not inconsistent' with the agreement (WTO, 1994).

The panel ruled that the gasoline rule promoted health objectives covered under the Article XX(b) exception, but that the differential baselines were not 'necessary' to its success. When faced with a choice among alternative measures, governments were obliged to impose consistent measures on domestic and foreign goods. Failing that, they were to use the least inconsistent ones available. In the case of the gasoline rule, the US was able to establish a uniform policy for domestic and foreign gasoline. Individual baselines were one option. Data and enforcement issues could be addressed. Labeling, tracking and other measures were employed customarily in international trade and had been dealt with in the EPA's May Proposal. The panel was not convinced that foreign refiners had incentives to manipulate the system. And, here too, a non-discriminatory remedy was available: the US could impose the statutory baseline on all refiners and eliminate concerns about air quality deterioration. In fact, the current program did not prevent such deterioration. Domestic refiners did not face 1990 volume caps and refiners of certain jet fuels were exempt from the requirement to produce gasoline at least as clean as that of 1990. The US had failed to demonstrate that it was 'necessary' to maintain different baselines to meet its clean air standards (WTO, 1996a).

Under Article XX(g), governments were permitted to seek exceptions for measures 'relating to the conservation of exhaustible natural resources if such measures are made effective in conjunction with restrictions on domestic production or consumption' (WTO, 1994). Venezuela asserted that renewable natural resources like clean air were not covered by the exception. The panel rejected that argument, citing a GATT dispute in which renewable stocks of fish were found to qualify as exhaustible natural resources (WTO, 1996a). However, on the basis of another ruling in the same dispute, the panel concluded that the differential baselines were not compatible with Article XX(g)'s 'related to' requirement because they were not 'primarily aimed' at conservation (WTO, 1996a, para. 6.40). There was 'no direct connection' between the desire to promote clean air and the imposition of different baselines for domestic and foreign refiners (WTO, 1996a, para. 6.40). The panel invoked judicial economy and did not rule on whether the gasoline rule imposed restrictions on domestic consumption or production as required by Article XX(g)'s final clause or satisfied the conditions specified in Article XX's preamble (known as the chapeau) (WTO, 1996a).

The differential baselines were also incompatible with the Article XX(d) exception for regulations 'necessary to secure compliance' with other measures that were consistent with GATT obligations (WTO, 1994). The panel held that the rules in dispute *established* baselines rather than *secured compliance* with the baseline program as a whole. The panel underscored the technical nature of its ruling by noting that the baseline program as a whole *might* be consistent with Article III's national treatment provisions. As that matter was not in dispute, the panel declined to address it (WTO, 1996a). Nevertheless, the clarification was important in light of the environmental goals pursued through the baseline program.

2.7 THE APPEAL

The panel's rulings provided grist for the mill on the 1996 campaign trail. Presidential candidate Pat Buchanan protested that, 'This decision of the WTO ... is a gross attack on the sovereignty' of the US (Bluestein, 1996, p. F3). He vowed to seek a plank in the Republican Party platform calling for US withdrawal from the WTO. Stung by Mr Buchanan's attacks against his US Senate vote approving the creation of the WTO, fellow candidate and future Republican presidential nominee, Bob Dole weighed in as well: 'Our laws should continue to be a matter for Americans, not international judges, to determine' (Borrus et al., 1996, p. 48). Representative George Miller (D-California) observed that, 'The WTO's gasoline decision proves that our concerns about so-called free trade agreements are genuine: US environmental and worker protection standards will be the first to go' (*Greenwire*, 1996).

These pressures were too significant to resist during an election year. USTR Mickey Kantor decided to appeal despite initially expressing reservations about that course of action (Bluestein, 1996), but the Clinton Administration filed a narrow appeal that addressed only the panel's conclusion that differential baselines did not qualify for the Article XX(g) exception (WTO, 1996b). Belatedly, the Administration realized that it was essential to make the compatibility of trade and environmental objectives, not the protection of domestic refiners, the centerpiece of its efforts at the WTO.

The US maintained that the baseline rules satisfied Article XX(g)'s 'related to' requirement. The Appellate Body agreed and overturned the panel's rulings. The Appellate Body faulted the panel for focusing on the discriminatory and unfavorable *effects* of the differential baselines rather than their *role* in the gasoline rule. Additionally, the panel overstated the 'related to' requirement. The Appellate Body emphasized that it was customary to interpret treaties using the ordinary meaning of the words employed.[2] Instead, relying partially on precedent, the panel employed the more demanding 'primarily aimed at' and 'direct connection'. The Appellate Body concluded that the baseline rules were 'related to' the conservation of clean air because they were 'related to' the tracking of gasoline emissions, a function that was not invalidated by differential baselines (WTO, 1996b).

Having ruled that the baseline rules satisfied the 'related to' criterion, the Appellate Body next examined whether the measures were 'made effective in conjunction with restrictions on domestic production or consumption' (WTO, 1994). The Appellate Body concluded that the baseline rules were compatible with that requirement. The Appellate Body stressed that the US was not required to treat domestic and foreign gasoline in an identical manner. The US was merely obliged to impose conservation restrictions on domestic as well as foreign gasoline (WTO, 1996b). Oddly, the Appellate Body characterized the requirement as one of 'even-handedness' (WTO, 1996b, p. 20). In fact, the baseline rules were not even-handed and Article XX(g) did not require them to be so; that matter was addressed by Article XX's preamble (chapeau).

The chapeau prohibited the implementation of regulations in 'a manner which would constitute a means of arbitrary or unjustifiable discrimination' or 'a disguised restriction on international trade' (WTO, 1994). The Appellate Body noted with considerable understatement that the 'text of the chapeau is not without ambiguity' (WTO, 1996b, p. 23). In suggesting that the requirements be 'read side-by-side' and that they 'impart meaning to one another', the Appellate Body introduced some ambiguity of its own and missed an opportunity to clarify the relationship among the requirement's components (WTO, 1996b, p. 24).

The Appellate Body was on stronger ground when it emphasized that the chapeau was intended to prevent governments from abusing the Article XX exceptions. The Appellate Body found that the differential baseline rules did not pass this test because the US did not provide a plausible rationale for differentiating between foreign and domestic producers. Individual baselines could have been established for foreign refiners had the US worked with its trade partners to address its data, verification and enforcement concerns. Congress's decision to deny funding to implement the May Proposal did not absolve the US of its responsibility to seek a collaborative solution. Alternatively, the US could have imposed the statutory baseline on domestic refiners. Instead, domestic refiners were granted a three-year transitional period to help them cope with the program's high implementation costs, while no relief was provided to foreign refiners (WTO, 1996b). For PDSVA, compliance was estimated to entail capital expenditures of $1billion (Bahree, 1995).

Citing these two issues, the Appellate Body ruled that the gasoline rule did not satisfy the requirements of Article XX's chapeau. The differential baseline rules had been applied in such a way as to constitute arbitrary and unjustifiable discrimination and a disguised restriction on trade. Consequently, the US was not entitled to invoke the Article XX(g) exception. The US was obliged to treat gasoline imports as favorably as domestic gasoline but had failed to do so by assigning different baselines to domestic and foreign refiners (WTO, 1996b).

Conscious of the wide interest in its findings and the controversy surrounding the dispute, the Appellate Body concluded its report with remarks that echoed those of the panel. The panel stated that 'WTO Members were free to set their own environmental objectives' (WTO, 1996a, para. 7.1). The Appellate Body remarked that 'it is of some importance' to 'point out what this does *not* mean' (original emphasis) (WTO, 1996b, p. 29). It did not mean that members were not able to set their own environmental objectives. Indeed, Article XX had been drafted to provide governments with the ability to pursue environmental, health and other goals in the manner that they thought best, yet members were required to do so in a way that did not interfere with their other obligations (WTO, 1996b).

Both sets of remarks were striking. Typically, reports ended with the bland injunction that members imposing offending measures bring them into conformance with their obligations under the various agreements subject to the dispute resolution process. The reports were designed to be read by government bureaucrats who were responsible for implementing them. This dispute was different. The reports (or at least parts of them) would be read by a large and diverse audience many of whom were convinced that the WTO prioritized trade at the expense of the environment, health and other objectives. For this audience, the conventional approach would not suffice. It might leave the erroneous impression that the rulings went against the gasoline rule rather than its discriminatory implementation. Such an impression was problematic. It called into question the organization's claim that trade and environmental objectives were compatible.

2.8 AFTERMATH

As the first dispute in which a ruling was issued, the gasoline case offered the first test of the WTO's ability to enforce its decisions. Would the US comply? The stakes were high. The compliance of the world's leading trading nation would give a huge boost to the new dispute resolution process. Failure to comply would send a strong signal that little had changed in the dispute resolution arena. The US and other powerful countries could reject WTO rulings just as they had flouted GATT rulings in the past.

Several factors promoted compliance. The US was the principal advocate for a stronger dispute resolution process and was the chief author of the changes made (Cunningham, 1995). Additionally, the US could not have been surprised by the rulings. Federal agencies had debated the pros and cons of differential baselines and were aware of the competitive advantages they provided to domestic refiners. Most concluded that they would not survive a WTO challenge (US House, 1995; US Senate, 1994). On the other hand, Congress had refused to fund the implementation of individual baselines for foreign refiners. Sentiment against individual baselines was strong, especially in the House, where some members remained convinced that air quality would decline. Others were willing to do the oil industry's bidding or resented the WTO's infringement on sovereignty (Kovski, 1996).

When the appellate decision was announced, the Administration's response was predictably mixed. The US welcomed the conclusion that the baseline rules met the requirements of Article XX(g). The rulings reversed the panel on that critical issue and suggested that trade and environmental pursuits were not incompatible. Although the US disputed that the baselines did not conform to the chapeau, the US agreed to comply with the Appellate Body's rulings. Acting USTR Charlene Barshefsky vowed to 'examine any and all options for compliance' (Woellert, 1996, p. B7). In fact, once the decision to comply was made, there was only one legitimate response: extend individual baselines to foreign refiners of reformulated gasoline and conventional gasoline, since the WTO rulings applied to both markets. At the end of a 15-month implementation period, the EPA took that course (WTO, 1997). Foreign refiners were permitted to apply for individual baselines for both reformulated and conventional gasoline; statutory baselines were reserved for those that could not meet the EPA's data and monitoring requirements (EPA, 1997).

The environmental community remained unconvinced. Public Citizen's Lori Wallach co-authored an article with Alan Tonelson of the US Business and Industrial Council Education Foundation. They objected to the ruling on the grounds that it required the US to permit the entry of 'more contaminated gasoline' into the country (Tonelson and Wallach, 1996, p. C4). Equal Exchange's Kevin Danaher characterized the decision as anti-environment and anti-democratic. Citizens no longer possessed the ability to hold polluters accountable; the WTO 'dictated' the nation's environmental agenda (Danaher, 1996, p. 25). Simon Retallack (1997, p. 136), a spokesperson for the International Forum on Globalization, complained that the WTO had helped a foreign government 'subvert the national democratic process'. The Sierra Club's Daniel Seligman opined, 'It's not so much that the sovereignty of the nation is being directly threatened. It's more that trade has become a kind of de facto global government serving only one constituent – transnational corporations' (Collier and Martin, 1999, p. A1).

In a revealing editorial, the *Oil & Gas Journal* suggested that, despite concerns about diminished competitiveness, US refiners might benefit. The 'EPA may find itself so distracted by the politics of foreign baselines that it loses its taste for even stricter regulation of US gasoline' (*Oil & Gas Journal*, 1996, p. 21).

The WTO rulings were greeted more favorably in developing nations. Venezuela and Brazil had triumphed over the US in the WTO, an institution that the US had done more than any other nation to create. Despite its size and economic power, the US was subject to the same trade rules as smaller, poorer and less influential nations. Unlike its GATT predecessor, the WTO's dispute resolution process had teeth. Its greater enforcement powers enhanced developing nations' confidence in the institution, as evidenced by a spate of disputes that poor nations had initiated and were likely to win against rich nations (Reddy, 1996).

The rulings received a mixed reception in the academic community. In a law journal article, Scott Daniel McBride (1998) praised the Appellate Body's understanding of environmental issues and the environmental movement. He went so far as to suggest that, if the gasoline rulings were any indication, environmentalists might 'find the WTO to be the best friend they have ever had' (McBride, 1998, p. 339). He reached this unconventional conclusion by challenging conventional wisdom. Environmentalists saw the executive branch and the WTO as twin threats to environmental standards. In their view, the executive branch's control over environmental policy had increased in recent years at the expense of Congress. At the same time, the Uruguay Round enhanced the WTO's influence over the environment and other non-trade matters. Closing the circle, the WTO strengthened the role of the executive branch over trade and environmental issues since only it could speak for the nation in the organization's proceedings. In this scenario, only Congress stood between high environmental standards and a race to the bottom (McBride, 1998).[3]

McBride argued persuasively that the entire chain worked in reverse. Congress was less trustworthy when it came to environmental protection because, in Tip O'Neil's well-known phrase, 'All politics is local.' Electoral concerns frequently compelled members of Congress to represent special interests rather than the general public welfare. Congressional riders like the one directed at the baseline rule tended to be anti-environment and anti-democratic. In most cases, they were attached to appropriations bills without debate (although this was not true for the baseline rider) and reflected the narrow interests of the members introducing them. By contrast, the executive branch was able to take the long and wide view basing environmental policy on national rather than local interests. Similarly, the Appellate Body's rulings in the gasoline dispute revealed that the WTO required members to consider the broader (cross-border) consequences of their policies and promoted consultation and cooperation on environmental matters (McBride, 1998).

Dartmouth economist Douglas Irwin also disagreed with environmentalists' interpretation of the rulings. He observed that the EPA was 'free to demand any standard of cleanliness it chose' as long as it applied the same one to domestic and foreign gasoline (Irwin, 2000, p. 193). Puzzled by Public Citizen's advocacy on the issue, he noted that 'Public Citizen, which decries corporate influence on government policy, put itself in the position of defending a rule that worked to the advantage of the domestic petroleum industry, one of the nation's most politically powerful special interest groups' (Irwin, 2000, p. 196).

Law lecturer Jennifer Schultz expressed more qualified approval of the rulings. She described the gasoline rule as a 'clear example' of green protection (protection under the guise of environmental objectives) (Schultz, 1996, p. 21). She disagreed with those who claimed the WTO was unsympathetic to the environment and suggested that the proper response to the rulings was to design laws that did not discriminate. Nevertheless, she observed that the Appellate Body lacked the expertise and legitimacy to rule on environmental matters. She proposed the formation of expert review groups and enhanced public participation to address these deficiencies (Schultz, 1996).

Others in the legal community rendered harsher assessments. Steve Charnovitz (1998, p. 912) criticized the Appellate Body for 'invent[ing] new requirements' in Article XX's chapeau and 'apply[ing] them arbitrarily'. He argued that it would be difficult for governments to design regulations that were consistent with the chapeau. Craig Dixon (2000, p. 119) remarked that the WTO merely paid 'lip service' to balancing trade and environmental objectives. The Appellate Body's interpretation of the chapeau would preclude nations from successfully exercising the exceptions for health and environmental regulations in Articles XX(b) and (g), respectively. Similarly, Martin McCrory and Eric Richards (1999, p. 44) worried that the Appellate Body's interpretation of the Article XX exceptions was 'overly hostile to domestic environmental concerns'.

2.9 RECONCILING TRADE AND THE ENVIRONMENT

The panel and Appellate Body rulings were open to criticism but not of the sort customarily made by the WTO's critics. It was true that the WTO impinged on national sovereignty. What treaty did not? In other contexts, environmentalists and consumer activists supported international arrangements that involved the loss of sovereignty. Indeed, most critics expressed outrage (with good reason) that the US had failed to sign on to treaties affecting global climate change, biodiversity and a host of other issues ranging from cigarettes to war crimes. This criticism can be dismissed, as can criticism that the rulings diminished US air quality. The EPA's own data demonstrated that gasoline 'as dirty or dirtier' than foreign gasoline was produced in the US. Equally, if not more compelling, the EPA's Assistant Administrator for Air and Radiation admitted in Congressional testimony that the differential baseline rules were designed to favor domestic refiners. And in oral arguments at the WTO, the US conceded that domestic refiners were afforded the more lenient individual baselines because the Administration wished to give them additional time to absorb the program's high financial and technical costs. Overall, it is hard to disagree with the WTO's conclusion that the differential baseline rules were driven by the desire to protect domestic refiners rather than to promote clean air.

Although the environmental community interpreted the decision as undermining clean air standards specifically and environmental policy in general, both the panel and Appellate Body reports suggested otherwise. Both emphasized that nations had the right to set their own standards but must not discriminate against imports as the US had so obviously and unnecessarily done in the case of the gasoline rule. Additionally, the Appellate Body broke new ground in finding that the baseline program was consistent with Article XX(g). This finding provided strong support for nations seeking to use this exception to justify measures designed to protect exhaustible natural resources. Importantly, the Appellate Body rejected an 'effects test', explaining that the results of conservation initiatives might not be apparent for years (WTO, 1996b, p. 21). In finding that the differential baseline rules were inconsistent with Article XX's chapeau, the Appellate Body demonstrated that nations were not permitted to use environmental policy to cloak protection. Ironically, this aspect of the ruling might have actually advanced the standing of environmental goals within the WTO by defusing the concerns of WTO members who feared that the environmental exception was open to abuse.

The Article XX rulings were less satisfactory in other respects. One overriding and troubling question lingered: was the panel's interpretation of Article XX(g) wrong? The panel examined whether the *differential* baseline rules were 'related to' conservation of clean air. The Appellate Body ruled that the panel should have examined whether the baseline program as a whole was 'related to' conservation of clean air. It is difficult to see why. Brazil and Venezuela did not dispute the baseline program. They disputed the differential baselines.

It is troubling that the panel and Appellate Body differed as to whether the offending regulations or the entire baseline program were the proper subject of the examination. It is also worrisome that the panel erred by relying on a ruling in a GATT dispute. In the past, panel rulings were not subject to appeal. As a result, errors would not necessarily have been identified or corrected, leaving some precedents of dubious value. In addition, Article XX's provisions are expressed in broad terms, which arguably lend themselves to varying interpretations. But errors and misunderstandings on such fundamental matters increase the burden on the Appellate Body, lengthen the dispute resolution process and reduce confidence in it. Although panel performance has improved over time as greater expertise has developed on the issues and treaty provisions in dispute, additional resources should be devoted to panels to improve the quality of their decisions, decrease the burden on the Appellate Body and enhance the credibility of the dispute resolution process. Additional suggestions to improve panel performance are explored in Chapter 9.

NOTES

1. Those opposing foreign refiner individual baselines were Senators: Baucus, Breaux, Cohen, Ford, Graham, Johnston, Lautenberg, Lieberman, Matthews, McConnell, Mikulski, Mitchell, Robb, Sarbanes, Sasser, Specter, Warner and Wofford; Representatives: Andrews, Barton, Bevill, Boucher, Brooks, Brown, Byrne, Chapman, Fields, Franks, Gallo, Greenwood, Hall, Hastert, Hochbruchkner, Machtley, Martin, McMillan, Mezvinsky, Mice, Moorhead, Oliver, Oxley, Pallone, Quillen, Richardson, Sisisky, Slattery, Smith, Tauzin and Zeliff.
    Those favoring foreign refiner individual baselines were Representatives: Frank, Manton, Markey, Studds and Synar.
2. See Waincymer (1996) for a discussion of alternative approaches to treaty interpretation.
3. For a more complete discussion of these issues, see Smith (1996).

REFERENCES

Bahree, B. (1995), 'Venezuelan case against US is test for WTO', *Asian Wall Street Journal*, 11 April, 2.

Bluestein, P. (1996), 'WTO ruling draws fierce criticism: Buchanan, Nader group assail decision against US on fuel imports', *Washington Post*, 19 January, F3.

Borrus, A., B. Javetski, J. Perry and B. Bremner (1996), 'Change of heart', *Business Week*, 20 May, 48.

Charnovitz, S. (1998), 'Environment and health under WTO dispute settlement', *The International Lawyer*, **32**(3), 901–22.

Choinski, A. (2002), 'Anatomy of a controversy: the balance of political forces behind the implementation of the WTO's gasoline decision', *Law and Policy in International Business*, **33**(4), 569–613.

Collier R. and G. Martin (1999), 'US laws diluted by trade pacts/rulings stir criticism across political spectrum', *San Francisco Chronicle*, 24 July, A1.

Cunningham, Richard (1995), 'Dispute settlement in the WTO: did we get what the United States wanted, or did we give up the only remedy that worked?', in Harvey Appelbaum and Lyn Schmitt (eds), *The GATT, the WTO and the Uruguay Round Agreements, Understanding the Fundamental Changes*, New York: Practicing Law Institute, pp. 549–78.

Danaher, K. (1996), 'Trade decision hurts environment', *Chicago Tribune*, 24 May, 28.

Dixon, C. (2000), 'Environmental survey of WTO dispute panel decisions since 1995: trade at all costs', *William & Mary Environmental Law & Policy Review*, **24**(1), 89–119.

EPA (Environmental Protection Agency) (1997), 'Regulation of fuels and fuel additives: baseline requirements for gasoline produced by foreign refiners, final rule (gasoline rule)', Washington, DC: *Federal Register*, **62**(167), 28 August, 45533–68.

Greenwire (1996), 'Worldview', 19 January.

Irwin, Douglas E. (2000), *Free Trade Under Fire*, Princeton: Princeton University Press.

Kovski, A. (1996), 'WTO's decision on gasoline regulation may receive split response on Capitol Hill', *The Oil Daily*, 25 January, 3.

McBride, S. (1998), 'Reforming executive and legislative relationships after reformulated gasoline: what's best for trade and environment?' *William & Mary Environmental Law & Policy Review*, **23**(1), 299–354.

McCrory, M. and E. Richards (1999), 'Clearing the air: the Clean Air Act, GATT and the WTO's reformulated gasoline decision', *UCLA Journal of Environmental Law & Policy*, **7**(1), 1–44.

Oil & Gas Journal (1996), 'The WTO's gasoline ruling', **28**(21), 8 July, 21.

Reddy, C. (1996), 'Hindu-editorial: dispute settlement: a WTO success story', *Hindu*, 10 November, NOPGCIT.

Retallack, S. (1997), 'The WTO's record so far – corporations: 3 / humanity and the environment: 0', *Ecologist*, **27**(4), July–August, 136–7.

Schultz, J. (1996), 'The demise of "green protectionism": the WTO decision on the US gasoline rule', *Denver Journal of International Law and Policy*, **25**(1), 1–24.

Smith, A. (1996), 'Executive-branch rulemaking and dispute settlement in the World Trade Organization: a proposal to increase public participation', *Michigan Law Review*, **94**(5), 1267–93.

Tonelson A. and L. Wallach (1996), 'We told you so, the WTO's first trade decision vindicates the warnings of critics', *The Washington Post*, 5 May, C4.

US House of Representatives (US House) (1995), *Reformulated Gasoline Hearing before the Subcommittee on Oversight and Investigations of the Committee on Energy and Commerce, 22 June 1994*, Washington, DC: Government Printing Office, 103rd Congress, Serial no. 103–155.

US Senate (1994), *Oversight of the Reformulated Gasoline Rule Hearing before the US Senate Committee on Environment and Public Works*, Washington, DC: Government Printing Office, 103rd Congress, Second Session, 22 April.

Waincymer, J. (1996), 'Reformulated gasoline under reformed WTO dispute settlement procedures: pulling Pandora out of a chapeau?', *Michigan Journal of International Law*, **18**(1), 141–81.

Woellert, L. (1996), 'US accepts defeat in WTO ruling on gas', *Washington Times*, 20 June, B7.

WTO (1994), *General Agreement on Tariffs and Trade* (GATT), Geneva: WTO.

WTO (1995a), *US – Standards for Reformulated and Conventional Gasoline, Request for Consultations* (Venezuela) (WT/DS2/1), Geneva: WTO, 24 January.

WTO (1995b), *US – Standards for Reformulated and Conventional Gasoline, Request for Consultations* (Brazil) (WT/DS4/1), Geneva: WTO, 10 April.

WTO (1996a), *US – Standards for Reformulated and Conventional Gasoline, Report of the Panel* (WT/DS2/R), Geneva: WTO, 29 January.

WTO (1996b), *US – Standards for Reformulated and Conventional Gasoline, Report of the Appellate Body* (WT/DS2/AB/R), Geneva: WTO, 29 April.
WTO (1997), *US – Standards for Reformulated and Conventional Gasoline, Status Report by the US* (WT/DS2/10/Add.7), Geneva: WTO, 26 August.

3. Shrimp–turtle

In 1996, India, Malaysia, Pakistan and Thailand challenged a US ban on shrimp imports from countries that did not employ turtle excluder devices (TEDs). The US claimed that the shrimp ban was necessary to conserve sea turtles, an endangered species protected under the Convention on International Trade in Endangered Species of Wild Fauna and Flora (CITES). The four Asian nations disagreed, noting their own status as signatories to CITES as well as other multilateral environmental agreements protecting sea turtles. The dispute galvanized opposition to the WTO in the environmental community in the US and other developed nations where the rulings were interpreted as undermining US environmental policy. At the same time, many in the developing world interpreted the rulings as permitting the US to force its trade partners to comply with its environmental agenda. Indeed, largely on those grounds, Malaysia contested the adequacy of US efforts to revise its regulations to comply with the rulings. Environmental organizations were also dissatisfied with US compliance measures and challenged them in the US Court of International Trade as too weak to offer adequate protection to sea turtles. The dispute had repercussions within the WTO as the Appellate Body's decision to admit amicus curiae (friend of the court) briefs submitted by environmental organizations provoked opposition from developing nations. For these reasons, the shrimp–turtle dispute provides a rich vehicle to explore developed and developing nations' conflicting environmental agendas and the influence of the WTO, multilateral environmental agreements (MEAs), non-governmental organizations (NGOs) and the courts on environmental policy.

3.1   SECTION 609

Found in tropical and subtropical habitats, sea turtles spend most of their lives at sea but reproduce on land. Efforts to protect sea turtles began during the early 1970s when it became apparent that human activities threatened sea turtles with extinction both directly through exploitation of eggs, tortoise shells and turtle meat as well as indirectly through habitat degradation and incidental capture in fisheries. By 1978, all six species of sea turtles found in US waters had been granted protected status under the Endangered Species Act (ESA) (Rudloe and Rudloe, 1989). Nevertheless, sea turtle mortality remained high as sea turtles continued to be caught as by-catch by shrimp trawlers in the Gulf of Mexico and the Atlantic Ocean off the southeastern US. In response, the National Marine Fishery Service (NMFS) developed turtle excluder devices (TEDs), trapdoors that permitted turtles and other large organisms to escape shrimp nets. Beginning in 1983, NMFS promoted TEDs on a voluntary basis (WTO, 1998a). NMFS pilot projects demonstrated that TEDs were highly effective: 97 percent of sea turtles encountered were released unharmed with minimal shrimp loss (2 percent) (Jones, 1993). But shrimp fishermen (shrimpers) vehemently opposed the program, claiming that TEDs reduced shrimp catch by 20 to 50 percent (Rudloe and Rudloe, 1989). Because most refused to participate in the voluntary program, a mandatory program was introduced in 1987. Shrimpers remained opposed to the program, launched a series of unsuccessful lawsuits, and eventually took their fight to Congress (Rudloe and Rudloe, 1989).

Congress decided to phase in the mandatory program over a three-year period ending in 1990. Initially, shrimp trawlers were permitted to choose between using TEDs and observing tow time restrictions. At the end of the three-year phase-in period, shrimp trawlers were required to use TEDs (with limited exceptions) in all US waters where sea turtles were likely to be found. To prevent the TED requirement from creating a competitive disadvantage for the US shrimp industry, Congress enacted legislation (Section 609 of Public Law 101-162) in 1989 requiring the State Department to negotiate sea turtle conservation agreements with other nations. More controversially, Section 609 imposed a ban on shrimp imports harvested with fishing technology that might harm sea turtles. Shrimp harvesting nations could avert the ban provided that the State Department certified their sea turtle conservation programs as comparable to the US program in design and effectiveness (WTO, 1998a).

Fearing that Section 609 would have an extraordinary impact on US trade partners because of the large number of nations exporting shrimp to the US, the State Department developed implementation guidelines in

1991 that restricted Section 609's scope to the Caribbean and western Atlantic and gave nations in the region three years to comply. The guidelines took a flexible approach to the comparability requirement. Certification could be achieved by programs mandating TEDs or other effective mortality reduction measures. The comparability requirement became more restrictive under the revised guidelines issued by the Clinton Administration in 1993. Effective 1 May 1994, certification was contingent upon the use of TEDs, although exceptions were permitted for shrimp harvested in waters that were not inhabited by sea turtles as well as for farm-raised (aquaculture) and manually harvested shrimp (US Department of State, 1996). Thanks to briefer tow times, vessels employing manual net collection (artisanal) methods were anticipated to experience lower rates of incidental sea turtle capture than trawlers employing mechanized retrieval systems (WTO, 1998a).

3.2   EARTH ISLAND INSTITUTE GOES TO COURT

Environmental organizations objected to the State Department's implementation of Section 609. Led by Earth Island Institute, they filed a lawsuit in federal district court. After the US Court of Appeals ruled that federal district courts did not have jurisdiction over trade policy, Earth Island Institute took the case to the Court of International Trade (CIT). The Court of International Trade (CIT) ruled that Section 609 contained no geographical limitations and ordered the State Department to impose the shrimp ban and related certification procedures globally effective 1 May 1996 (US Court of International Trade, 1999). In April 1996, the State Department issued new guidelines, which extended the ban and certification procedures to all waters inhabited by sea turtles. In addition, the 1996 guidelines permitted shrimp imports from uncertified nations provided that the exporter and a government official attested that the shrimp had been harvested with TEDs or under other conditions that did not adversely affect sea turtles (US Department of State, 1996).

Earth Island Institute charged that the revisions obliterated Section 609 and returned to the Court of International Trade. The State Department took the position that permitting imports of TED-caught shrimp from uncertified countries increased the program's flexibility while satisfying Section 609's TED requirement. Earth Island Institute maintained that Section 609 required US trade partners to employ TEDs on all of their shrimp harvesting vessels. In the absence of such a requirement, fleets would have little incentive to adopt TEDs other than on vessels serving the US market. Worse, the requirement could easily be evaded altogether by fleets claiming falsely to employ TEDs. Congressional intent would be frustrated: Section 609 would neither protect sea turtles nor level the playing field for US shrimp trawlers. The court agreed with Earth Island Institute. Since US trawlers were required to use TEDs, foreign programs seeking certification were required to demonstrate that their fleets employed TEDs. Exceptions were permitted for shrimp harvested in aquaculture, by artisanal methods, or in waters uninhabited by sea turtles, conditions that did not adversely affect sea turtles (US Court of International Trade, 1999).

The federal government and Earth Island Institute sparred in court for the next several years. The next round went to the federal government, which appealed the Court of International Trade's (CIT) ruling to the US Court of Appeals for the Federal Circuit. The Federal Circuit court vacated the CIT's rulings on procedural grounds in June of 1998 (US Court of Appeals for the Federal Circuit, 2002)

By January 1998, the US had certified 43 nations. Nineteen, predominantly Latin American and Caribbean, nations were certified as operating programs comparable to that of the US (Belize, Brazil, China, Colombia, Costa Rica, Ecuador, El Salvador, Fiji, Guatemala, Guyana, Honduras, Indonesia, Mexico, Nicaragua, Nigeria, Panama, Thailand, Trinidad & Tobago, and Venezuela). Sixteen nations were certified on the grounds that sea turtles were not present in their cold waters (Argentina, Belgium, Canada, Chile, Denmark, Finland, Germany, Iceland, Ireland, Netherlands, New Zealand, Norway, Russia, Sweden, United Kingdom and Uruguay). Eight countries were certified as artisanal shrimp harvesters (Bahamas, Brunei, Dominican Republic, Haiti, Jamaica, Oman, Peru and Sri Lanka) (WTO, 1998a).

3.3   THE WTO DISPUTE

In October 1996, India, Malaysia, Pakistan and Thailand jointly requested consultations with the United States on Section 609 and the 1996 implementation guidelines. The parties were unable to resolve the dispute through negotiations. In February 1997, the parties agreed that one panel would undertake a joint investigation of the disputes. Testifying to the wide interest in the matter, 16 countries, including many of those receiving certification, participated as third parties

(Australia, Colombia, Costa Rica, Ecuador, El Salvador, European Union, Guatemala, Hong Kong, Japan, Mexico, Nigeria, Philippines, Senegal, Singapore, Sri Lanka and Venezuela).[1] The panel met the parties in June and September of 1997 and issued its report in April 1998. Lasting 14 months, the panel proceedings significantly overshot the nine-month timeline set in the Dispute Settlement Understanding (DSU) (WTO, 1998a).

India, Malaysia, Pakistan and Thailand challenged Section 609 as incompatible with the General Agreement on Tariffs and Trade's (GATT or General Agreement hereafter) Article XI, which prohibited most quotas, bans and other quantitative restrictions. They claimed that Section 609 also violated Article I's prohibition against discrimination among like products. They maintained that product likeness was determined by product characteristics, not process or production methods (PPMs) such as TEDs. Consequently, the US was required to treat shrimp from uncertified countries as favorably as those from certified countries regardless of the manner of harvest. The US was also required to treat new and original program participants in an equally favorable manner. But the four Asian nations were granted just three or four months to phase in their programs while the original participants had three years to comply. The original participants also benefited from technical and financial assistance from the US through the Inter-American Convention for the Protection and Conservation of Sea Turtles (IAC). The US had not entered into sea turtle conservation agreements with the four nations or provided them with technical and financial assistance. For the same reasons, Section 609 violated Article XIII, which prohibited discriminatory application of product restrictions (WTO, 1998a).

The US acknowledged that Section 609 imposed an import ban on shrimp from uncertified countries and declined to contest the complainants' challenge under Article X1. Instead, the US invoked Article XX, which provided exceptions to obligations under the General Agreement. The US argued that Section 609 qualified for two exceptions: the Article XX(g) exception for conservation measures and the Article XX (b) exception for measures necessary to protect animal life and health. The four Asian nations contended that the US was not permitted to apply the exceptions beyond its borders or to impose unilateral environmental measures on its trade partners. As the parties agreed that Section 609 violated Article XI's prohibition on quantitative restrictions, the panel decided that it was unnecessary to explore their arguments under Articles I and XIII. Section 609's fate hinged on Article XX (WTO, 1998a).

Measures seeking to qualify as exceptions under Article XX were required to pass a two-part test: (1) satisfy the terms of one of Article XX's sub-paragraphs (in this case either (g) or (b)); (2) meet the conditions set out in the introduction to Article XX (known as the chapeau). To prevent governments from abusing the exceptions, the chapeau prohibited regulations that were implemented in a manner that created arbitrary or unjustifiable discrimination among trade partners or constituted disguised restrictions on trade (WTO, 1994a).

In an unusual step, the panel reversed the customary order of the investigation and examined the chapeau first. The panel began its analysis with the observation that states were obliged to avoid actions that would frustrate the object and purpose of the agreements to which they were parties. The panel acknowledged that the WTO Agreement addressed environmental goals but stressed that its principal objective was to spur economic development through liberalized trade. Permitting members to impose unilateral conservation measures would jeopardize that pursuit because the multilateral trading system could no longer guarantee members predictable access to other markets. Instead, exporting nations would face numerous and possibly conflicting policy requirements. Soon the entire multilateral trading system would cease to exist. The regulation in dispute might not pose a significant threat on its own, nevertheless, there was still the potential for serious harm should the imposition of the measure encourage other governments to impose similar ones. Unilateral measures like Section 609 that posed such a risk constituted unjustifiable discrimination and were inconsistent with the requirements of Article XX's chapeau (WTO, 1998a).

The panel also faulted the US for failing to make a serious effort to negotiate with the four nations before imposing Section 609. As signatories to the Convention on International Trade in Endangered Species (CITES), all five nations agreed to refrain from trade in sea turtles and to develop sea turtle conservation programs. Rather than mandating any specific measures, CITES delegated program development and implementation to participating governments, as did Agenda 21, the Fish Stocks Agreement and the LOS Convention, three UN-sponsored initiatives that encouraged governments to reduce the incidental capture of non-target species during fishing and trawling. These agreements encouraged governments to develop collaborative solutions to cross-border environmental problems and discouraged unilateral initiatives.

Additionally, Section 609 required the US to negotiate sea turtle conservation agreements with its trade partners, but the US limited its efforts to nations in the Americas. Further, if sea turtles were a shared global resource as claimed by the US, their protection could best be achieved by negotiating a joint strategy with other nations sharing a common interest in their survival. Finally, as implemented, Section 609 failed to address the diverse economic, social and environmental factors affecting sea turtle conservation in the four Asian nations. However, the preamble to the WTO Agreement obliged members to pursue environmental objectives in ways that took into account members' diverse situations and varying levels of economic development. Similarly, the experts consulted by the panel recommended that sea turtle conservation programs reflect local conditions and priorities (WTO, 1998a).

On appeal, the Appellate Body rejected the panel's decision to reverse the order of its Article XX investigation. The Appellate Body concluded that the panel erred by examining the conditions in the chapeau prior to those detailed in the exceptions themselves. The first order of business was to investigate whether the shrimp ban was provisionally qualified under either the Article XX(g) or (b) exception. The Appellate Body went on to speculate that the panel's decision to invert the Article XX analysis led it to err in its examinations of the chapeau. Instead of examining the application of Section 609, the panel examined its design and purpose and concluded erroneously that they were in conflict with those of the entire GATT/WTO system. The Appellate Body reversed the panel, explaining that the deployment of the Article XX exceptions necessarily entailed the imposition of unilateral measures conditioning market access. The exceptions had been included in the agreement to insure that governments could pursue conservation and other activities 'recognized as important and legitimate in character' (WTO, 1998b, para. 121). The panel's interpretation 'render[ed] most, if not all, of the specific exceptions of Article XX inutile' (WTO, 1998b, para. 121).

As the US had invoked the Article XX(g) and (b) exceptions, Section 609's design and purpose were properly explored in an analysis of those provisions. Although the panel had not ruled on the exceptions, the Appellate Body proceeded to perform the analysis, observing that it felt obliged to do so in order to determine whether Section 609 was entitled to an Article XX exception. The Appellate Body had taken a similar course in several other disputes, including the gasoline case where it had also been necessary to rule on legal matters not addressed by the panel (WTO, 1998b).

Invoked successfully for the first time in the gasoline dispute, Article XX(g) allowed members to seek exceptions for measures 'relating to the conservation of exhaustible natural resources if such measures be made effective in conjunction with restrictions on domestic production and consumption' (WTO, 1994a). The US argued that Section 609 was 'related to' sea conservation in as much as shrimp trawling posed the most significant global threat to sea turtles and TEDs were recognized as the most effective method for reducing trawl-related mortality. As an endangered species, sea turtles qualified as an exhaustible natural resource. Finally, the TED requirement entailed restrictions on domestic as well as foreign vessels (WTO, 1998a, 1998b).

Reprising arguments made by Venezuela and Brazil in the gasoline dispute, the four Asian nations contended that the Article XX(g) exception did not apply to sea turtles. Drafted in 1947, sub-paragraph (g) was intended to apply to non-living, non-reproducible resources such as minerals. As living natural resources, sea turtles were capable of reproduction; hence, they were renewable rather than exhaustible. In addition, TEDs failed to satisfy the 'related to' requirement. The requirement entailed a substantial relationship between TEDs and sea turtle conservation. However, shrimp trawling was not the greatest danger facing sea turtles in their jurisdictions. Direct exploitation of sea turtles for food, pollution, coastal development and fish trawling were far more significant threats in Asia. As a result, it was not apparent that the adoption of TEDs would enhance turtle conservation in their waters. Finally, TEDs failed the even-handedness test. TEDs might be appropriate in the US where shrimp trawling posed the most significant danger to sea turtles, but different conditions in the four Asian nations necessitated alternative measures, including restrictions on fishing and shrimping near nesting areas, monitoring of nesting areas, placement of eggs in hatcheries and release of hatchlings to the sea (WTO, 1998a).

The Appellate Body rejected most of the complainants' arguments and concluded that Section 609 was provisionally justified under the Article XX(g) exception. On the matter of whether sea turtles qualified as exhaustible natural resources, the Appellate Body noted that the text did not exclude living resources. Moreover, renewability and exhaustibility were not 'mutually exclusive' concepts as the complainants claimed (WTO, 1998b, para. 128). Although living resources were capable of reproduction, they nevertheless could be exhausted and were 'just as "finite"' as minerals and other non-living resources (WTO, 1998b, para. 128). Moreover, the text must be interpreted in view of current environmental concerns. WTO members had embraced these concerns during the Uruguay Round when they adopted language promoting sustainable development and environmental protection in the preamble to the WTO Agreement. In addition, the multilateral environmental agreements referenced throughout the dispute, including the LOS Convention, Convention on Biological Diversity (CBD) and the Convention on the Conservation of Migratory Species of Wild Animals (CMS) all recognized the importance of protecting living natural resources. Finally, as signatories to CITES, all of the parties to the dispute had acknowledged that sea turtles were endangered (WTO, 1998b).

In order to satisfy the 'related to' aspect of Article (g), the Appellate Body ruled that Section 609 would have to satisfy the 'substantial relationship' test that it had articulated in the gasoline case (WTO, 1996, p. 19). Section 609's design and structure were required to have a strong relationship with its purpose; means were to be closely related to ends. In the case of Section 609, the Appellate found that the means were 'reasonably related' to the ends as shrimp trawling posed a major threat to sea turtles and the use of TEDs mitigated that threat (WTO, 1998b, para. 141). Further, Section 609 was not 'disproportionately wide in its scope and reach' because it included exceptions that waived the TED requirement for shrimp that were harvested under conditions that did not adversely affect sea turtles (WTO, 1998b, para. 141). Section 609 satisfied the even-handed requirement because it imposed similar requirements on domestic and foreign shrimp fleets (WTO, 1998b).

Having provisionally justified Section 609 under Article XX(g), the Appellate Body ruled that it was not necessary to examine the disputants' claims under Article XX(b). Instead, the Appellate Body revisited the chapeau. Here, it emphasized that it was required to examine the application of Section 609. For such an examination, it was not possible to claim, as the US did, that the conservation purposes pursued through Section 609 justified differential treatment. Measures could be provisionally justified under Article XX(g) but nevertheless be incompatible with the chapeau's requirements. The role of the chapeau was to insure that a balance was preserved between members' right to claim exceptions and their duty to respect the rights of other members (WTO, 1998b). The Appellate Body's task was to define a 'line of equilibrium' between those rights and duties as they related to the shrimp ban (WTO, 1998b, para. 159).

The Appellate Body concluded that the implementation of Section

609 failed to satisfy the conditions set out in the chapeau. As applied, Section 609 required other nations to adopt turtle conservation programs that were virtually identical to that of the US regardless of differing local conditions. The inflexibility of the regime created two types of discrimination. First, TED-harvested shrimp from uncertified countries were treated less favorably than those from certified countries even though the same harvest method was employed in both types of countries. Second, by imposing the TED requirement on countries facing different circumstances, the US had discriminated against countries where different conditions prevailed (WTO, 1998b). With this latter ruling, the Appellate Body extended the definition of discrimination beyond the terms expressed in the chapeau, which addressed only arbitrary and unjustifiable discrimination between countries where the same conditions prevailed.

Like the panel, the Appellate criticized the US for its failure to negotiate a turtle conservation agreement with the complainants. The Appellate Body emphasized that this failure constituted unjustifiable discrimination because the US had negotiated an agreement with other WTO members. Moreover, the various multilateral environmental agreements that the US had invoked during the proceedings urged signatories to develop multilateral responses to cross-border environmental problems, as did the WTO's Committee on Trade and the Environment (CTE). As the US had negotiated a turtle conservation agreement with nations in the Americas, it was apparent that negotiations posed an alternative to the unilateral imposition of Section 609. The more generous phase-in periods made available to nations in the Americas added to the ban's discriminatory effect. The Appellate Body acknowledged that the differential phase-in periods resulted from the Court of International Trade's rulings but explained that WTO members were responsible for the activities of all branches of their governments (WTO, 1998b).

In addition, the absence of procedural safeguards resulted in arbitrary discrimination between certified and uncertified nations. Shrimp-harvesting nations had no opportunity to advocate for their programs or to respond to concerns about them. The State Department did not notify applicants once a certification decision was made. It merely posted certification decisions in the *Federal Register*. Countries denied certification were not provided with a written explanation of their program's deficiencies and were not given an opportunity to appeal. Greater transparency and accountability were needed to insure that uncertified nations were not denied due process (WTO, 1998b).

The Appellate Body concluded that the shrimp ban violated the chapeau's prohibition against arbitrary and unjustifiable discrimination. The Appellate Body did not examine whether Section 609 was applied in a manner that constituted a disguised restriction on trade. As in the gasoline case, the Appellate Body felt that it was necessary to explain what it had and had '*not* decided' (original emphasis) owing to the broad interest in the dispute (WTO, 1998b, para. 185). It had *not* decided that WTO members could not take measures to preserve sea turtles and other endangered species on their own or in collaboration with other governments inside or outside of the WTO. According to the Appellate Body, 'Clearly, they can and should' (WTO, 1998b, para. 185). However, they were required to do so in ways that complied with their obligations under the various GATT/WTO agreements. Section 609 failed in this regard because it had been implemented in ways that created arbitrary and unjustifiable discrimination among WTO members. However, the environmental purposes pursued by Section 609 were compatible with the Article XX(g) exception for conservation measures.

3.4   COMPLIANCE

The Dispute Settlement Body (DSB) accepted the panel and Appellate Body reports in November 1998 and recommended that the US bring Section 609 into conformity with its WTO obligations. Shortly thereafter, the parties agreed that the US would have until December 1999 to comply with the recommendations (WTO, 2001c). The State Department issued revised regulations in July 1999. As in the past, the regulations promoted the adoption of TEDs. However, certification of foreign programs was no longer limited to those requiring TEDs. Certification was also available to governments that could demonstrate that other conservation programs were as effective as the US TED-based program. When reviewing programs that did not employ TEDs, the State Department was obliged to take into account the varying circumstances of the countries seeking certification. The revised regulations also introduced several procedural safeguards. US officials would visit nations seeking certification to meet officials and to review their programs. Foreign governments would receive a written preliminary decision indicating remedial measures necessary for certification. US officials would consider additional information submitted in response to the preliminary decision and would provide a written explanation of the final certification decision. Governments denied certification would be permitted to re-apply at any time (US Department of State, 1999).

In October 2000, Malaysia challenged US compliance on the grounds that it was insufficient to modify the import ban. In light of the Appellate Body's preference for cooperative, cross-border conservation efforts, the US was required to lift the ban until a regional consensus could be achieved. However, a regional sea conservation agreement (Indian Ocean – South-East Asian Marine Turtle Memorandum of Understanding (IOSEA MOU)) had yet to be finalized. US efforts to improve the flexibility of the certification process were also deficient. Despite the changes, the US continued to compel other nations to adopt programs that were comparable to its program and failed to take local conditions into account. Malaysia declined to submit to such interference and chose not to seek certification or technical assistance from the US (WTO, 2001c).

The original panel revisited the matter and rejected virtually every aspect of Malaysia's complaint against US compliance measures. Using the Inter-American Convention for the Protection and Conservation of Sea Turtles (IAC) as a benchmark, the panel ruled that US efforts to negotiate with the complainants individually and regionally through the IOSEA MOU constituted serious, good faith efforts envisioned by the Appellate Body. The 1999 guidelines were sufficiently flexible to satisfy the requirements of the chapeau. As revised, the guidelines permitted imports of TED-caught shrimp from uncertified as well as certified countries. The modified comparability requirement insured that local conditions would be taken into account as foreign programs were no longer required to be identical to the US program. The US had transferred technology and provided training and other types of aid to various countries, including Australia, Bahrain and Pakistan, and through regional fora. New procedural safeguards removed the due process problems that existed under the 1996 guidelines (WTO, 2001c). Undaunted, Malaysia appealed the panel's finings. The Appellate Body upheld the panel on every point: the US had addressed the comparability, technical assistance and due process problems and had made a serious, good faith effort to negotiate a regional agreement. The US was not obliged to conclude that agreement before imposing the shrimp ban, as Malaysia contended. Requiring the US to do so would give any party to the negotiations 'in effect, a veto over whether the US could fulfill its WTO obligations' (WTO, 2001d, para. 123).[2]

3.5   AMICUS BRIEFS

Because the dispute resolution rules limited participation to members, WTO panels had refused to consider amicus curiae (friend of the court) briefs submitted by individuals and organizations interested in disputes that preceded shrimp–turtle. As discussed below, the Appellate Body attempted to widen the scope for amicus submissions in the shrimp–turtle dispute but encountered opposition from members that escalated in the asbestos dispute (Chapter 5).

The shrimp–turtle panel received two unsolicited briefs from environmental organizations. One was submitted by the Worldwide Fund for Nature and the other was submitted jointly by the Center for Marine Conservation (CMC) and the Center for International Environmental Law (CIEL). India, Malaysia, Pakistan and Thailand opposed consideration of the briefs. The US encouraged the panel to make use of the briefs, noting that the dispute resolution rules authorized panels to seek information from relevant sources. The panel disagreed, explaining that the rules gave parties and third parties the exclusive right to make submissions. The panel would consider only briefs that were incorporated into member government submissions. The US responded by attaching a portion of the brief submitted jointly by the Center for Marine Conservation (CMC) and Center for International Environmental Law (CIEL) (WTO, 1998a).

The Appellate Body reversed the panel, explaining that the dispute resolution rules not only authorized panels to seek information from any 'relevant source' but also obliged them to adopt procedures with 'sufficient flexibility so as to ensure high-quality panel reports' (WTO, 1994b, Article 13.2 and Article 12.2 cited in WTO 1998b, paras. 104 and 105). Together, these provisions gave panels 'broad authority' to oversee the information gathering aspects of their investigations (WTO, 1998b, para. 107). Consistent with that authority, panels had the option of accepting or rejecting any information received, regardless of whether it was solicited. The Appellate Body stressed that panels retained discretion over the matter. Since individuals and organizations had no standing within the dispute settlement process, they had no right to make submissions or to have them considered by panels. Those rights were limited to members who participated as parties or third parties to disputes (WTO, 1998b).

The US included three amicus briefs prepared by Earth Island Institute, the Center for International Environmental Law (CIEL) and the Worldwide Fund for Nature as appendices in its submission to the Appellate Body. Later a revised version of the CIEL brief was submitted directly to the Appellate Body. India, Malaysia, Pakistan and Thailand objected that the dispute settlement rules limited appeals to matters of law and legal interpretation addressed in panel reports. The briefs raised two problems in that they addressed factual matters that were beyond the scope of the appeal and, in some instances, took positions that differed from those of the US. The US explained that it was proper to share the briefs with the Appellate Body because of the environmental organizations' interest in and expertise on the matters in dispute. At the same time, the US qualified its support for the briefs. The US accepted the arguments in the briefs only to the extent that they were consistent with its positions. Although the Appellate Body accepted the briefs as part of the US submission, it declined to consider their arguments because of the US's conditional acceptance of them (WTO, 1998b).

When the panel and appellate reports were adopted by the Dispute Settlement Body in November 1998, several governments criticized the amicus rulings. Thailand complained that the Appellate Body had exceeded its authority and infringed member prerogatives by expanding the scope for NGO submissions. India asserted that the Appellate Body erred by considering the briefs before the US had articulated their relationship to its submission. Malaysia argued that the dispute resolution rules limited participation to parties and third parties. Hong Kong agreed, remarking that it was unfair to allow NGOs to participate but to exclude governments that were not parties or third parties to the disputes. Mexico complained that the participation of external actors created the possibility that political rather than legal issues might be decisive. Hong Kong and Malaysia called for the matter to be addressed in the upcoming review of the dispute settlement rules (WTO, 1998c).

These arguments were voiced by a larger number of members with greater intensity at a General Council Meeting held two years later for the sole purpose of addressing the Appellate Body's decision to expedite the acceptance of unsolicited briefs in the asbestos dispute. At the end of the General Council meeting, it was clear that only the US unqualifiedly approved the Appellate Body's efforts to facilitate the submission of amicus briefs (WTO, 2001a). In the face of vocal and widespread opposition from the membership, the Appellate Body took a step backward. While it did not suspend the application procedure implemented in the asbestos dispute, it rejected all of the briefs submitted under it (WTO, 2001b).

The briefs controversy was revisited the following year in the compliance phase of the shrimp–turtle dispute. The compliance panel received unsolicited amicus briefs from the National Wildlife Federation and the Earth Justice Legal Defense Fund. Malaysia maintained that the dispute settlement rules did not permit panels to accept unsolicited briefs. Further, members had expressed their broad opposition to unsolicited amicus submissions at the previous fall's special meeting of the General Council. The US held that the panel had the authority to accept both submissions but recommended that it consider only the National Wildlife brief as the Earth Justice brief was less germane. To insure that the National Wildlife brief was considered, the US attached it to its submission. Following the lead of the US, the panel declined to accept the Earth Justice brief and accepted the National Wildlife brief as part of the US submission (WTO, 2001c). Two additional briefs figured in the dispute when Malaysia appealed the panel's compliance rulings. The US attached a brief jointly submitted by the American Humane Society and the Humane Society International to its appellate submission. University of Michigan Law Professor Robert Howse submitted a brief directly to the Appellate Body. As the US maintained the same sort of qualified support for the Humane Society brief that it had expressed for the portion of the CMC/CIEL brief attached to its submission to the original panel, the Appellate Body again considered only the arguments presented by the US. Using ambiguous language, the Appellate Body stated that it had 'not found it necessary to take into account' Professor Howse's brief (WTO, 2001d, para. 78). The Appellate Body used the same language to describe the disposition of a brief that it received in the hot-rolled lead dispute (WTO, 2000). Chastened by the member opposition expressed at the General Council meeting, the Appellate formulated a less than satisfying compromise. While affirming members' right to attach briefs to their submissions and seemingly accepting unsolicited briefs, the Appellate Body would not draw upon them in its analysis of the issues in dispute.

3.6   IMPLICATIONS FOR SOVEREIGNTY, PPMS AND MEAS

Among the key players in the shrimp–turtle dispute, the US government, the apparent 'loser', was the most satisfied with its outcome. Upon the release of the initial appellate rulings, US Trade Representative Charlene Barshefsky remarked, 'We disagree with the Appellate Body's assessment that we have not implemented the law in an even-handed manner.' But 'the Appellate body has rightly recognized that our shrimp–turtle law is an important and legitimate conservation measure' (*Gazette*, 1998). In addition to acknowledging environmental goals, the shrimp–turtle rulings approved the extraterritorial application of a unilateral environmental measure and expanded the range of permissible environmental measures to include process and production methods (PPMs). Conventional wisdom held that import restrictions affecting the manner in which products were produced or processed were impermissible (Charnovitz, 2002). Since environmental protection was frequently advanced by regulations that affected how products were produced or processed, the prohibition was seen as drastically limiting the scope for environmental policy. Although the US blocked the adoption of the GATT-era tuna–dolphin rulings, they reinforced the conventional wisdom by rejecting a regulation that permitted only dolphin-safe tuna to be sold in the US. Like the shrimp ban, the tuna ban required domestic and foreign fishermen to reduce the incidental capture of a vulnerable, non-target species. The Appellate Body's shrimp–turtle rulings defied the conventional wisdom and gave approval to a conservation program based on the use of TEDs, a PPM.

Thus it was perplexing that environmentalists viewed the shrimp–turtle rulings as a defeat. According to the World Wildlife Fund's David Schorr, the shrimp turtle rulings demonstrated that the WTO was 'biased against the environment and in favor of trade at any cost' (Selinger, 1998). Matthew Stilwell, a spokesperson for the Center for International Environmental Law (CIEL) acknowledged that, unlike the panel rulings, the appellate decision had recognized the admissibility of NGO briefs and the right of governments to use trade measures to promote environmental protection. The appeal had produced 'better law' but the result was the 'same': an environmental measure had been deemed incompatible with WTO obligations (Swardson, 1998). Friend of the Earth's David Waskow observed that the compliance ruling, 'although on its face a victory, really in many ways undercuts countries' abilities to protect endangered species' because 'it requires countries to jump through diplomatic hoops before taking any action' (*Record*, 2001). Daniel A. Seligman, a trade policy analyst with the Sierra Club, articulated the most troubling aspect of the outcome for many in the environmental community: the administration's compliance measures 'radically weakened' Section 609, compromising sea turtle recovery throughout the world (Peterson, 1999).

This last criticism cannot be dismissed. The changes unequivocally weakened the program. As environmentalists predicted, relaxing the comparability requirement reduced the incentive for governments to mandate TEDs. In 1998, 19 nations were certified on the basis of their mandatory TED programs. By 2005, the number had declined to 13. Overall, 37 of the 70 nations exporting shrimp to the US in 2005 were certified by the State Department: fleets in eight nations employed artisanal methods and 16 nations' cold waters were not inhabited by sea turtles. In addition, Australia and Brazil took advantage of the 'TED-caught exception' for uncertified nations that were able to demonstrate that their segregation and enforcement procedures insured that only TED-caught shrimp were exported to the US. These 39 nations accounted for one-third of US shrimp imports in 2005.[3] Two-thirds of US shrimp imports were admitted under the more porous shipment declaration process, which relied on exporters and local officials to certify that each shipment of shrimp exported to the US was harvested in a manner that was not detrimental to sea turtles (in cold waters, from aquaculture or with turtle-safe fishing techniques (National Marine Fisheries Service, 2006; US Department of State, 2005).

Six nations accounted for nearly all (97 percent) of the shrimp imported under the shipment declaration process. Thailand alone held a whopping 27 percent share of US shrimp imports in 2005. Its share was more than double Viet Nam's (12 percent), Indonesia's (10 percent) and India's (9 percent). Bangladesh and Malaysia held shares in the 3 to 4 percent range. Thailand and Indonesia operated TED-certified programs as recently as 2001 and 2003, respectively (US Department of State, 2001, 2003). Had they retained their certifications, more than 70 percent of US shrimp imports would have been certified in 2005. Had the other four nations joined Thailand and Indonesia on the State Department's 2005 certification list, 98 percent of US shrimp imports would have been certified under Section 609 (National Marine Fisheries Service, 2006; US Department of State, 2005).

Clearly, regional conservation efforts were less successful in the Indian Ocean and South-East Asia region (IOSEA) than in the Americas. While 12 nations in the Americas operated TED certified programs in 2005, Pakistan was the only Asian nation to do so. China, Fiji, Hong Kong, Oman and Sri Lanka were certified as manual harvesting nations (US Department of State, 2005). However, only China accounted for a substantial share of US imports (6 percent) (National Marine Fisheries Service, 2006). Moreover, the Indian Ocean and South-East Asian regional agreement encouraged but did not mandate sea turtle conservation measures. Further, participation was not universal. As of May 2006, India and Malaysia had yet to sign on (IOSEA, 2006).

Nevertheless, the shrimp–turtle rulings were reasonable and necessary. The US was permitted to prohibit the sale of shrimp that was harvested in a manner detrimental to sea turtles. In order to do so, it could require foreign fleets seeking access to the US market to use turtle-friendly techniques. By refusing to allow the US to impose the requirement on other producers, the decision insured that India, Malaysia, Pakistan and Thailand were able to determine their own sea turtle conservation programs. A contrary decision, one favored by the environmentalists and the Court of International Trade, would have trampled on the four nations' sovereignty over environmental policy.

The other assessments from environmentalists ignored the favorable implications of the rulings for multilateral as well as unilateral environmental initiatives. Both the panel and Appellate Body observed that the preamble to the WTO Agreement espoused commitments to sustainable development and environmental protection that were compatible with the environmental objectives pursued through multilateral environmental agreements (MEAs). While the panel suggested that those commitments were subordinate to trade goals, the Appellate Body strongly rejected that view. In addition, the Appellate Body used the commitments to protect endangered species embodied in CITES and other MEAs to justify the shrimp ban under Article XX(g). Seemingly innocuous, in fact that aspect of the Appellate Body's rulings was potentially significant for governments seeking to impose environmental measures as it implied that measures taken to comply with MEAs were likely to qualify for an exception under Article XX (Scott, 2004). Because that possibility was controversial within the WTO membership, particularly among developing nations, who were less likely to impose such measures, clarifying the relationship between WTO rules and MEA obligations was added to the agenda for the Doha round of trade talks, although little progress was made on the issue during the round.

Both the panel and Appellate Body deployed MEAs to make the case that multilateral measures were preferred to unilateral measures. Nonetheless, the Appellate Body's rulings provided emphatic support for the right of governments to impose unilateral environmental measures. The Appellate Body stressed that the unilateral imposition of restrictions conditioning market access was 'a common aspect' of measures qualifying for an exception under Article XX (WTO, 1998b, para. 121). In its compliance rulings, the Appellate Body noted that 'it was one thing to prefer' international consensus and 'another to require' that measures be taken under multilateral agreements (WTO, 2001d, para. 124). On that basis, the Appellate Body rejected Malaysia's claim that the US was required to lift the shrimp ban while negotiations promoting sea turtle conservation in the Indian Ocean and Southeast Asia region were going on. Indeed, some criticized the Appellate Body for not giving greater weight to consensus-based multilateral measures (De La Fayette, 2002). However, the Appellate Body's approach was likely to be superior from an environmental perspective as unilateral measures tend to stimulate multilateral initiatives (Chang, 2000). The Appellate Body was also criticized for failing to delineate fully the relationship between the WTO and MEAs (De La Fayette, 2002). As the first WTO dispute to involve multilateral environmental agreements, shrimp–turtle began the process of clarifying the relationship among WTO rules, domestic law and MEAs. No more could be expected as the rulings properly addressed the relationship between the specific issues in dispute and relevant MEAs rather than the general relationship between the WTO and MEAs.

The apparent 'winners,' the governments of India, Malaysia, Pakistan and Thailand, objected to the rulings. In a striking irony, their conclusions were the obverse of those voiced by the environmentalists. Pakistan's representative to the WTO complained that the Appellate Body had 'elevated environmental concerns' beyond the level contemplated in the Uruguay Round (WTO, 1998c, p. 6). A spokesperson for the government of Thailand predicted that the rulings would result in an 'explosive growth in the number of environmental (and perhaps labor) measures . . . justified pursuant to Article XX' (Pruzin, 1998). Malaysia's *Business Times* (2001) opined that the compliance ruling 'signals yet another victory for powerful developed nations to practice double standards and selective protectionism, in the name of conservation and the environment'.

The apparent 'winners' in the shrimp–turtle dispute were not persuaded that the Appellate Body's approach accommodated the interests of both developing and developed countries, even though its rulings constrained the ability of the US to impose the shrimp ban by requiring it to consider the ban's impact on US trade partners and the specific circumstances faced by foreign producers. Nevertheless, only Malaysia challenged US compliance measures. Although India, Pakistan and Thailand did not agree with the rulings, they recognized that the US had complied with the Appellate Body's recommendations. Since Malaysia faced essentially the same conditions, Malaysia's challenge could be interpreted as obstructionist, especially given the scrupulous nature of US compliance. Further, after the compliance panel rejected each one of Malaysia's complaints, Malaysia appealed the panel rulings to the Appellate Body, which upheld the panel on every issue. Ultimately, Malaysia's actions served only to prolong the resolution of the dispute. The most important development during the compliance phase was the decision by the US to comply with the Appellate Body's recommendations. As we will see in several of the other disputes investigated in this volume, compliance cannot be taken for granted.

3.7 DEVELOPMENTS AT THE WTO

These varying responses played out in future developments at the WTO. The US and EU attempted to respond to the perception in the environmental community that the organization was inhospitable to environmental concerns. They were instrumental in organizing an environmental symposium in 1999 that was intended to reinvigorate the quiescent efforts of the WTO's Committee on Trade and the Environment. Since developing nations did not embrace the idea of advancing the organization's environmental agenda, the environmental meeting was paired with a development symposium. However, developing nations sent few non-Geneva-based officials to the environmental meeting where representatives from NGOs in the developed world far outnumbered those from their sister organizations in the developing world. The discussion at the meeting underscored the gulf between developed and developing nations as developing nations indicated their desire to confine consideration of environmental issues to the CTE and opposed the imposition of new environmental commitments in the upcoming round of trade negotiations (*Hindu*, 1999a, 1999b).

Later that year, the inability of developed and developing nations to agree on an agenda for the next round of negotiations contributed to the collapse of the WTO Ministerial Meeting in Seattle. For developing countries, it was imperative to exclude environmental, labor and other issues that were seen as inhibiting trade and economic development in their nations. Of course, these were the very same issues that mobilized NGOs in developed nations to organize street protests at the Seattle meeting. The shrimp–turtle decision figured prominently in that effort as the fate of sea turtles had become a cause célèbre in the aftermath of the rulings. At Seattle, hundreds of protesters clad in turtle costumes came to symbolize the broad opposition to the organization in the developed world, based on the perception that it advanced trade at the expense of the environment and other social goals. Ironically, the ubiquity of the turtle protesters suggested just the opposite to critics in developing nations, who saw environmentalists and other activists as exercising undue influence on the WTO's agenda.

In view of these tensions, it is important to keep in mind that, although environmental organizations based in the developed world took the lead in activism related to the shrimp–turtle dispute, they were joined by environmental organizations from developing nations. Eleven NGOs based in the developing world were parties to the amicus briefs submitted in the dispute: Mangrove Action Project, Philippine Ecological Network, Red Nacional de Acción Ecológica, Sobrevivencia, Centro Ecoceanos, Kenya Sea Turtle Committee, Marine Turtle Preservation Group of India, Operation Kachhapa, Project Swarajya, Visakha Society for the Prevention of Cruelty to Animals and Fiscalía Del Medio Ambiente (WTO, 1998b, 2001c). Local chapters of the World Wildlife Federation and the World Conservation Union operated conservation programs with the government of Pakistan. The Indian NGO CIFNET developed a TED for local use. Environmental organizations participated in pilot projects that promoted TEDs in India, Malaysia and Thailand (WTO, 1998a). Their efforts garnered attention and support from the media and the broader public. When Turtle Island Restoration Network bombarded the Indian embassy in the US with emails urging that nation to adopt TEDs, Indian officials demurred, observing that large, foreign vessels were responsible for the sea turtle deaths occurring in Indian waters not small, domestic fishing boats (*News India-Times*, 1999). However, that view was not pervasive. The *Hindu* (1999b) castigated the Indian government and others in the region for failing to promote reasonable conservation measures, observing that 'shrimp trawling will not kill turtles if inexpensive "turtle excluder devices" are attached to the nets'.

3.8   NGOS AND THE COURTS

The environmental community was the principal constituency advocating for sea turtle conservation in the US and around the world. Their efforts resulted in domestic legislation and international agreements outlawing capture of and trade in sea turtles. Once these measures went into effect, environmental organizations worked with international, federal, state and local regulators to insure that they were implemented and enforced (Rudloe and Rudloe, 1989; Sea Turtle Restoration Project, 1994; Shore, 1998). When it became apparent that shrimp trawling posed the most significant threat to sea turtles in US waters, they insisted that shrimp trawlers use TEDs and, along with shrimp producers, convinced Congress to extend the requirement to shrimp imports (Rudloe and Rudloe, 1989). When they objected to the manner in which the State Department implemented the TED requirement, they initiated the legal action that led the Court of International Trade (CIT) to reject the department's implementation guidelines. When the matter reached the WTO, environmental organizations submitted the briefs that triggered the amicus curiae controversy. After the US Court of Appeals for the Federal Circuit vacated the CIT rulings, the US reverted to the practice of permitting imports of TED-caught shrimp from uncertified countries. That decision infuriated the environmental community, prompting Earth Island Institute, the Humane Society and the Sierra Club, among others, to return to the Court of International Trade. The CIT reiterated its previous rulings and the Administration appealed yet again to the US Court of Appeals (US Court of Appeals for the Federal Circuit, 2002; US Court of International Trade, 1999).

In March 2002, several months after the Appellate Body issued its compliance report, the US Court of Appeals for the Federal Circuit (2002) reversed the CIT. The court reasoned that the revised regulations were compatible with Congressional intent because they limited US shrimp imports from uncertified nations to those harvested with TEDs. One last appeal remained: environmentalists led by Turtle Island Restoration Network sought redress at the US Supreme Court, but it decided not to review the case (Murphy, 2003).[4]

The Court of International Trade's rulings put US policy at odds with WTO obligations. Similarly, in the gasoline dispute, Congressional pressure contributed to the EPA's decision to use the baseline rules to favor domestic producers. Later, after the EPA decided to reverse course and accord like treatment to both foreign and domestic refiners, Congress prevented it from doing so by denying funding for foreign refiner individual baselines. The CIT proved more formidable than Congress, as the latter did not oppose the EPA's decision to comply with the WTO rulings in the gas dispute. By contrast, when environmental organizations challenged US compliance measures, the CIT affirmed its ruling, although later the US Court of Appeals reversed the CIT. Ultimately, Congressional and judicial intervention complicated the resolution of the two disputes but did not alter their outcomes. However, they might easily have done so. All that was lacking was more determined Congressional opposition in the gasoline dispute and an appellate court that shared the CIT's interpretation of Section 609 in the shrimp–turtle dispute.

As additional environmental measures come before the WTO, we can expect non-state actors to exploit and exacerbate conflicts among the executive, legislative and judicial branches about the direction of environmental and trade policy. As discussed in Chapter 2 (gasoline), there is not an obvious way to defuse legislative–executive conflicts. Electoral considerations compel members of Congress to focus on the local implications of environmental concerns, while the WTO requires the executive branch to consider their international implications. In the case of the courts, tensions of this sort could be mitigated if the judiciary were to attempt to minimize conflicts between domestic and international law (Morrill, 2000). In the shrimp–turtle dispute, the US Court of Appeals proved more amenable to that approach than the Court of International Trade. While that outcome was desirable, its impact on future disputes is unclear because they are likely to involve different issues and to be decided by different courts.

3.9   PANEL CONSULTATIONS WITH SCIENTIFIC EXPERTS

The shrimp–turtle panel consulted five experts: Dr John A. Eckert, Hubbs Sea World Research Institute, United States; Dr John G. Frazier, Centro de Investigación y Estudios Avanzados, Mexico; Mr Michael Guinea, Northern Territory University Australia; Mr Hock-Chark Liew, University of Putra Malaysia, Malaysia and Dr Ian Poiner, Commonwealth Scientific and Industrial Research Organization, Australia. Despite devoting a substantial part of its report (roughly 200 pages of the 431 page report) to the experts' testimony, the testimony did not figure prominently in the panel rulings owing to the panel's decision to explore the chapeau before Article XX(g). Once the panel concluded that the shrimp ban was incompatible with the chapeau, it was not necessary to explore Article XX(g) for which the experts' testimony was most relevant. However, the experts' testimony proved invaluable in illuminating the key issues in dispute and provided more than sufficient evidence to adjudicate the conflicting claims made by the US and the four Asian nations regarding sea turtles' endangered status, the threats posed by shrimp trawling and other activities, and the efficacy of TEDs and other conservation efforts (WTO, 1998a).

According to the experts, sea turtles were vulnerable to a variety of human and non-human threats over the course of their lives and were in danger of extinction despite the conservation efforts made by the five nations and others. These threats varied across species and nations as well as within nations because of socio-economic and other factors. The consumption of turtle eggs and direct harvest of sea turtles for their meat, shells and oil continued to pose major threats in Asia. Those activities were insignificant in the US where the available evidence suggested that shrimp trawling posed the most significant threat to three species (green, kemp's ridley and loggerhead). Comparable data were not available for India, Malaysia, Pakistan and Thailand, where by-catch monitoring was not a priority. However, Dr Frazier opined that intensive shrimp trawling imperiled sea turtles in every shrimping nation except Australia, which managed its fisheries tightly. Dr Eckert and Mr Liew noted that sea turtles were captured routinely by shrimp trawlers in Malaysia and Thailand and that shrimp trawling was believed to have caused the deaths of thousands of sea turtles on India's Orissa Coast (WTO, 1998a).

The experts found TEDs to be highly effective. In the US, TEDs had reduced sea turtle strandings by 44 percent with minimal shrimp loss (0–2 percent). Varying socio-economic conditions were not likely to affect TED use as the skills required were similar to those used in trawling. TEDs could be adapted to diverse conditions, as was borne out by local versions developed in Thailand (Thai Turtle Free Device (TTFD)) and Australia (AusTED). Tests of the AusTED in Australia's Northern Prawn Fishery were highly successful. No sea turtles were caught and fish by-catch declined by as much as 30 percent. Shrimp yields actually rose (by 4–7 percent) along with shrimp quality as fewer shrimp were damaged from contact with by-catch in the net collection process (WTO, 1998a).

The experts expressed disagreement on the desirability of mandating TEDs. In light of the compliance problems in the US, Mr Liew recommended further study, noting that other measures might be more effective as compliance was likely to be weaker elsewhere. Drs Eckert and

Frazier disagreed, observing that TEDs were more effective and less costly than other measures. Seasonal and area restrictions did not adjust with migration. Tow-time restrictions were impractical because sea turtles could drown in as few as 30 minutes. Tow-time restrictions were also unenforceable and probably ineffective because they exposed sea turtles to multiple captures (WTO, 1998a).

As this brief discussion reveals, the experts made important contributions to the panel process. As we will see in Chapters 4, 5, 6 and 8, scientific experts made equally valuable contributions in the asbestos, hormones, salmon, apples, agricultural products and GMOs disputes. And, unlike the shrimp–turtle panel, the other panels made extensive use of the experts' testimony in their rulings.

3.10   PANEL AND APPELLATE PERFORMANCE

The shrimp–turtle panel erred on several fundamental matters. Its decision to invert the sequence of the Article XX investigation and its misinterpretation of role of the chapeau led it to conclude erroneously that Section 609 posed an impermissible threat to the multilateral trading system. These errors were especially troubling because they created confusion in the environmental community and the broader public about the standing of environmental goals and regulations within the WTO. As discussed in the following chapters, panel performance has improved over time. However, significant errors continue to occur, increasing the length of the process and casting doubt on its credibility. Chapter 9 discusses suggestions to improve panel performance.

Although the Appellate Body corrected the panel's errors, it made two questionable decisions of its own. First, the Appellate Body declined to rule explicitly on whether regulations justified under the Article XX(g) exception could be applied extra-jurisdictionally. Instead, it ruled that there was a 'sufficient nexus' between the US and sea turtles for the 'purposes of Article XX(g)' (WTO, 1998b, para. 133). The Appellate Body went on to justify the shrimp ban under Article XX(g) and, in effect, approved the imposition of the shrimp ban extra-territorially. In the rest of its analysis, the Appellate Body underscored the importance of adhering to the treaty text, yet there was no textual basis for the sufficient nexus criterion. As the text imposed no territorial limit, it would have been more straightforward to conclude that there was no textual basis for a jurisdictional limit on the shrimp ban. Second, in its analysis of Article XX(g)'s 'related to' requirement, the Appellate Body concluded that the shrimp ban satisfied the requirement in part because TEDs were 'directly connected to' sea turtle conservation (WTO, 1998b, para. 140). However, in the gasoline case, the Appellate Body ruled that the panel had overstated the 'related to' requirement by requiring differential baselines to have a 'direct connection' to clean air (Mavroidis, 2000). The Appellate Body would do well to follow its advice to avoid straying from the text. By adhering strictly to the provisions of Article XX(g), the Appellate Body has been able to provide strong support for environmental measures (Chang, 2000). Because that support has been controversial within the membership, it is crucial that the Appellate Body establish a sound legal foundation for it.

The Appellate Body's rulings drew criticism on the grounds that they were more politically savvy than legally satisfying (Appleton, 1999; Bhagwati, 2001; Jackson, 2000; Knox, 2004). These critics complained that the Appellate Body's desire to build support for its decisions led it to exceed its authority. Its decision to rule on issues of law that were not addressed by the original shrimp–turtle panel was seen as an attempt to placate the environmental community (Appleton, 1999). If that was the intention, it was most unsuccessful, as the environmental community perceived US compliance measures designed to respond to the Appellate Body's rulings as weakening Section 609. Because the Court of International Trade had issued rulings previously that were at odds with the WTO rulings, it was more likely that the Appellate Body intended to clarify the issues in dispute for the US and other governments as well as for external constituencies including the courts. Recall that the Appellate Body identified several flaws in the application of Section 609 that had eluded the panel. During the compliance phase, the US corrected each of these flaws. Had the Appellate Body not identified those deficiencies, it was unlikely that the US would have corrected them at that stage and the dispute would have dragged on unresolved. The Appellate Body's approach was preferable. Its detailed critique of Section 609's application addressed the issues fueling the dispute and provided guidance for the US and other WTO members on how to satisfy their obligations under the chapeau.

In the briefs controversy, the Appellate Body was criticized for seeking to be 'all things to all people' (Appleton, 1999, p. 488). The attempt backfired as the Appellate Body's handling of the NGO briefs satisfied few. Its ruling that panels may choose at their discretion to accept unsolicited briefs drew praise from those seeking to enhance the scope for public participation in the dispute resolution proceedings. But proponents of greater public participation perceived the Appellate Body as 'retreat[ing] to a do nothing stance' during the compliance phase because it declined to address the arguments in the NGO brief attached to the US submission and did not consider an unsolicited brief that it received (De La Fayette, 2002, p. 689). The Appellate Body provoked harsher criticism from member governments, most of whom charged that it had exceeded its authority under the dispute resolution rules and impinged on member rights by permitting the submission of unsolicited NGO briefs (WTO, 1998c, 2001a). At the dispute's end, the Appellate Body appeared committed to an unsatisfactory compromise. It had incorporated amicus briefs into the dispute resolution process but it had not actually made use of any of the briefs. This compromise proved contentious but surprisingly durable. In the asbestos dispute (Chapter 5), member opposition stymied an effort by the Appellate Body to take additional steps to facilitate amicus briefs. In the GMOs dispute (Chapter 8), the panel accepted amicus submissions but 'did not find it necessary to take' them 'into account' (WTO, 2006, para. 7.11). Reforms addressing amicus submissions and other measures to improve the transparency and accountability of the dispute resolution process are discussed in Chapter 9.

NOTES

1. The Philippines also filed a complaint against the US (US – Import Prohibition of Certain Shrimp and Shrimp Products (WT/DS61)) but decided to participate as a third party in this dispute instead of pursuing that complaint.
2. Malaysia also objected to the scope of the panel's review. The Appellate Body ruled that the panel's investigation had properly emphasized US obligations under the chapeau. However, the panel had not neglected the broader issue of whether the steps taken by the US were compatible with other provisions of the General Agreement.
3. Market shares discussed in this section were calculated by the author, based on National Marine Fisheries Service shrimp import data for 2005.
4. Turtle Island Restoration Network was spun off from Earth Island Institute to take the lead in the organization's sea turtle advocacy initiatives.

REFERENCES

Appleton, A. (1999), 'Shrimp/turtle: untangling the nets', *Journal of International Economic Law*, **2**(3), 477–96.
Bhagwati, Jagdish (2001), 'After Seattle: Free Trade and the WTO', in R.B.

Porter, P. Sauvé, A. Subramanian and A.B. Zampetti (eds), *Efficiency, Equity, and Legitimacy, The Multilateral Trading System at the Millennium*, Washington, DC: Brookings Institution Press, pp. 50–62.

Business Times (Malaysia) (2001), 'Turning turtle the environment', 25 October, 6 (Trends).

Chang, H. (2000), 'Toward a greener GATT: environmental trade measures and the shrimp–turtle case', *Southern California Law Review*, **74**(1), 31–47.

Charnovitz, S. (2002), 'The law of environmental "PPMs" in the WTO: debunking the myth of illegality', *Yale Journal of International Law*, **27**(1), 59–110.

De La Fayette, L. (2002), 'WTO – GATT – trade and environment – import restrictions – endangered species', *The American Journal of International Law*, **96**(3), 685–92.

Gazette (1998), 'WTO raps the US over shrimp law', 13 October, C2.

Hindu (1999a), 'EU, US push environment at WTO', 16 March, 1.

Hindu (1999b), 'Chasms remain on trade–environment issue', 18 March, 1.

IOSEA (Indian Ocean – South-East Asian Marine Turtle Memorandum of Understanding Secretariat) (2006), 'Official texts' and 'Membership', Bangkok, Thailand (website accessed during May).

Jackson, J. (2000), 'Comment on shrimp/turtle and the product/process distinction', *European Journal of International Law*, **11**(2), 303–7.

Jones, J. (1993), 'US shrimp import ban and sea turtle loss', *TED Case Studies: An Online Journal*, **2**(1), 1–6.

Knox, J. (2004), 'The judicial resolution of conflicts between trade and the environment', *Harvard Environmental Law Review*, **28**(1), 1–77.

Mavroidis, P. (2000), 'Trade and the environment after shrimps–turtle litigation', *Journal of World Trade*, **14**(1), 73–88.

Morrill, J. (2000), 'A need for compliance: the shrimp turtle case and the conflict between the WTO and the US Court of International Trade', *Tulane Journal of International and Comparative Law*, **11**(1), 413–46.

Murphy, S. (2003). 'Unsuccessful challenge to Department of State shrimp–turtle guidelines', *The American Journal of International Law*, **97**(3), 691.

National Marine Fisheries Service (2006), '2005 Product data, shrimp', Silver Springs, MD: Fisheries Statistics and Economics Division (website accessed during May).

News India-Times (1999), 'Embassy flooded with e-mail to use anti-turtle devices', 17 December, 10.

Peterson, J. (1999), 'WTO summit in Seattle: activists bring turtles' cause to WTO fishbowl', *Los Angeles Times*, 3 December, A1.

Pruzin, D. (1998), 'WTO formally adopts shrimp–turtle ruling as Thailand fears victory may be pyrrhic', *International Trade Reporter*, 11 November, 1884–5.

Record (2001), 'WTO upholds US law that protects sea turtles', 16 June, A8.

Rudloe, J. and A. Rudloe (1989), 'Shrimpers and lawmakers collide over move to save the sea turtles', *Smithsonian*, **20**(9), 1–6 (web version).

Scott, J. (2004), 'International trade and environmental governance: relating rules and standards in the EU and WTO', *European Journal of International Law*, **15**(2), 307–54.

Sea Turtle Restoration Project (STRP) (2004), 'WTO sea turtle/shrimp time-line', Forest Knolls, CA: STRP, Programs and Campaigns (website accessed during March 2006).

Selinger, M. (1998), 'WTO fishing decision both good, bad for US', *Washington Times*, 13 October, B7.

Shore, T. (1998), 'Sea turtle deaths mount in Texas', *Earth Island Journal*, **13**(3), 10.

Swardson, A. (1998), 'Trade group overturns US sea turtle law', *Advocate*, 13 October, 14A.

US Court of Appeals for the Federal Circuit (2002), '*Turtle Island Restoration Network* v. *Donald L. Evans*', (00-1569, -1581, -1582), 21 March, 1-31.

US Court of International Trade (1999), '*Earth Island Institute* v. *William M. Daley*', (Slip Op. 99–32), 2 April, 1–39.

US Department of State (1996), 'Revised notice of guidelines for determining comparability of foreign programs for the protection of turtles in shrimp trawl fishing operations' (1996 guidelines), Washington, DC: *Federal Register*, **61**(77), 19 April, 17342–4.

US Department of State (1999), 'Revised guidelines for the implementation of Public Law 101-162 relating to the protection of sea turtles in shrimp trawl fishing operations' (1999 guidelines), Washington, DC: *Federal Register*, **64**(130), 8 July, 36949–52.

US Department of State (2001, 2003, 2005), 'Shrimp turtle conservation and shrimp imports', Washington, DC: Office of the Spokesperson, *Media Note*, May.

WTO (1994a), *General Agreement on Tariffs and Trade* (GATT), Geneva: WTO.

WTO (1994b), *Understanding on Rules and Procedures Governing the Settlement of Disputes* (DSU), Geneva: WTO.

WTO (1996), *US – Standards for Reformulated and Conventional Gasoline, Report of the Appellate Body* (WT/DS2/AB/R), Geneva: WTO, 29 April.

WTO (1998a), *US – Import Prohibition of Certain Shrimp and Shrimp Products, Report of the Panel* (WT/DS58/R), Geneva: WTO, 15 May.

WTO (1998b), *US – Import Prohibition of Certain Shrimp and Shrimp Products, Report of the Appellate Body* (WT/DS58/AB/R), Geneva: WTO, 12 October.

WTO (1998c), *Minutes of Dispute Settlement Body, 6 November 1998* (WT/DSB/M/50), Geneva: WTO, 14 December.

WTO (2000), *US – Imposition of Countervailing Duties on Certain Hot-Rolled Lead and Bismuth Carbon Steel Products Originating in the United Kingdom* (WT/DS/138/AB/R), Geneva: WTO, 10 May.

WTO (2001a), *Minutes of General Council Meeting, 22 November 2000* (WT/GC/M/60), Geneva: WTO, 23 January.

WTO (2001b), *EC – Measures Affecting Asbestos and Products Containing Asbestos, Report of the Appellate Body* (WT/DS135/AB/R), Geneva: WTO, 12 March.

WTO (2001c), *US – Import Prohibition of Certain Shrimp and Shrimp Products, Recourse to Article 21.5 by Malaysia, Report of the Panel* (WT/DS58/RW), Geneva: WTO, 15 June.

WTO (2001d), *US – Import Prohibition of Certain Shrimp and Shrimp Products,*

Recourse to Article 21.5 by Malaysia, Report of the Appellate Body (WT/DS58/AB/RW), Geneva: WTO, 22 October.

WTO (2006), *EC – Measures Affecting the Approval and Marketing of Bitotech Products, Report of the Panel* (WT/DS291/R, WT/DS292/R, WT/DS293/R), Geneva: WTO, 29 September.

4. Hormones

Chapter 4 takes up the dispute between the EU and Canada and the US regarding the EU's ban on imports of beef treated with growth hormones. The hormones dispute dated to 1987 when the US issued a GATT challenge to the ban under the Tokyo Round Agreement on Technical Barriers to Trade (TBT). The GATT dispute resolution process was not able to resolve the matter and the ban remained in place. In 1989, the US retaliated by imposing 100 percent duties on certain EU agricultural products. Later that year, the EU agreed to permit imports of hormone-treated pet food and certified hormone-free meat from the US. In response, the US reduced the number of EU products facing retaliatory tariffs (Vogel, 1995). No further developments occurred until 1996, when the US and Canada challenged the ban at the WTO.[1]

The case not only pitted the world's two trade superpowers against one another, it also involved the first test of the new Sanitary and Phytosanitary (SPS) Agreement. The long-simmering hormones dispute was a catalyst for the agreement. Negotiated during the Uruguay Round (1986–94), the SPS Agreement was designed to prevent governments from using food safety regulations to impede access to their markets. The agreement sparked controversy by promoting the adoption of international standards (Articles 3.1 and 3.2) and requiring nations that choose higher standards (Article 3.3) to support them with scientific evidence (Article 2.2) and the results of a risk assessment (Article 5.1).

Critics charged that the provisions compromised the environment, public health and sovereignty and were outraged that the hormones ban was found to be incompatible with them (Retallack, 1997; Wallach and Woodall, 2004). But critics tended to overlook the careful and narrow nature of the Appellate Body's rulings. The Appellate Body concluded that the ban was not supported by the scientific evidence examined in the EU's risk assessment but it relaxed the panel's more restrictive interpretation of the risk assessment and scientific justification requirements. The Appellate Body also rejected the US and Canadian claims that the ban was a protectionist measure masquerading as a health regulation.

Although the Appellate Body attempted to sidestep ruling on the precautionary principle, the hormones rulings addressed potential health risks and shed light on the precautionary principle's status in the WTO. As the first set of rulings to make significant use of testimony from scientific experts, the rulings provided insight on the extent to which panel members with expertise in trade and diplomacy were able to address the scientific matters in dispute as well as the effectiveness of their consultations with scientific experts. The chapter explores the EU's options at the implementation phase and their implications for sovereignty and the efficacy of the dispute resolution process. The chapter concludes with a discussion of new initiatives during the compliance phase promoting greater transparency in the dispute resolution process.

4.1   THE HORMONES BAN

By 1980, there was widespread concern that European livestock producers were abusing growth hormones. The synthetic hormone DES (dimethylstilbene), a suspected carcinogen, had been used illegally in French veal production, and Italian children who had consumed hormone-treated veal were reported to have developed abnormal sexual organs (Vogel, 1995). In response to these reports, the French Federal Consumer Union called for a veal boycott. Veal consumption declined by 70 percent in France within a month's time. The boycott spread throughout Europe under the auspices of the European Bureau of Consumers Union, a federation of national consumer organizations (Hunter, 1988).

At the time, growth hormones were regulated by EU member states. Germany and Luxembourg permitted natural hormones but banned synthetic hormones. Belgium, France, Ireland and the United Kingdom permitted the use of natural hormones and some synthetic hormones. Denmark, Greece, Italy and the Netherlands banned growth-promoting hormones in livestock production (Caduff, 2002). The public outcry necessitated a Union-wide response. Because Belgium, Ireland and the United Kingdom objected to a complete ban, the EU enacted a partial ban in 1981 that prohibited all but five hormones for use in growth promotion: three natural hormones (estrogen (oestradiaol-17^2), progesterone, and testosterone) and two synthetic hormones (trenbolone acetate (trenbolone) and zeranol).[2] Under new regulations issued in 1988, the ban was extended to the five hormones, although the three natural hormones were permitted to be used for therapeutic purposes. In 1996, the previous directives were replaced by regulations that maintained the ban with respect to growth promotion and further restricted the therapeutic use of the three natural hormones (WTO, 1997a).[3]

4.2   THE WTO DISPUTE

Canada and the US challenged the ban with respect to six growth hormones: estrogen (oestradiaol-17[2]), progesterone, testosterone, trenbolone, zeranol and melengestrol acetate (MGA) (WTO, 1997a, 1997b).[4] MGA was included in cattle feed. The other hormones were implanted as pellets in cow ears and timed to release over a period of weeks. At slaughter, the ears were discarded to prevent the pellets from entering the food chain (WTO, 1997a). The hormones provided a return of about $80 per animal by reducing the fattening period by 20 to 25 days and producing higher quality (leaner) meat. US and Canadian meat exports to the EU declined sharply after the ban went into effect and producers feared that the ban could threaten their access to other markets should other governments follow the EU's lead (Vogel, 1995).

Canada and the US charged that the ban violated several provisions of the new Sanitary and Phytosanitary (SPS) Agreement. Under Article 3.1, members were required to base their sanitary measures on international standards. While Article 3.3 permitted members to adopt regulations achieving a level of sanitary protection, they were required to provide scientific justification (Article 2.2) or support from a risk assessment (Article 5.1). But the available evidence demonstrated the safety of the hormones in dispute. In light of this evidence, the EU's attempt to invoke the precautionary principle was misguided. Article 5.7 permitted temporary precautionary measures only where the scientific evidence was unclear or conflicting. Moreover, it was contradictory for the EU to cite potential health risks to justify the hormones ban while permitting swine producers to use two carcinogenic feed additives, carbadox and olaquindox. The EU's inconsistent regulation of these health risks suggested that the hormones ban was a disguised restriction on trade (Article 5.5) that was designed to eliminate chronic surpluses in the beef market. The ban was also more trade-restrictive than necessary; regulation and oversight could assure the safe use of the hormones in growth promotion (Article 5.6) (WTO, 1997a).

The EU maintained that it had met its obligations under the SPS

Agreement. The ban was the product of a risk assessment as required by Article 5.1 and based on scientific principles as mandated by Article 2.2. The evidence suggesting that the hormones could be used safely in growth promotion was not conclusive. In any case, the three natural hormones were known to pose cancer risks when used or consumed for purposes other than growth promotion.[5] New studies suggested that these risks were greater than was assumed previously. Under experimental conditions, high doses of the six hormones had been found to induce cancer in animals. Many questions remained about the hormones' carcinogenicity. As a result, the ban was justified under the precautionary principle even though Article 5.7's provisions for precautionary measures did not apply to permanent measures. In the face of scientific uncertainty, responsible governments were obliged to protect their citizens from potential health threats (WTO, 1997a).

The EU emphasized that it was not obliged to adopt international standards that did not meet its level of safety (Article 3.3). As the EU was unwilling to accept *any* risk posed by hormones *added to* meat, the ban was the only measure capable of achieving its desired level of safety. The ban was not a disguised restriction on trade (Article 5.5); it was a response to health concerns raised by the widespread abuse of hormones in the livestock industry. Given the scale of the abuse, consumer confidence in meat safety and regulatory control could not be restored without a total ban. Additionally, the ban was consistent with the EU's desire to harmonize hormone regulations in member states in order to create a common beef market (WTO, 1997a).

4.3   INTERNATIONAL STANDARDS

As the first dispute to involve international food safety standards, the hormones dispute provided the first test of the SPS Agreement's harmonization provisions. Article 3.1 obliged members 'to base' their sanitary regulations on 'international standards, guidelines, or recommendations where they exist' (WTO, 1994a). Under Article 3.2, sanitary regulations that 'conformed to international standards' were 'presumed' to be in compliance with the agreement (WTO, 1994a). Article 3.3 allowed governments to impose higher standards as long as they could provide scientific support. Annex A identified the standards set by the Codex Alimentarius Commission (Codex) as the international standards governing food additives and veterinary drugs (WTO, 1994a).

In 1995, Codex adopted standards for five of the six hormones in dispute (all but MGA). Codex acted on the basis of recommendations from the Joint Food and Agriculture Organization (FAO)/World Health Organization (WHO) Expert Committee on Food Additives (JECFA), an independent body responsible for developing safe acceptable daily intake (ADI) and maximum residue limits (MRL) for veterinary drugs. In 1987, JECFA examined the three natural hormones (estrogen, progesterone and testosterone) and two of the synthetic hormones (trenbolone and zeranol). JECFA decided that it was not necessary to set ADI and MRL levels for the three natural hormones. Estrogen, progesterone and testosterone were produced by cows over the normal course of their development and occurred naturally (endogenously) in their meat products. These endogenous hormones were indistinguishable from residues of estrogen, testosterone and progesterone introduced exogenously for growth promotion. Since the natural hormones also occurred endogenously in human beings, the additional residues occurring in meat from treated animals were not likely to pose a health risk. In particular, the small amount of the residues remaining in meat at the point of consumption precluded a hormonal effect in human beings. Absent a hormonal effect, the residues posed no risk to consumers (WTO, 1997a).

JECFA set acceptable daily intake (ADI) and maximum residue limits (MRL) for zeranol and trenbolone. The former performed the same functions as estrogen and the latter the same as testosterone, but they did not share the same compositions or withdrawal rates. As with the natural hormones, potential toxic effects were linked to hormonal responses in consumers. Consequently, the ADI and MRL were set conservatively to assure that the residues present in meat were not large enough to produce a hormonal effect. As was customary, these limits were determined by extrapolating from animal tests using a safety factor of 100. JECFA's recommendations for the five hormones were limited to their use for growth promotion in cattle. JECFA did not investigate MGA and Codex made no recommendations with respect to it (WTO, 1997a).

As the first panel to examine the harmonization provisions, the hormones panel developed its interpretation without the benefit of precedent and misconstrued the relationship among Articles 3.1, 3.2 and 3.3. The panel interpreted Article 3.1 as imposing a general obligation to adopt international standards. The Appellate Body found no support in the SPS text for that interpretation. Citing the preamble, Article 3.1 and other provisions, the Appellate Body concluded that the SPS Agreement promoted but did not require the use of international standards (WTO, 1998a). Harmonization of sanitary regulations was 'a goal, yet to be realized in the future' rather than an obligation facing members in the 'here and now' (WTO, 1998a, para. 165). Article 3.2's presumption in favor of measures conforming to international standards provided an incentive for members to adopt such standards but did not establish a presumption against measures that differed from international standards (WTO, 1998a). Governments possessed an 'autonomous right' under Article 3.3 to impose sanitary measures that achieved a higher level of sanitary protection than international standards (WTO, 1998a, para. 104).

The Appellate Body went on to reverse the panel's ruling that the ban was not based on international standards as required by Article 3.1. The Appellate Body attributed the panel's error on that matter to its decision to equate Article 3.1's and Article 3.3's 'based on' requirements with Article 3.2's 'conform to' requirement. The Appellate Body explained that a regulation based on an international standard would have to reflect some but not necessarily all aspects of the standard, but a measure conforming to an international standard would have to comply in all respects. The panel ignored that distinction and concluded erroneously that the ban failed to comply with Article 3.1 because it did not conform to the level of sanitary protection achieved by the Codex standards (WTO, 1998a).

But since the EU was seeking a level of safety higher than was achievable under the Codex standards, it would have to justify the ban under Article 3.3. In order to do so, the ban would have to satisfy Article 5.1's risk assessments requirements. Although the opening paragraph of Article 3.3 seemed to create two distinct exceptions for measures justified by scientific evidence (Article 2.2) or a risk assessment (Article 5.1), the Appellate Body observed that the distinction between the two exceptions was 'more apparent than real' citing a footnote that defined scientific justification as the product of a risk assessment satisfying the agreement's requirements (WTO, 1998a, para. 176).

With these rulings, the Appellate Body strongly affirmed WTO members' sovereignty over sanitary regulations. The Appellate Body emphasized that governments were free to adopt any level of sanitary protection they deemed appropriate as long as they could provide scientific justification for the regulations imposed. Importantly, the Appellate Body reversed the panel's decision to impose the burden of proof on countries seeking to justify a departure from international standards. As the Appellate Body noted, the panel's decision penalized the EU for seeking a higher level of sanitary protection. While some saw the decision as impeding the harmonization effort (Cottier, 2001), the Appellate Body recognized that international standards were not an end but a means for preventing protectionist measures from serving as disguised restrictions on trade. The Appellate Body's reliance on the ordinary meaning of the words employed in Articles 3.1 and 3.2 eased the path for governments seeking to invoke Article 3.1. Regulations 'based on' internationals need not comply in every respect. But regulations seeking a higher level of safety required the support of a risk assessment.

4.4   RISK ASSESSMENT, SCIENTIFIC EVIDENCE AND THE PRECAUTIONARY PRINCIPLE

Unfortunately, the EU's risk assessment did not support the ban. In 1982, the EU convened the Scientific Group on Anabolic Agents in Animal Production to examine the safety of hormones for growth promotion. Chaired by Professor G.E. Lamming, the group concluded that estrogen, progesterone and testosterone 'would not present harmful effects to the health of the consumer when used under the appropriate conditions as growth promoters in farm animals' (EC Scientific Group, 1982, cited in WTO, 1997a, para. 2.28). The Lamming Group decided that the safety of zeranol and trenbolone required additional study but was unable to issue a conclusion before it disbanded. In the meantime, the Office International des Epizootics' (OIE) 1983 Scientific Report concluded that zeranol and trenbolone were safe for growth promotion provided that residue levels were insufficient to produce hormonal activity (WTO, 1997a).[6] These results were affirmed at the 1995 EC Scientific Conference convened to study the matter. The conference concluded that residue levels arising from trenbolone and zeronal used for growth promotion were 'well below the levels regarded as safe' (EC Scientific Conference, 1995, pp. 20–21, cited in WTO, 1997a, para. 2.33). With respect to the three natural hormones, the conference found that there was 'no evidence for possible health risks to the consumer' because residue levels in treated animals were comparable to those observed in untreated animals (EC Scientific Conference, 1995, pp. 20–21, cited in WTO, 1997a, para. 2.33). Safety was further enhanced by the hormones' low bioavailability, that is, only a small amount of hormones ingested in food was likely to survive metabolism (WTO, 1997a).

The panel concluded that the EU had not provided any evidence that the use of growth hormones posed actual risks to human health. While the International Agency for Research on Cancer (IARC) had tied the three natural hormones to real or potential cancer risks, it had not examined their use for growth promotion and resulting residues arising in food. Moreover, carcinogenic risks were linked to the production of a hormonal effect. But the JECFA studies concluded that residue levels in food were far below the levels necessary to induce hormonal activity. Similarly, the results of new research that suggested that estrogen might be genotoxic (able to induce tumors) involved doses that were too high to be comparable scientifically to the minute residues remaining in meat from cows treated with growth hormones. Four of the five scientific experts advising the panel testified that the results of the new studies did not warrant reconsideration of the conclusions reached by the Lamming Group, JECFA and the 1995 EC Scientific Conference (WTO, 1997a). The dissenting expert emphasized the possibility of risk but agreed with the others that there was no evidence that the five hormones posed an 'identifiable' health risk when used for growth promotion (WTO, 1997a, para. 8.124).

Although the EU cited potential health risks arising from unforeseen long-term effects and unanticipated interaction effects, the Lamming Report, JECFA and the 1995 EC Scientific Conference found that these risks did not arise with proper use. The EU suggested that the potential for abuse was significant enough to warrant the ban but the panel disagreed, explaining that the EU had not shown that it was more difficult to prevent the abuse of hormones than other veterinary drugs. Further, these hypothetical risks reflected the limits of science. As the experts explained, one could not exclude the *possibility* that growth hormones posed a risk. As a result, the EU's desire to achieve a zero-risk level was unattainable even theoretically. Moreover, the zero-risk objective was compromised on a practical level by the EU's decision to permit the use of the three natural hormones for therapeutic purposes. Finally, the precautionary principle could not be deployed to justify the ban. Article 5.7 permitted governments to enact temporary sanitary regulations on a precautionary basis in cases of scientific uncertainty but the EU declined to seek a defense under Article 5.7 because of the permanent nature of the ban. Equally important, the precautionary principle did not supersede the EU's obligation to meet the SPS Agreement's risk assessment requirements (WTO, 1997a).

The Appellate Body upheld the panel explaining that the EU was not required to support the ban with a preponderance of evidence. Nor was it required to subscribe to prevailing views within the scientific community (WTO, 1998a). But its risk assessment was required to 'sufficiently warrant' or 'reasonably support' the ban (WTO, 1998a, para. 193). The EU's risk assessment failed in this regard. The available evidence indicated that five of the hormones could be used safely in growth promotion. The EU had not examined the safety of the sixth hormone (MGA) (WTO, 1998a).

The Appellate Body observed that it was 'unnecessary, and probably imprudent' to take a position on the precautionary principle as its standing in international law was the subject of considerable controversy (WTO, 1998a, para. 123). Nevertheless, it proceeded to do so. The precautionary principle was not limited to Article 5.7's provisions for temporary precautionary measures. It was also reflected in the preamble and Article 3.3, which authorized members to set safety levels that were higher (more cautious) than international standards. And it was relevant for the risk assessment process in cases of inconclusive or conflicting evidence (WTO, 1998a). In the presence of scientific uncertainty, governments could take action against potential health risks especially where failing to act would expose the public to 'imminent' or 'life-threatening' dangers (WTO, 1998a, para. 194). But the precautionary principle could not 'override' the results of a risk assessment, which yielded no evidence of risk to consumers (WTO, 1998a, para. 125).

Importantly, the Appellate Body relaxed the panel's narrow interpretation of the risk assessment requirements. The panel erred by ruling that the risk assessment must produce an identifiable or scientifically identified risk. Both terms implied that the risk assessment process must identify a quantifiable risk of 'a certain magnitude or a threshold level' but the SPS Agreement imposed no such requirement (WTO, 1998a, para. 186). Similarly, there was no basis for the panel's decision to limit the risk assessment to scientific matters and to those that could be explored under laboratory conditions. Consumer anxieties about growth hormones and the effectiveness of regulatory measures and other non-scientific factors were relevant for the risk assessment process, but consideration of those factors did not relieve the EU of its obligation to provide scientific support for the ban (WTO, 1998a).

4.5   DISGUISED RESTRICTIONS ON TRADE

The panel identified two arbitrary and unjustifiable inconsistencies in the EU's sanitary regulations that constituted disguised restrictions on trade that were incompatible with Article 5.5. First, it was inconsistent to permit unlimited consumption of natural hormones present endogenously in meat and other foods but to prohibit any consumption of hormone residues in treated meat. Second, it was contradictory to allow two carcinogenic feed additives (carbadox and olaquindox) to be used in swine production but to prohibit growth hormones to be used in cattle production. These differences in sanitary treatment suggested that the ban was a disguised restriction on trade, as did their effects on North American producers and the EU's beef surplus (WTO, 1997a).

The Appellate Body overruled the panel, explaining that the differential treatment of endogenous hormones and those added for growth promotion was not arbitrary and unjustifiable. As a practical matter, it was not feasible to ban endogenous hormones owing to the large number of food items containing them, including meat, eggs and milk. The varying treatment of the growth hormones and carbadox and olaquindox was arbitrary and unjustifiable but it did not constitute a disguised restriction on trade. The Appellate Body was persuaded that the ban was motivated primarily by the EU's desire to protect the health of its citizens. A wealth of evidence documented the public's concern about meat safety and the adequacy of regulatory measures. By contrast, there was no evidence that domestic producers advocated on behalf of the ban. The ban's disproportionate effect on US and Canadian producers was not surprising since growth hormones were permitted in those nations but not in the EU. As a consequence of the EU's harmonization effort, beef surpluses were likely to fall, benefiting not only EU producers but also hormone-free beef exporters seeking access to the EU market (WTO, 1998a).[7]

4.6 CONSULTATIONS WITH SCIENTIFIC EXPERTS

After seeking nominations from Codex and the International Agency for Research on Cancer (IARC), the panel invited the parties to choose two experts from those nominated, or other sources. The panel planned to select two additional experts but added a third upon the EU's request for one with expertise in the carcinogenicity of hormones. The five experts selected were: Dr Francoise André, Laboratoire des Dosages Hormonaux, France; Dr Dieter Arnold, Federal Institute for Health Protection of Consumers and Veterinary Medicine, Germany; Dr George Lucier, National Institute of Environmental Health Sciences, United

States; Dr Jock McLean, Division of Science, Engineering and Design, Swinburne University of Technology, Australia; Dr Len Ritter, Canadian Network of Toxicology Centres, University of Guelph, Canada. The parties expected the panel to form an expert review group (WTO, 1997a). The panel declined to do so, explaining that an expert review group would be 'required to reach a consensus view' of the health risks posed by growth hormones (WTO, 1997a, para. 8.7). The panel 'considered it more useful to leave open the possibility of receiving a range of opinions' (WTO, 1997a, para. 8.7) and decided to consult with the experts as individuals. In light of the evidence, the panel's desire to 'hear all views' appeared to favor the EU (WTO, 1997a, para. 8.9), but the EU insisted that the dispute resolution rules required the formation of expert review groups to insure that panels were not in a position to choose freely among divergent views (WTO, 1998a). Perhaps the EU was hoping to establish a precedent that would be helpful in the asbestos dispute (Chapter 5). In the case of asbestos, there was consensus within the scientific community that no level of exposure was free of health risk.

The EU rested its case on provisions in the Dispute Settlement Understanding (DSU), addressing the formation of expert review groups and permitting panels to request reports from expert review groups (WTO, 1997a). But the EU ignored other provisions that allowed panels to consult virtually anyone on any terms. For example, Article 13.1 authorized panels to 'seek information and technical advice from any individual or body which it deems appropriate' (WTO, 1994b). Article 13.2 empowered panels to 'seek information from any relevant source' and to 'consult experts to obtain their opinion' (WTO, 1994b). Article 11.2 of the SPS stated that, in disputes 'involving scientific or technical issues, a panel should seek advice from experts' and 'may, when it deems it appropriate' form an expert review group (WTO, 1994a). The Appellate Body concluded that the panel's individual consultations were compatible with those provisions (WTO, 1998a).

The EU challenged the panel's interpretation of much of the scientific evidence. The Appellate Body upheld the panel's findings despite noting a couple of instances when the panel misquoted or misinterpreted the experts' opinions (WTO, 1998a). The Appellate Body explained that panels were not required to defer to the disputants' interpretation of the evidence but to make an objective assessment of the facts. Panels were presumed to fulfill that obligation unless they made 'egregious' errors such as deliberately disregarding or distorting evidence (WTO, 1998a, para. 133).

Wirth (1998, p. 758) objected that this ruling made the panels' weighing of scientific evidence 'virtually unreviewable.' This criticism went too far because egregious errors could be overturned on appeal. But the Appellate Body did grant panels considerable discretion over scientific matters and, consequently, raised the stakes riding on the outcome of the consultation process. Some held that panel members, typically trade, diplomatic and legal experts working at the WTO or doing business in Geneva, lacked the expertise to address scientific matters and to benefit sufficiently from consultations with experts (Guzman, 2004; Harlow, 2004). Others suggested that expert review groups would be more effective than individual consultations in disputes in which the parties presented conflicting evidence or the experts expressed divergent views (Carruth and Goldstein, 2004).

The hormones panel was vulnerable to this criticism. The panel consisted of a law professor and two diplomats (Charnovitz, 1997), encountered conflicting evidence and consulted individual experts who occasionally expressed varying views. But its rulings, the first to make significant use of scientific evidence and expert testimony, indicated that these concerns were exaggerated.[8] Overall, the hormones panel deployed the experts' testimony and other evidence properly despite making a few minor errors. One error received considerable attention but neither it nor the other errors affected the outcome of the dispute. The panel stated that the total dietary intake of estrogen posed a breast cancer risk of between 0 and 1 in a million. In fact, Dr Lucier testified that the breast cancer risk attributable to total dietary intake of estrogen was several thousand times greater. It was the consumption of meat from cows treated with estrogen that posed a breast cancer risk of between 0 and 1 in a million (WTO, 1997a). The EU claimed that this estimate demonstrated that growth hormones posed a health risk (WTO, 1998a). The Appellate Body disagreed, observing that a 'single divergent opinion' did not 'overturn' the scientific evidence establishing the safety of the hormones in growth promotion (WTO, 1998a, para. 198). Both the EU and the Appellate Body misinterpreted Dr Lucier's statement.[9] Dr Lucier could not rule out the possibility that growth hormones posed a risk to consumers, but, *if* there was a risk, it was small, close to zero, a fraction of the risks posed by normal dietary intake. This view did not diverge from the other testimony. According to Dr Ritter, science was incapable of 'testing to a certainty' that hormone-treated meat was free of risk (WTO, 1997a, 6.92). For the same reason, the Appellate Body concluded that risk assessments must address real as opposed to hypothetical risks (WTO, 1998a).

We will return to the efficacy of panel consultations with scientific experts in Chapter 6, where we investigate three other food safety disputes, each of which hinged on the panel's interpretation of scientific evidence.

4.7   COMPLIANCE

The EU's compliance record in the hormones dispute raised concerns about how best to reconcile sovereignty over health policy with a binding dispute resolution process. The EU sought a lengthy implementation period (four years) to address the inadequacies of its risk assessment. The matter went to arbitration and, after the expiration of a much briefer implementation period (15 months), the EU announced its intention to retain the ban and to continue its risk assessment process (WTO, 1998b, 1999a). Choosing that course had several undesirable effects. Canadian and US meat producers did not obtain access to the European market so the underlying dispute remained unresolved. Punitive tariffs were imposed on European exporters who were not parties to the dispute, reducing their access to markets in Canada and the US. Thus the remedy further restricted trade and failed to compensate US and Canadian exporters harmed by the ban (Ambrose, 2000).

The EU's Scientific Committee on Veterinary Measures Relating to Public Health continued to assess the risks posed by growth hormones and confirmed previous conclusions supporting the ban in 2000 and 2002. In 2003, the EU placed a permanent ban on the use of estrogen for growth promotion and imposed a provisional ban on the five other hormones involved in the dispute (WTO, 2003). The permanent ban reflected estrogen's status as a 'complete carcinogen', one that had tumor-initiating and tumor-promoting effects (WTO, 2003, Annex I, p. 4). As there was less complete information on the health risks posed by the other hormones, a provisional ban was imposed while the EU sought additional information. The legislation phased out the therapeutic use of estrogen but retained therapeutic exemptions for testosterone and progesterone (WTO, 2003).

With the adoption of the amended legislation in 2003, the EU contended that it had complied with the dispute resolution rulings. The US and Canada disputed that claim, continued to impose retaliatory tariffs and blocked the EU's efforts to re-examine compliance. In response, the EU initiated two new disputes against Canada and the US alleging wrongful imposition of the retaliatory tariffs (WTO, 2005a, 2005b). A joint panel was formed to address these disputes. Its rulings were unavailable at the time of writing (April 2007) so one could only speculate on the outcome of this phase of the dispute. But it was unlikely that the permanent ban on estrogen would survive the panel's review unless new evidence validated the health risks posed. The provisional ban was also on shaky ground. According to the panel and appellate rulings in the agricultural products and apples disputes (Chapter 6), sanitary measures may be imposed on a provisional basis in cases of insufficient scientific evidence, provided that governments sought additional information to validate the measures imposed. The five hormones subject to the 'provisional' ban were prohibited for nearly 20 years. During that period, none of the evidence gathered by the EU demonstrated a health risk when the hormones were used in growth promotion. Moreover, the EU examined a good deal of evidence suggesting that five of the six hormones (all but MGA) could be used safely for growth promotion. It was unlikely that the provisional ban would be upheld in the absence of new evidence demonstrating a health risk.

For the dispute resolution process to be credible, it must produce binding outcomes. Consequently, the dispute resolution rules encouraged members to remove offending regulations. However, members were permitted to retain non-conforming measures provided that they compensated the parties challenging the measures or permitted them to suspend trade concessions (WTO, 1994b). The suspension of concessions was designed to rebalance the parties' commitments during a brief period in which 'losers' might be unable to comply with their obligations. But it was more commonly viewed as retaliation. Generally, 'winners' imposed exorbitant tariffs on exports of political or economic significance to 'losers' in an attempt to maximize the cost of non-compliance (Lawrence, 2003).

The hormones dispute illustrated the unfairness and ineffectiveness of this system. In August 1999, Canada and the US began imposing 100 percent tariffs worth C$11.3 and $116.8 million, respectively, on a variety of exports from the EU, including meat, vegetables, fruit, cheese and chocolate (WTO, 1999a, 1999b). Thus producers and consumers of Roquefort cheese, Belgian chocolate and French wine bore the burden of the EU's decision to retain the hormones ban. It would have been preferable for the EU to compensate Canada and the US with a payment or by liberalizing trade concessions. Unlike retaliatory tariffs, monetary compensation did not restrict trade or impose the burden of non-compliance on those who were not parties to the dispute. Monetary compensation also provided a mechanism to provide financial assistance to producers harmed by non-compliance. Alternatively, the EU could have compensated the US and Canada by reducing trade barriers against non-beef exports. Liberalizing trade concessions would have enhanced trade, thereby offsetting the trade restricting effects of non-compliance (Lawrence, 2003).

Both forms of compensation ameliorated the asymmetric aspects of the retaliatory system, which favored large countries over smaller ones. Large economies like the EU could absorb trade penalties like those in the hormones dispute with relative ease. But smaller countries had limited capacities to withstand retaliation because they were likely to result in real harm to the domestic economy through lower export earnings. Similarly, small country 'winners' were reluctant to retaliate for non-compliance through punitive tariffs because it burdened the domestic economy with higher import costs and could lead to retaliation from the 'loser' in other markets (WTO, 2005c). Of course, a compensation system did not eliminate the 'buy out' problem; large countries would always be in a better position to opt out of their obligations than small ones (Jackson, 2004, p. 121). Another difficulty was that the compensation system depended on cooperation from the 'loser' while the retaliatory system did not (Lawrence, 2003). Suggestions to improve compliance are further explored in Chapter 9.

In the case of the hormones ban, the negative aspects of non-compliance could have been avoided had the EU lifted the ban and adopted a labeling scheme. Product labels would have allowed consumers who were not persuaded that growth hormones were safe to shun hormone-treated meat in favor of hormone-free meat. This approach would have allowed the EU to respond to the public's concerns while abiding by trade rules. The hormones panel signaled its support for product labels as a solution to the dispute in its concluding remarks, which noted that some WTO members used labeling standards to achieve the EU's objectives (WTO, 1997a). In negotiations during the implementation period, the US agreed to labels identifying hormone-treated beef as a 'product of the USA' although the US rejected labels stating that hormone levels were higher in US beef than in European beef (Josling, Roberts and Orden, 2004, p. 121).

From a purely technical perspective, the case for product labels is dubious in circumstances like these where there is no scientific basis for distinguishing between products. In fact, the use of product labels tends to reinforce the perception that the products pose differing health risks. However, over the long term, product labels combined with educational campaigns should more closely align actual and perceived risks (Viscusi, 1990). In the meantime, product labels provide consumers with the information they need to make choices that reflect their tolerance of risk.

Of course, citizens make better decisions and social welfare is higher in societies where citizens are able to distinguish between real and imaginary risks. The scientific justification and risk assessment guidelines may be helpful in this regard. By compelling governments to establish a rational basis for their sanitary regulations, the requirements promote greater understanding of health risks and their control, which in turn improves decision making and enhances social welfare (Howse, 2000). The requirements might also serve to foster greater public participation in and democratic control over health policy by subjecting government policy to greater scrutiny (Howse, 2000). These benefits are especially valuable in situations where domestic producers seek to disguise protectionist measures as health regulations (Chang, 2004).

The EU's unwillingness to replace the ban with labeling standards was puzzling in light of its subsequent decision to institute labeling standards for food containing genetically modified organisms (GMOs) (Chapter 8). Initially, by choosing to retain the ban and to face retaliation, the EU affirmed its sovereignty over health policy without undermining the dispute resolution process. But the EU's decision to initiate a new dispute challenging the continued imposition of the retaliatory tariffs raised questions about its willingness to abide by the hormones rulings. In the absence of new scientific evidence to support the ban, the new dispute could look more like an effort to obstruct implementation of an adverse ruling than one designed to promote food safety.

4.8 TRANSPARENCY OF THE DISPUTE RESOLUTION PROCESS

On a more positive note, progress was made on improving the transparency of the dispute resolution process during the panel proceedings examining the EU's challenge to the retaliatory tariffs. At the urging of Canada, the EU and the US, the panel became the first to open its proceedings to the public, albeit in a limited fashion. After applying for seats on a first-come-first-serve basis, 400 trade officials, NGO representatives, academics and members of the media observed two days of the proceedings via a closed-circuit television broadcast at the WTO in September 2005 (ICTSD, 2005). The panel's meeting with scientific experts in September 2006 and its meeting with disputants in October 2006 were televised in the same manner (ICTSD, 2006).

Unfortunately, many WTO members continue to oppose opening the dispute resolution proceedings to the public, as was apparent in the dispute. Owing to member opposition, the panel's meeting with third party participants in 2005 was not televised (ICTSD, 2005).[10] As discussed in Chapters 3 (shrimp–turtle) and 5 (asbestos), developed nations tend to favor a more transparent dispute resolution process. Developing countries object that opening the proceedings to the public is incompatible with their intergovernmental character. Because of this division in the membership, it is likely that broadcasts will be the exception rather than the rule for the foreseeable future. Despite the limitations of this approach, it moves the transparency agenda forward while accommodating the disparate views of the WTO's members (Esserman and Howse, 2005). Additional suggestions to improve the transparency of the dispute resolution process are explored in Chapter 9.

4.9   CONCLUSION

The hormones case shared several features with the gasoline and shrimp–turtle disputes (Chapters 2 and 3). In all three disputes, the panels narrowly interpreted the provisions permitting members to establish environmental and sanitary regulations and erroneously restricted governments' right to set policy affecting those matters. In each case, the Appellate Body reversed the panel and provided strong support for governments seeking to implement environmental or health policies. In a further parallel, the Appellate Body acknowledged the goals pursued but concluded that the regulations at issue were applied or crafted in ways that were incompatible with WTO obligations. The administrative deficiencies were glaring in each case. As applied by the US, the reformulated gas standards favored domestic producers and the shrimp ban favored some foreign producers over others. In the case of the hormones ban, the EU's risk assessment did not produce any evidence that hormones were harmful when used for growth promotion. In its first three rulings on environmental and sanitary measures, the Appellate Body bolstered sovereignty over the environment and public health while affirming governments' traditional obligation to avoid trade discrimination and illuminating the new role of the scientific evidence and risk assessment requirements in providing support for sanitary measures.

This view was by no means pervasive. Wallach and Woodall (2004, p. 69) complained that the risk assessment requirements were so onerous that it was 'nearly impossible' to establish safety regulations that exceeded international standards. Sykes (2002, p. 364) emphasized that governments faced possibly 'insurmountable' obstacles in demonstrating the existence of 'low level' risks like those associated with hormone residues in meat. Charnovitz (1997, p. 1784) observed that the ban was probably 'irrational' but the rulings reinforced criticism that the WTO advanced trade at the expense of public health. Guzman (2000) argued that the WTO should defer to members' risk assessments to insure that governments retained sovereignty over health policy.

Anticipating criticism of this sort, the Appellate Body explained that the SPS Agreement not only liberalized trade but also 'safeguard[ed], at the same time, the right and duty of Members to protect the life and health of their people' (WTO, 1998a, para. 177). The scientific evidence and risk assessment requirements were necessary to maintain the 'delicate and carefully negotiated balance' between these 'shared, but sometimes competing, interests' (WTO, 1998a, para. 177). Without the requirements, the organization would be unable to prevent governments from disguising protectionist measures as health regulations. This was not a hypothetical concern. As agricultural quotas and tariffs were reduced or eliminated, sanitary regulations proliferated (Henson and Loader, 2001). At the WTO, 35 (10 percent) of the 352 complaints filed as of January 2007 involved food safety regulations purporting to protect animal, human or plant health (WTO, 2007). While most of these complaints were withdrawn or resolved through consultations, nearly all involved disguised restrictions on trade. As we will see in Chapter 6, the salmon, apples and agricultural products disputes illustrate this phenomenon and the key role that the SPS Agreement's scientific justification and risk assessment requirements play in distinguishing between protectionist and legitimate health measures.

As in the shrimp–turtle dispute, some criticized the Appellate Body for issuing rulings that were more politically savvy than legally sound (Quick and Bluthner, 1999). Victor (2000) opined that the Appellate Body's decision to require a rational relationship between the results of the risk assessment and the measure in dispute created an ill-defined standard that would be difficult to interpret and apply. Quick and

Bluthner (1999) worried that the Appellate Body improperly broadened the range of factors considered in the risk assessment process. Harlow (2004) asserted that the Appellate Body muddied the distinction between risk assessment and risk management. Ambrose (2000) feared that permitting governments to base sanitary policies on divergent scientific opinion created the possibility that governments would impose regulations supported by a single, rogue scientist. Wagner (2000, pp. 856–7) held the contrary view that the Appellate Body's references to 'qualified and respected sources' and 'life-threatening' risks meant that it merely 'paid lip service' to the right of governments to rely on minority scientific opinion. Although disparate, these critiques objected implicitly to the practical, results-oriented, case-by-case approach that the Appellate Body took towards the resolution of the dispute. On balance, despite the limitations captured by the critiques, the approach was effective. By adhering closely to the language of the SPS Agreement, the Appellate Body fulfilled its mandate to resolve the dispute at hand while declining to establish a one-size-fits-all precedent for future disputes.

NOTES

1. Canada and the US filed separate complaints against the ban. Although the hormones panel conducted two separate investigations (WTO, 1997a, 1997b), it addressed the same issues, consulted with one group of scientific experts and issued nearly identical rulings in both disputes. Both sets of rulings were appealed to the Appellate Body, which considered the matters jointly and issued a single report (WTO, 1998a).
2. The three synthetic hormones performed the same functions as the natural hormones. Zeranol affected female sex characteristics and was a substitute for estrogen. Like testosterone, trenbolone affected male sex characteristics. MGA and progesterone helped sustain pregnancies. For more insight on the roles of the hormones, see WTO (1997a, paras 2.6–2.10).
3. Directive 96/22/EC went into effect 1 July 1997 replacing directives 81/602/EEC, 88/146/EEC and 88/299/EEC. For a more complete discussion of the hormones regulations, see WTO (1997a, paras 2.1–2.5).
4. The hormones were employed in cattle and lamb production in the US and Canada but the dispute was limited to meat and meat products from cattle because no evidence was presented with respect to lamb.
5. The International Agency for Research on Cancer (IARC) classified estrogen as a Group 1 carcinogen (carcinogenic to humans). Testosterone was identified as Group 2A (probably carcinogenic to humans) and progesterone was listed as Group 2B (possibly carcinogenic to humans).
6. The Office International des Epizootics (OIE) is also known as the World Organization for Animal Health.
7. The panel and Appellate Body exercised judicial economy on whether the ban was more trade restrictive than necessary (Article 5.6).
8. The shrimp–turtle panel consulted scientific experts but made little use of their contributions in its report.

9. For a contrary view, see Sykes (2002).
10. The third parties were Australia, Brazil, China, India, Mexico, New Zealand and Taiwan.

REFERENCES

Ambrose, K. (2000), 'Part II: review of key substantive agreements: panel IId: Agreement on Technical Barriers to Trade (TBT) and Agreement on the Application of Sanitary and Phytosanitary Measures (SPS): science and the WTO', *Law & Policy in International Business*, **31**(4), 861–8.

Caduff, L. (2002), 'Growth hormones and beyond', Center for International Studies, Zurich, Working Paper 8-2002.

Carruth R. and B. Goldstein (2004), 'The asbestos case: a comment on the appointment and use of nonpartisan experts in World Trade Organization dispute resolution involving health risk', *Risk Analysis*, **24**(2), 471–81.

Chang, H. (2004), 'Risk regulation, endogenous public concerns and the hormones dispute: nothing to fear but fear itself?', *Southern California Law Review*, **77**(4), 743–75.

Charnovitz, S. (1997) 'The World Trade Organization, meat hormones and food safety', *International Trade Reporter*, **14**(41), 1781–7.

Cottier, Thomas (2001), 'Risk management experience in WTO dispute settlement', in David Robertson and Aynsley Kellow (eds), *Globalization and the Environment, Risk Assessment and the WTO*, Cheltenham, UK and Northampton, MA, USA: Edward Elgar, pp. 41–62.

EC Scientific Conference (1995), 'Assessment of Health Risk – Working Group II', *EC Scientific Conference Proceedings*, Brussels: EC Scientific Conference on Growth Promotion and Meat Production, 29 November–1 December, cited in WTO (1997a), para. 2.33.

EC Scientific Group (1982), *Lamming Report*, Brussels: EC Scientific Group on Anabolic Agents in Animal Production, 22 September, cited in WTO (1997a), para. 2.28.

Esserman, S. and R. Howse (2005), 'The creative evolution of world trade', *Financial Times*, 23 August, 11.

Guzman, A. (2004), 'Food fears: health & safety at the WTO', *Virginia Journal of International Law*, **45**(1), 1–39.

Harlow, S. (2004), 'Science-based trade disputes: a new challenge in harmonizing evidentiary systems of law and science', *Risk Analysis*, **24**(2), 443–7.

Henson, S. and R. Loader (2001), 'Barriers to agricultural exports from developing countries: the role of sanitary and phytosanitary requirements', *World Development*, **29**(1), 85–102.

Howse, R. (2000), 'Democracy, science and free trade: risk regulation on trial at the World Trade Organization', *Michigan Law Review*, **98**(7), 2329–57.

Hunter, M. (1988), 'Francois Lamy: how France's Nader won ban on hormone-treated meat', *The Washington Post*, 25 December, H3.

ICTSD (International Centre for Trade and Sustainable Development) (2005), 'First public WTO dispute settlement hearing under way', *Bridges Weekly Trade News Digest*, **9**(30), 14 September, 4.

ICTSD (International Centre for Trade and Sustainable Development) (2006), 'Beef hormones dispute panel holds second public hearing', *Bridges Weekly Trade News Digest*, **10**(32), 4 October, 8.

Jackson, J. (2004), 'Editorial comment: international law status of the WTO dispute settlement reports: obligation to comply or option to "buy out"?', *American Journal of International Law*, **98**(1), 109–25.

Josling, Tim, Donna Roberts and David Orden (2004), *Food Regulation and Trade, Toward a Safe and Open Global System*, Washington, DC: Institute for International Economics.

Lawrence, Robert Z. (2003), *Crimes and Punishments? Retaliation Under the WTO*, Washington, DC: Institute for International Economics.

Quick, R. and A. Bluthner (1999), 'Has the Appellate Body erred? An appraisal and criticism of the ruling in the WTO hormones case', *Journal of International Economic Law*, **2**(4), 603–40.

Retallack, S. (1997), 'The WTO's record so far – corporations: 3 / humanity and the environment: 0', *The Ecologist*, **27**(4), July–August, 136–7.

Sykes, A. (2002), 'Exploring the need for international harmonization: domestic regulation, sovereignty, and scientific evidence requirements: a pessimistic view', *Chicago Journal of International Law*, **3**(2), 353–67.

Victor, D. (2000), 'The Sanitary and Phytosanitary Agreement of the World Trade Organization: an assessment after five years', *New York University School of Law Journal of International Law and Politics*, **32**(4), 865–937.

Viscusi, W. (1990), 'Sources of inconsistency in societal responses to health risks', *American Economic Review*, **80**(2), Papers and Proceedings of the 102nd Annual Meeting of the AEA, May, 257–61.

Vogel, David (1995), *Trading Up, Consumer and Environmental Regulation in a Global Economy*, Cambridge, MA: Harvard University Press.

Wagner, J. (2000), 'The WTO's interpretation of the SPS Agreement has undermined the right of governments to establish appropriate levels of protection against risk', *Law and Policy in International Business*, **31**(4), 855–9.

Wallach, Lori and Patrick Woodall (2004), *Whose Trade Organization? A Comprehensive Guide to the WTO*, New York: The New Press for Public Citizen.

Wirth, D. (1998), 'International decisions: EC – measures concerning meat and meat products (hormones)', *The American Journal of International Law*, **92**(4), 755–9.

WTO (1994a), *Agreement on the Application of Sanitary and Phytosanitary Measures* (SPS), Geneva: WTO.

WTO (1994b), *Understanding on Rules and Procedures Governing the Settlement of Disputes* (DSU), Geneva: WTO.

WTO (1997a), EC – *Measures Concerning Meat and Meat Products (Hormones)*, Complaint by the US, Report of the Panel (WT/DS26/R/USA), Geneva: WTO, 18 August.

WTO (1997b), *EC – Measures Concerning Meat and Meat Products (Hormones)*, Complaint by Canada, Report of the Panel (WT/DS48/R/CAN), Geneva: WTO, 18 August.

WTO (1998a), *EC – Measures Concerning Meat and Meat Products*

(Hormones), Report of the Appellate Body (WT/DS26/AB/R and WT/DS48/AB/R), Geneva: WTO, 16 January.

WTO (1998b), *EC – Measures Concerning Meat and Meat Products (Hormones)*, Arbitration Under Article 21.3 of the DSU, Award of the Arbitrator (WT/DS26/15 and WT/DS48/13), Geneva: WTO, 29 May.

WTO (1999a), *EC – Measures Concerning Meat and Meat Products (Hormones), Original Complaint by the United States, Recourse to Arbitration under 22.6 of the DSU, Decision by the Arbitrators* (WT/DS26/ARB), Geneva: WTO, 12 July.

WTO (1999b), *EC – Measures Concerning Meat and Meat Products (Hormones) Original Complaint by Canada, Recourse to Arbitration under 22.6 of the DSU, Decision by the Arbitrators* (WT/DS48/ARB, Geneva: WTO, 12 July.

WTO (2003), *EC – Measures Concerning Meat and Meat Products (Hormones), Communication from the European Communities* (WT/DS26/22 and WT/DS48/20), Geneva: WTO, 28 October.

WTO (2005a), *US – Continued Suspension of Obligations in the EC Hormones Dispute, Request for the Establishment of a Panel* (WT/DS320/6), Geneva: WTO, 14 January.

WTO (2005b), *Canada – Continued Suspension of Obligations in the EC Hormones Dispute, Request for the Establishment of a Panel* (WT/DS321/6), Geneva: WTO, 14 January.

WTO (2005c), *The Future of the WTO, Addressing Institutional Challenges in the New Millennium, Report by the Consultative Board to the Director General Supachai Panitchpakdi*, Geneva: WTO.

WTO (2007), *The Disputes*, Geneva: WTO (website accessed during January).

5. Asbestos

In July 1996, France announced a ban on asbestos production, use and trade. With no domestic asbestos production since 1965, virtually all of the asbestos used in France was imported chrysotile. Two-thirds was imported from Canada, the world's second largest chrysotile asbestos producer. For the long-troubled Canadian asbestos industry, the ban posed not only the immediate loss of the French market but also the disturbing possibility that the French measure might strengthen global efforts to ban chrysotile. Concentrated in Quebec, the Canadian asbestos industry had considerable support within the Canadian government despite its small size, declining fortunes, and the hazardous nature of its production. Canadian officials charged that the ban was a hasty and ill-considered response to irrational fears among the French public regarding asbestos health risks in the wake of the mad cow disease and tainted blood scandals. Canada challenged the ban at the WTO, arguing that it was an unwarranted infringement on asbestos trade since modern extraction, production and use standards reduced health risks to undetectable levels. Citing asbestos' carcinogenicity, France asserted that the ban was necessary to impede asbestos-related disease. Setting these contrasting views against one another, the asbestos dispute involved the most significant health risks to be addressed by the WTO and provided a crucial test of the organization's ability to reconcile commercial and health objectives.

5.1   ASBESTOS REGULATION

During 1995, extensive media coverage of the health risks arising from occupational exposure to asbestos alarmed the French public. That summer, the French government requested that the Institut National de la Science et de la Recherche Médicale (INSERM), the nation's premier science institute, study the matter. In late June 1996, INSERM submitted an executive summary of its findings to the French government. Four days later, the National Association of Protection for Asbestos

Victims (Association Nationale de Défense des Victimes de L'Aminate (ANDEVA) instituted legal proceedings against the government alleging that it had failed to protect the public. In early July, the French government announced its decision to ban asbestos. The government approved the asbestos ban (Decree No. 96-1133) in late December and the ban went into effect on 1 January 1997 (WTO, 2000a).

INSERM released its final report in November 1997. The report tied asbestos to three diseases: asbestosis, mesothelioma (a pleura cancer) and lung cancer. The diseases were associated primarily but not exclusively with occupational exposure. Overall, asbestos claimed 2000 lives in France in 1995, 1200 from lung cancer and 750 from mesothelioma. A hundred and sixty-six new cases of asbestosis were documented in the same year. Dormant for on average 30 years, mesothelioma was terminal typically within a year of the onset of symptoms. The building trades accounted for one-quarter of the mesothelioma cases; sheet-metal workers, carpenters and plumbers experienced the highest incidence of the disease. Asbestosis, a pulmonary fibrosis, was linked to prolonged asbestos exposure. After exposure had terminated, the condition stabilized or advanced, leading to potentially life-threatening respiratory problems. There was no cure for the disease, which developed over seven or eight years on average. While lung cancer was linked to tobacco use and other factors, exposure to asbestos was the only known cause of mesothelioma and asbestosis (WTO, 2000a).

In making the case for the ban, France emphasized health risks to secondary users, including construction, service and maintenance workers and do-it-yourselfers, who cut and drilled pipes and other products containing asbestos. Since asbestos's presence in these materials was not discernible, many secondary users were unaware of their exposure and took no precautionary measures. Others were unwilling to purchase the expensive safety equipment necessary for controlled use. As no level of asbestos exposure was free of health risk, the ban was necessary to insure the safety of occupational users, do-it-yourselfers and others who might otherwise be exposed to asbestos (WTO, 2000a).

France first regulated asbestos in the late 1970s, when it set limits for workplace exposure to asbestos dust and banned the spraying of asbestos fibers. At the time, occupational health risks arising from the inhalation of crocidolite (blue asbestos) raised the greatest concern. In 1986, the International Labor Organization's Asbestos Convention (Convention 162) banned the spraying of all forms of asbestos, prohibited the use of crocidolite and recommended that other forms of asbestos be replaced by safer substitutes. By 1988, France had placed a complete ban on production, use and trade in crocidolite and had imposed a partial ban on chrysotile (white asbestos). Chrysotile continued to be used in cement-based building products, brake linings and roofing materials for its fire-resistant properties. Workplace safety regulations set exposure limits, required the use of protective equipment and prohibited untrained and casual employees from working with chrysotile (WTO, 2000a).

In 1980, the European Union began to regulate asbestos with the twin goals of promoting public health and harmonizing disparate asbestos regulations among member nations. In the early 1980s, the European Union's asbestos initiatives emphasized reducing occupational exposure by establishing exposure limits and safety procedures. During the same period, the EU instituted mandatory labeling of all asbestos products, banned asbestos spraying and prohibited the use of crocidolite (with limited exceptions). By 1985, partial bans were imposed on other forms of asbestos. In 1990, the EU mandated that employers replace carcinogenic substances with safer substitutes. In 1991, the EU classified all forms of asbestos as category 1 carcinogens (substances that caused cancer in human beings). But, initially, subsequent regulations maintained the practice of differentiating between chrysotile and other forms of asbestos. For example, legislation adopted in 1991 prohibited the use of chrysotile in 14 specific product types but imposed a complete ban on the sale and use of all other forms of asbestos. Nevertheless, with the enactment of the replacement principle and the classification of chrysotile as a carcinogen along with other forms of asbestos, chrysotile's days in the EU were numbered. The differential treatment of chrysotile was a temporary reprieve designed to accommodate nations requiring additional time to transition to a complete ban. In 1999, the EU extended its asbestos ban to chrysotile and set an effective date of 1 January 2005 (WTO, 2000a).

Elsewhere, Iceland and Norway imposed bans on asbestos in the 1980s while permitting some exceptions that were tightened during the 1990s. In 1989, Switzerland banned crocidolite, chrysotile and a third form of asbestos (amosite) while allowing some exceptions. In accordance with EU mandates, Belgium (1998), the UK (1999), Ireland (2000), Luxembourg (2002) and Spain (2002) banned chrysotile, having previously banned other forms of asbestos. EU aspirants, Poland (1997) and Latvia (2001), enacted complete bans while Slovenia (1996) and Lithuania (1998) imposed partial bans. Asbestos bans remained largely a European phenomenon until Kuwait (1995) and Saudi Arabia (1998) imposed total bans. In 1995, Japan banned crocidolite and amosite (Kazan-Allen, 2005). Since 1991, the US has imposed a partial ban on asbestos that prohibited its use in paper and flooring products as well as for any new uses (Global Environment & Technology Foundation, 2003).

5.2 CANADIAN AND GLOBAL ASBESTOS PRODUCTION

Facing an increasingly hostile regulatory environment, the asbestos industry has been in decline since the 1970s, when global production reached 5.2 million tonnes (WT0, 2000a).[1] By 1997, production world-wide had shrunk to 1.9 million tonnes. The Canadian industry shared a similar fate. Canadian asbestos production totaled 750 000 tonnes in 1985 but declined substantially over the next decade, reaching 506 000 tonnes by the end of 1996. In the next two years, Canadian asbestos production plummeted, registering decreases of 86 000 tonnes in 1997 and 100 000 tonnes in 1998. At the end of 1998, production stood at 320 000 tonnes, 40 percent lower than two years previously. Production rose slightly in 1999 but fell to just 240 000 tonnes in 2002, less than one-third of the 1985 level (Natural Resources Canada, 2003).

As European governments tightened asbestos regulation during the 1970s and 1980s, Canada's exports to the region declined and it increasingly sought other markets. By 1988, Asian markets had become more important to the Canadian asbestos industry than those in Europe. Exports to Europe fell dramatically over the next several years. Canada's European exports had declined to just 46 000 in 1996, with France accounting for about 14 000 tonnes or 30 percent of the European market. When the ban became effective in 1997, the French market evaporated. Canada's exports to France fell to 21 tonnes in 1997, while its European exports declined to 22 000 tonnes. The ban accounted for about 60 percent of the reduction in the European market in 1997 and 16 percent of the total reduction in Canadian asbestos exports that year. It did not contribute materially to the sharp decrease in Canadian asbestos exports in 1998 (Natural Resources Canada, 2003; WTO, 2000a).

The Asian financial crisis was the key factor contributing to the precipitous decline in Canadian asbestos exports during the period 1997 to 1998. Canada's asbestos exports to Asia had surged to the neighborhood of

300 000 tonnes in the early 1990s but fell below 200 000 by 1998. Despite this decline, markets in the region accounted for 57 percent of the industry's exports in 1998. The downturn in Asia compounded the long-term decline affecting other markets. During the period 1994 to 1997, asbestos exports to the Americas, European Union, Mideast and Africa decreased by nearly 40 percent (Natural Resources Canada, 2003).

The Canadian industry also faced unfavorable changes in its competitive landscape. In 1997, Canada retained its traditional position as the world's second largest asbestos producer and accounted for 23 percent of global production. Its production was exceeded only by Russia's, which amounted to 685 000 tonnes or 36 percent of the global total. China (13 percent) and Brazil (11 percent) were the third and fourth largest producers with production levels of 250 000 and 208 000 tonnes, respectively. By 1998, Canada's production was surpassed by Russia's and China's. Global production rose by just 30 000 tonnes to 1.94 million tonnes in 1998. Production was stable or declining everywhere except China where production nearly doubled. China's advance came at the expense of Russia and, especially, Canada. By the end of 1998, Russia's and Canada's shares of global production had fallen to 32 percent and 16 percent, respectively, while China's share had climbed to 23 percent. Russia's large internal market, which absorbed 60 percent of its production, insulated it to some degree from competition with China. By contrast, Canada, the world's leading chrysotile exporter, exported 98–99 percent of its production. Russia was also better able to compete with China on price. By the late 1990s, the surge in Chinese production, its lower cost, and proximity to Canada's Asian markets placed new pressures on the long-troubled Canadian asbestos industry (Natural Resources Canada, 2003).

Following the closure of an asbestos mine in Newfoundland in 1994, Canadian production was limited to three mines in Quebec. The mines were operated by two companies, LAB Chrysotile, Inc. (Black Lake and Bell mines) and JM Asbestos, Inc. (Jeffrey mine). Production declined at both companies during the late 1990s, leading to layoffs and periodic shutdowns. In 1998, LAB Chrysotile produced about 195 000 tonnes of asbestos and employed 1100 workers. JM Asbestos produced roughly 115 000 tonnes and employed 400 (Natural Resources Canada, 2003). The Canadian government estimated that another 2500 individuals were employed in asbestos processing, manufacturing and related activities (WTO, 2000a). Canada's 1998 asbestos exports were valued at approximately C$199 million (Natural Resources Canada, 2003).

5.3 CANADA AND THE POLITICS OF ASBESTOS

By the late 1990s, the Canadian asbestos industry's long-term decline had turned into a downward spiral. The value of the industry's production and the number of jobs that it generated were trivial in the context of the nation's total production and employment. The prospects for a turnaround in international markets were remote. Within Canada, health, environmental, labor and other activists stridently opposed the industry and the government's controlled use asbestos policy. However, the government's commitment to the industry and controlled use did not waver.

The number of businesses and jobs affected was small but they were located in Quebec. Issues of concern in Quebec loomed large in Canadian politics owing to the strength of separatist sentiments in the province.[2] In addition, the industry was prominent in the province, as indicated by the identification of the product with the community (town of Asbestos) and producers (JM Asbestos, Inc. and LAB Chrysotile, Inc.). The industry had benefited from the support of leading political figures for decades. Quebec's Premier Lucien Bourchard, one of the leaders of the 1995 separatist campaign, promoted asbestos as 'a safe product if it is used safely' (Dougherty, 2000, p. D5). As Prime Minister, Jean Chrétien, a native of Quebec, advocated controlled use at home and abroad during the period 1993 to 2004 (Kazan-Allen, 2002). During the late 1970s, Quebec's Premier René Levesque called for nationalization of the industry as a way to promote new uses for asbestos and enhance the industry's competitiveness on international markets. Although the proposal was dropped, nonetheless it suggested the significance of the industry in the province. In 1949, university professor and future Prime Minister Pierre Trudeau catapulted to national prominence when he supported striking asbestos miners in the province (Dougherty, 2000).

During the 1980s, the Canadian government adopted controlled use of chrysotile as its asbestos policy. According to the government, the modern industry was distinct from the traditional industry in several ways. In the past, crocidolite and other amphiboles had been the dominant forms of asbestos in use. Respiratory disorders including lung cancer, mesothelioma and asbestosis had been linked to occupational exposure in mining, manufacturing and processing where workers faced high-intensity and prolonged exposure to amphiboles in a largely unregulated environment (WTO, 2000a). In the modern industry, the use of chrysotile and the dissemination of controlled use practices reduced occupational disease risks to 'undetectable' levels (WTO, 2000a, para. 3.50). Chrysotile did not penetrate as deeply into the respiratory tract or endure as long as amphibole asbestos. Since disease risks were tied to inhalation of asbestos particles, primary users were required to use wet processing, air purification systems, masks and other measures to reduce emissions to levels approved by the International Organization for Standards (ISO 7337). Secondary users encountering chrysotile in construction, plumbing and related activities did so safely because chrysotile fibers were bonded to or encapsulated in cement, plastics, resins and other materials that reduced dust emissions to a minimum when pipes and other products were cut or drilled. Do-it-yourselfers faced no health risks since their exposure to chrysotile was low and sporadic. However, low-speed tools, water-immersion, suction suits, masks and other measures could be employed as further precautions reducing inhalation risks virtually to nil. By contrast, the safety of substitute products had yet to be established, thus they posed indeterminate and potentially higher risks than chrysotile (WTO, 2000a).

During the 1990s, Canadian producers joined producers in other nations in promoting controlled use in asbestos consuming nations. In March 1997, the Canadian government signed a memo of understanding with the industry's Asbestos Institute agreeing to aid its efforts to promote controlled use internationally. Later that year, the Asbestos Institute began to hold training seminars in developing nations using a safe use program developed in conjunction with Canada's Resource Ministry. In 1998, the Resource Ministry collaborated with the governments of Brazil, Russia, South Africa, Swaziland and Zimbabwe, as well as producer and labor organizations in those countries to promote asbestos use and oppose asbestos bans (Natural Resources Canada, 2003).

Over the years, the industry received considerable governmental support, including subsidies totaling C$40 million from national and provincial governments from 1984 to 1993 (Schiller, 2000). Subsequently, the government of Quebec guaranteed 70 percent of a $65 million loan that JM Asbestos, Inc. secured from private lenders to undertake a C$135 million expansion project. The project was expected to extend the mine's life to 2020, yielding 250 000 tonnes of asbestos annually (Natural Resources Canada, 2003). The expansion plans were ambitious to say the least – the firm's production had been declining for years. JM president, Bernard Coulombe's plans to create 'niche markets' for the company's production were even more grandiose: 'Our mine has a capacity of 600 000 tonnes per year, but we are only mining about 140 000 tonnes so there is a lot of potential if we can promote the safe and practical uses of our product' (*Mealey's Litigation Report*, 2000).

LAB Chrysotile also undertook significant capital projects in the 1997–99 period, although apparently without direct public support. Its capital expenditures totaled C$70 million and were anticipated to extend production at its mines for at least another ten years. Redevelopment plans for the mining towns also hinged on safe use. Noranda, Inc. had opened a factory that was extracting magnesium from asbestos in Asbestos. Mayor Laurent Lessard of neighboring Thetford Mines hoped to attract similar investment in the town's asbestos industry (Dougherty, 2000).

Despite adverse market trends during the 1990s, the asbestos industry devised aggressive expansion and promotional strategies that were strongly supported by the Canadian government. Having made these commitments, it was essential to turn back the anti-asbestos tide. In addition to challenging the French ban at the WTO, Canadian officials intervened when other nations proposed bans – perhaps most publicly in the case of Chile. When Chile announced its ban, Canada's Ambassador created an uproar by denouncing Chilean health authorities as 'in the thrall of American environmental[ists]' (Dobbin, 2001, FP 13). Canadian Prime Minster Jean Chrétien spoke to Chilean President Ricardo Lagos on the matter and felt compelled to release an official statement indicating that he had 'forcefully made the Canadian case – based on clear scientific evidence – that chrysotile asbestos can be used safely' (Kazan-Allen, 2002, p. 1). Chilean authorities disagreed. The Chilean Medical Association's Andrei Tchermitchin said, 'There are some types of asbestos that are more toxic than others, but every type of asbestos has been proved to cause cancer' (Kazan-Allen, 2002, p. 1). Bernardo Reyes, the leading proponent of Chile's asbestos ban, accused the Canadians of hypocrisy: 'They [Canadian officials] claim to be worried about the environment – but when their exports are threatened they try to overturn Chile's laws for their self-interested advantage' (Kazan-Allen, 2002, p. 2).

Healthcare workers and environmentalists criticized the controlled use policy, emphasizing health risks to developing nations (Schiller, 2000). Since nearly all of the asbestos mined and milled in Canada was exported to other countries, there was little to no threat to the Canadian citizenry as a whole. Asbestos workers and unions accepted and promoted the safe use policy. The Director of the Syndicat des Métallos

du Québec (metalworkers' union) described the French ban 'as
completely at odds with the experience of chrysotile miners in Quebec'
(Fédération des Travailleurs et Travailleuses du Québec, 1996). He
claimed that conditions in asbestos mines and mills were as safe as those
in other fiber and chemical industries. While his claim was most likely
hyperbolic, there was some evidence that workers in Quebec's mines
and mills experienced lower rates of asbestos-related disease than
comparable workers in other nations (WTO, 2000a). Thus it was possible that controlled use reduced the health threats arising from asbestos
exposure. However, it had not eliminated these risks as the incidence of
asbestos-related disease was significantly higher in Quebec than in the
rest of Canada (WTO, 2000a). Further, because the incidence of
asbestos-related disease differed so dramatically for asbestos workers in
Quebec as compared to asbestos workers in other nations, additional
investigation was necessary to substantiate the results for Quebec.

5.4   THE WTO DISPUTE

In May 1998, Canada requested consultations at the WTO with the
European Union on the French ban. In October, Canada concluded that
dispute could not be resolved through consultations and requested that
the WTO establish a panel to hear the dispute. The parties agreed on
panel members in March 1999 and, soon after, Brazil, the United States
and Zimbabwe joined the dispute as third parties. Brazil and Zimbabwe
presented arguments that supported Canada. The US took positions
similar to the EU's (WTO, 2000a).

Canada argued that the ban violated provisions of both the General
Agreement on Tariffs and Trade (GATT) and the Agreement on Technical
Barriers to Trade (TBT). While the GATT's Article III prohibited discrimination against like products, France treated asbestos imports less favorably than substitute products of domestic origin.[3] As a technical
regulation, the ban fell under the domain of the TBT and was incompatible with several of its provisions. The European Union countered that
asbestos imports were treated no less favorably than domestic asbestos:
both were banned. Further, asbestos was not 'like' substitute products
because it posed a health risk, while they did not. For the same reason, the
ban was justified under the Article XX(b) exception for measures necessary to protect human health. The TBT did not apply because the ban was
not a technical regulation as defined by that agreement (WTO, 2000a).

5.5 ARTICLE III

By GATT/WTO convention, the likeness of products was determined by examining four factors: (1) properties, nature and qualities; (2) end-uses; (3) consumer taste and habits; and (4) tariff classifications. Despite acknowledging asbestos's unique chemical and physical properties, the panel concluded that chrysotile's properties were 'equivalent if not identical' to substitute products' because they shared a 'small number' of end-uses (WTO, 2000a, para. 8.125). The panel was not troubled that its analysis of tariff classifications contradicted this finding. Although the tariff classifications for asbestos (mineral) and the substitutes (vegetables and synthetics) differed because of varying product natures, the panel observed that products with different natures could share the same properties and end-uses in certain situations. Using this dubious interpretation of the properties criterion, the panel ruled that asbestos and substitute materials were like products within the meaning of Article III. As a result, the ban violated Article III because asbestos imports were treated less favorably than 'like' domestic substitutes, which were not subject to the ban (WTO, 2000a).

The panel rejected the notion of addressing health considerations in the 'likeness' determination, explaining that to do so 'would largely nullify' the Article XX(b) health exception (WTO, 2000a, para. 8.130). The decision was strongly criticized. As Friends of the Earth's David Waskow explained, the likeness rulings created the perverse result that 'a carcinogenic product is the same as a non-carcinogenic product' (Knight, 2000). The Earth Justice Legal Defense Fund's Martin Wagner questioned why the ban had to '"earn" an exception' to be compatible with trade rules (Knight, 2000).[4]

The Appellate Body rejected the panel's deployment of the four-part likeness criteria. Rather than producing a collective assessment after weighing each factor, the panel made a premature conclusion based on an improper examination of one criterion, properties, that excluded consideration of health risks and conflated the properties and end-use criteria. Despite acknowledging asbestos' unique properties, the panel concluded that asbestos and substitute products shared like properties because they shared certain end-uses. The Appellate Body disagreed, observing that the equivalence of end-uses did not change varying chemical and physical properties (WTO, 2001b). In the case of asbestos, carcinogenicity was a 'defining aspect' of these properties (WTO, 2001b, para. 114). The panel erred by failing to incorporate health considerations into its analysis.

The Appellate Body went on to reverse the panel's likeness determination, concluding that Canada had not met the burden of proof necessary to demonstrate the likeness of asbestos and substitute products. The Appellate Body remarked that the evidence presented on physical properties, health risks and tariff classifications suggested that the products were 'not like' but it stopped short of reaching that conclusion. No evidence had been presented on consumer tastes and insufficient evidence had been presented on end-uses. In the absence of additional information on these two factors, the Appellate Body concluded that it could not complete the likeness determination (WTO, 2001b).

The Appellate Body's reasoning was flawed. In light of chrysotile's carcinogenicity, it would have been reasonable to accept the EU's position that consumers were likely to prefer substitutes even though no evidence was presented. Similarly, the existence of a large number of non-shared end-uses should have provided an adequate basis for making a 'not like' finding under the end-use criterion even though the evidence reviewed by the panel was limited to a few shared end-uses. Thus each of the four criteria supported a 'not like' finding. Moreover, there was more than sufficient evidence to support a 'not like' finding regardless of the outcomes on the consumer taste and end-use criteria. Health considerations alone should have been decisive given the health risks posed by chrysotile. One of the three members of the Appellate Body shared this view and criticized the other members for giving greater weight to commercial than to public health objectives (WTO, 2001b).

5.6   ARTICLE XX(B)

Since the panel ruled that the ban violated Article III's prohibition against discrimination among like products, the EU was forced to invoke the Article XX(b) exception for measures 'necessary to protect human, animal, or plant life or health' (WTO, 1994). Although the parties had presented conflicting evidence, the panel did not set out to 'settle a scientific debate' (WTO, 2000a, para. 8.181). Instead, it would merely determine whether there was enough evidence to substantiate a health risk and to support the measures undertaken. Because of the scientific nature of the issues in dispute, the panel decided to consult four scientific experts: Dr Nicholas H. de Klerk, Department of Public Health, University of Western Australia; Dr Douglas W. Henderson,

Department of Anatomical Pathology, Flinders University of South Australia; Dr Peter F. Infante, Health Standards Program, US Occupational Health and Safety Administration and Dr Arthur W. Musk, Clinical Professor of Medicine and Public Health, University of Western Australia. During the expert selection process, the panel conferred with the EU and Canada and solicited nominations from the World Health Organization (WHO), International Labor Organization (ILO), International Program on Chemical Safety (IPCS), International Agency for Research on Cancer (IARC) and International Organization for Standardization (ISO) (WTO, 2000a).

Citing the experts' testimony and the recommendations of international organizations, the panel concluded that the ban was necessary to achieve France's objective of arresting asbestos-related disease. Since 1977, the International Agency for Research on Cancer (IARC) has classified all forms of asbestos as carcinogens. According to the experts, chrysotile posed serious health risks to occupational users and the broader public. In the past, the incidence of asbestos-related diseases was greatest for primary users engaged in mining and processing activities. More recent data indicated that workers engaged in construction, maintenance, service and other secondary activities experienced high rates of asbestos-related morbidity and mortality. Although disease risks increased with the intensity and duration of exposure, there was no level below which exposure was free of risk (WTO, 2000a).

Controlled use had not been shown to be effective in addressing these disease risks. Dr Infante characterized controlled use as a 'misnomer' and stated that it 'was not realistic in workplace situations' (WTO, 2000a, paras. 5.358, 5.343). In the US, there had been 4000 workplace safety violations in 1996–98 alone, despite 20 years of asbestos regulation and control. Deliberate non-compliance, accidents, human error, incomplete knowledge of exposure risks, poor judgment and training and communication failures were contributing factors. Controlled use was even less effective in non-occupational settings (WTO, 2000a).

The panel rejected Canada's claim that the ban was incompatible with the International Organization for Standards' dust exposure standards (ISO 7337). The panel explained that WTO members were entitled to establish their own risk levels and to implement the measures necessary to achieve them. As the ISO standards were not acceptable to France, it was not obliged to adopt them. Owing to the severity of asbestos disease risks, the International Labor Organization (ILO) recommended the use of substitutes, as did the WHO and the experts. France was not required to postpone taking action until the safety of the substitutes could be proved conclusively. The available evidence was limited but suggested that the substitutes were safer than chrysotile. These varying health risks motivated the ban and were reflected in its implementation. As applied, the ban neither discriminated nor created a disguised restriction on trade. Thus the ban satisfied Article XX's preamble (chapeau) as well as the requirements of Article XX(b) (WTO, 2000a).

The panel's Article XX(b) rulings were precedent-setting. Previous efforts to invoke the Article XX(b) exception had failed, leading critics to question whether it could be invoked successfully. When Canada appealed the rulings, the Appellate Body strongly affirmed the panel. Like the EU in the hormones dispute, Canada charged that the panel neither weighed the scientific evidence appropriately nor assessed it objectively. As in the hormones dispute, the Appellate Body ruled that panels had the discretion to weigh the evidence before them. Additionally, the asbestos panel's conclusions with respect to chrysotile and controlled use were supported by the available scientific evidence, the experts' testimony and international organizations' recommendations. However, WTO members were not required to conform to prevailing views within the scientific community as long as they relied on competent and reputable science (WTO, 2001b).

5.7   TBT

As with Article III, the panel emphasized that the TBT (Agreement on Technical Barriers to Trade) was designed to promote market access. With this goal in mind, the panel reasoned that the TBT applied to regulations permitting the sale of specific products with identifiable technical characteristics. As a general prohibition, the ban was not subject to the TBT because it neither identified particular products nor specified technical characteristics, nor permitted products to be sold. On the other hand, the temporary exceptions to the ban were subject to the TBT because they identified a specific list of products and the conditions under which they could be sold. But the panel did not examine the exceptions because Canada had not presented arguments on them (WTO, 2000a).

The Appellate Body discarded virtually every aspect of the panel's reasoning and concluded that the ban was subject to the TBT. As complementary aspects of a unified program, the ban and the exceptions were to be analyzed together, not separately. It was not necessary for specific products to be identified in technical regulations as long as they were identifiable. This was the case for the products subject to the ban since asbestos was their defining characteristic. Finally, regulations permitting and prohibiting the sale of products qualified as technical regulations. However, the Appellate Body was not able to rule on whether the ban violated the TBT because the panel made no factual findings with respect to Canada's claims (WTO, 2001b).

5.8 AMICUS BRIEFS

The asbestos panel received four unsolicited amicus briefs from non-governmental organizations and forwarded them to Canada and the EU for review. The EU attached two briefs to its submission, those from the Collegium Ramazzini and the American Federation of Labor–Congress of Industrial Organization (AFL–CIO). The EU characterized the briefs from the Ban Asbestos Network and Instituto Mexicano de Fibro Industrias AC as irrelevant and declined to incorporate them in its submission. Canada urged the panel to refuse to accept all four briefs but desired an opportunity to respond to them should the panel decide to accept the briefs (WTO, 2000a).

With the parties disagreeing on this matter, what was the panel to do? The panel split the loaf. It accepted the Collegium Ramazzini and AFL–CIO briefs as part of the EU submission. The panel indicated that it considered the briefs to be on the same footing as the other documents submitted by the EU, included them in the material presented to the experts, and gave Canada the opportunity to reply to them. On the other hand, the panel rejected the briefs submitted by the Ban Asbestos Network and Instituto Mexicano de Fibro Industrias AC. A fifth brief arrived several months later from the Indian non-governmental organization, Only Nature Endures. Although the panel forwarded the brief to the parties, the panel decided that it had arrived too late to be incorporated in the proceedings and noted that any additional briefs would be treated in the same manner (WTO, 2000a).

Expecting that it too would receive amicus submissions, the Appellate Body decided 'in the interests of fairness and orderly

procedure' that it would be desirable to issue new regulations governing the submission of amicus briefs in the case (WTO, 2000b, p. 1). The
Appellate Body consulted the parties and third parties who expressed
varying views on the matter. Surprisingly, the principals, Canada and
EU, were in agreement and held that the matter should be addressed by
WTO members rather than the Appellate Body. Among the third
parties, Brazil agreed with the EU and Canada. Zimbabwe expressed no
objections. The US supported the proposal. Several days later the
Appellate Body instituted an application procedure for individuals and
organizations desiring to submit amicus briefs (WTO, 2001b).

At this point, it might be useful to contrast the different approaches
taken by the panel and Appellate Body. The panel's main concern was
member governments. Taking a conservative approach, the panel
produced a compromise that satisfied the principals. Declining to
accept the briefs submitted by the Ban Asbestos Network and Instituto
Mexicano, the panel slighted these external constituents but accommodated Canada and the EU. By accepting the Collegium and AFL–CIO
briefs as part of the EU submission, the panel neutralized objections
from Canada. Additionally, as requested, Canada was afforded the
opportunity to respond to them. In short, the panel's actions favored its
internal constituency at the expense of non-governmental organizations, an external constituency. This approach did little to dispel criticism from external constituencies that non-governmental organizations
were excluded from participation in the dispute resolution process. But
it did have the virtue of having the support of the members.

The Appellate Body's priorities were exactly the opposite.
Concerned that insufficient NGO participation compromised the standing of the dispute resolution process with external constituents, the
Appellate Body wished to enhance the legitimacy of its rulings by
accepting unsolicited amicus briefs. In doing so, it lost sight of the preferences of its internal constituency and provoked outrage among WTO
members. Developing nations were especially vocal in their opposition.
Led by Egypt, the Informal Group of Developing Countries (IGDC)
called for a General Council meeting to address the matter. At the meeting, however, developing and developed countries were nearly unani-
mous in their opposition to the Appellate Body's initiative. Uruguay
and Egypt objected that the Appellate Body lacked the authority to
change the regulations. While the Appellate Body was empowered to
revise its working procedures to meet unforeseen situations that arose,
only the General Council had the authority to address substantive

issues. India and Colombia charged that the new procedure undermined the intergovernmental nature of the organization (WTO, 2001a). Singapore's ambassador agreed, explaining, 'as the rules stand, only parties and third parties have the right to participate in disputes' (Kanth, 2000). Hong Kong complained that poor nations might not have sufficient resources to respond to the large number of NGO briefs that might be submitted. Canada's representative distinguished between transparency and participation. Canada advocated greater transparency in the dispute resolution process but opposed the participation of external actors through amicus briefs. Only the US approved the Appellate Body's decision to adopt an application procedure for the amicus briefs (WTO, 2001a).

At the conclusion of the meeting, the Chair of the General Council remarked that additional clarification was needed on the substantive and procedural aspects of the rules governing amicus briefs. In the meantime, it was advisable for the Appellate Body to 'exercise extreme caution' (WTO, 2001a, para. 123). The Appellate Body compromised: it did not suspend the procedure but it did not accept any of the 17 briefs submitted under it. Six applications failed to meet the submission deadline. The remaining 11 were rejected for unspecified deviations from the submission criteria (WTO, 2001b).

5.9 AFTERMATH

The EU's Trade Commissioner Pascal Lamy greeted the Appellate Body's actions with approval: 'This ruling shows that the WTO is responsive to our citizens' concerns. Legitimate health issues can be put above pure trade concerns' (*Xinhua News Agency*, 2001). Canada stood by controlled use. Natural Resource Minister Ralph Goodale commented, 'In Canada, we can achieve the same health protection objectives through our policy of controlled use of certain specific applications of chrysotile asbestos' (*Gazette*, 2001). The Asbestos Institute's Denis Hamel feared that anti-asbestos forces including suppliers of substitute products would use the rulings to 'distort public opinion' in support of their efforts to achieve a global chrysotile ban (*Gazette*, 2001).

His concerns were well founded. Chile imposed a complete asbestos ban shortly after the Appellate Body's ruling. Argentina banned chrysotile in 2001 after banning crocidolite and amosite in 2000. In Brazil, cities and states representing 70 percent of the asbestos market banned it during the period 2000 to 2001. In 2002, Uruguay banned asbestos production and trade and New Zealand banned imports of asbestos fibers. In 2003, Australia banned chrysotile; crocidolite and amosite had been banned previously. Japan prohibited the use of chrysotile in building and friction products as of 2004 (Kazan-Allen, 2005). However, the industry secured an important victory at the multilateral level in 2004 when it blocked the inclusion of chrysotile in the Rotterdam Convention (Chrysotile Institute, 2004). The convention required exporters of hazardous substances to secure prior informed consent from the governments of importing nations. Previously, crocidolite had been included in the Convention (Food and Agriculture Organization, 2004).

5.10   RECONCILING HEALTH AND COMMERCIAL VALUES

The asbestos case featured the most serious health issues to figure in a WTO dispute, yet it has received the least attention – possibly because the WTO upheld the asbestos import ban. It is worth emphasizing that both the panel and Appellate Body upheld the ban. Although the panel ruled that the asbestos ban violated the GATT's anti-discrimination provisions, it concluded that the ban was justified under the agreement's Article XX(b) health exception.

The Appellate Body went beyond the panel by reversing its troubling conclusion that asbestos and substitute materials were like products despite differing health risks. Once the Appellate Body struck the panel's likeness determination, there was no basis for Canada's claim that the ban discriminated among like products. The ruling was important because it upheld the ban as compatible with the GATT's core anti-discrimination principles rather than as a health exception to those principles (Horn and Weiler, 2004). As a result, the Appellate Body could have decided to provide a perfunctory review of the issues appealed under Article XX(b). Instead, in its analysis of the Article XX(b) health exception, the Appellate Body strongly affirmed governments' right to regulate health risks (Howse and Tuerk, 2001). By doing so, the Appellate Body demonstrated its desire to uphold the panel's precedent-setting support for non-trade goals as well as to communicate clearly with the broader public about the extent of the organization's support for those goals.

The Appellate Body's Article XX(b) rulings contrasted sharply with the more cautious conclusion to its likeness rulings. Although the Appellate Body expanded support for non-trade goals by incorporating health considerations into the likeness determination, it could not conclude that asbestos and substitute products were 'not like' despite recognizing the deadly health risks associated with the former. Health risks alone were not decisive. Instead, health considerations were one among several factors affecting the competitive relationship between asbestos and substitute fibers, a relationship that could not be ruled out in the absence of additional information on the major commercial aspects of the relationship, consumer tastes and end-uses (Horn and Weiler, 2004). Ultimately, trade weighed more heavily than health even within a decision that advanced the status of non-trade goals within the WTO.

Howse and Tuerk (2001) offered a more favorable interpretation of the Appellate Body's likeness rulings. In their view, the Appellate Body adroitly balanced the interests of its internal and external constituencies. For the internal constituents, the ruling emphasized market access, the principal benefit that the organization provided to member governments. For the external constituents, the Appellate Body reversed the panel's decision to exclude health considerations from its analysis of commercial relations and implied that broader social goals would factor in future deliberations.

Goldstein and Carruth (2004) contrasted the Appellate Body's rulings with those in the hormones dispute. They contended that the asbestos rulings 'reopened the door' for the precautionary principle by 'allowing risk perception to supplant risk assessment' (Goldstein and Carruth, 2004, p. 494). This interpretation ignored key differences between the asbestos and hormones disputes. In the hormones dispute, the Appellate Body concluded that there was insufficient evidence to support the EU's claim that hormone-treated beef posed a health risk to consumers. In the case of asbestos, there was overwhelming evidence that exposure led to asbestos-related morbidity and mortality. It was this evidence, accumulated internationally over decades, that led the Appellate Body to conclude that the ban was justified. Where evidence was less conclusive, the Appellate Body was much more wary, as in its 'not like' rulings, leading some to question whether governments can rely on its support in situations where health risks are less apparent (Wirth, 2002).

5.11   PLAYING TO WIN

The asbestos dispute provides a vivid illustration of the substantial influence that politically connected special interest groups exert on government policy. Under pressure from the asbestos industry, the Canadian government adopted controlled use, continued to adhere to it, and challenged regulations that protected the public from serious health risks. That governments respond to such pressures is not news, but the asbestos dispute reveals that governments will do so even where the economic stakes are quite small, the prospects for success are rather low, and the goals pursued conflict with other more significant ones.

The dispute also demonstrates that, once a WTO dispute reaches the panel phase, governments play to win. Legal action is inherently adversarial so it is not unusual for disputants to present their cases in the most favorable light. However, Canada systematically misrepresented the key issues in dispute. Despite abundant evidence to the contrary, Canada touted the efficacy of controlled use, claimed that chrysotile posed no detectable health risks and asserted that substitutes posed unknown and potentially greater health risks. In short, Canada's arguments obscured rather than clarified the issues in dispute. The panels and Appellate Body are equipped to sort through the disputants' conflicting claims about the issues in dispute and benefit from the assistance of experts and WTO legal staff. The impact on the broader public is less clear. There is a risk that, when governments pursue their cases in self-serving and deceptive ways, they create confusion about the issues in dispute and contribute to the controversy surrounding the WTO.

5.12   TRANSPARENCY AND PUBLIC
PARTICIPATION

Because the dispute resolution proceedings have been closed to the public, the dispute resolution process has accentuated the potential for misconceptions to develop and propagate. As discussed in Chapter 4, the WTO began to experiment with closed-circuit television broadcasts in the panel proceedings addressing the EU's complaint against the retaliatory tariffs imposed by the US and Canada in the hormones dispute (WTO, 2005a, 2005b). While this was a positive step, it was not embraced by the membership. Some of the third party participants opposed the initiative and refused to permit their meeting with the panel to be included in the broadcast. Because their opposition reflects the majority view within the membership, it is likely that broadcasts will occur only on an occasional and experimental basis for the foreseeable future. This is unfortunate. Opening panel and appellate hearings to the public along the lines of court proceedings would enhance understanding of the dispute resolution process and the issues in dispute. Additional measures promoting greater transparency are discussed in Chapter 9.

The amicus brief incident earned the Appellate Body harsh and nearly universal criticism from WTO members and scholars.[5] In this rare instance, the panel demonstrated a more deft touch than the Appellate Body. Although the Appellate Body was well-intentioned, it was hard to escape the conclusion that it should have anticipated and thus prevented the ensuing uproar. It proved to be more attuned to its external than to its internal constituency despite the latter's evident and determined opposition. Canada and the EU, along with one of the third parties, opposed the Appellate Body's application procedure. This should have been enough to send the Appellate Body in another direction, given the controversy surrounding the amicus issue. Once the membership voiced its opposition in an unprecedented General Council Meeting called to address the matter, the Appellate Body had no choice but to backpedal. While maintaining that it had the authority to review and accept unsolicited briefs, nevertheless, the Appellate rejected all of the briefs submitted in the asbestos case. Paradoxically, by seeking to widen the scope for NGO participation and to facilitate the submission of amicus briefs, the Appellate Body diminished its room to maneuver on the issue at least in the short term.

Although the Consultative Board appointed by the WTO's Director-General suggested that the acceptance of amicus submissions could enhance the organization's external legitimacy, the membership seemed very far from that realization (WTO, 2005c). Instead, it was inordinately absorbed with concerns that a right to submit amicus briefs would impinge on governmental prerogatives and diminish the intergovernmental character of the dispute resolution proceedings. These concerns were misplaced. As the Appellate Body stressed in its amicus rulings, only governments had the right to participate in the proceedings. Members would retain their exclusive right to participate in the proceedings as complainants, respondents and third parties. Members would continue to choose whether and how to pursue or respond to complaints. For these reasons, the amicus furor seems exaggerated. By offering affected constituencies an opportunity to voice their concerns and share their expertise, the submission of amicus briefs opens an otherwise closed process to external actors affected by WTO disputes and enhances the accountability of the WTO and member governments without jeopardizing the intergovernmental character of the dispute resolution proceedings and unduly burdening the governments that participate in it.

NOTES

1. One metric tonne equals 1000 kilograms. The 'short' ton employed in the United States equals 907.2 kilograms (Wikipedia, 2006).
2. In 1995, voters narrowly rejected a referendum establishing Quebec as an independent state.
3. Canada also argued that the ban, a quantity restriction, violated the GATT's Article XI. The panel declined to rule on Article XI, stating that it was unnecessary to do so in light of its ruling that the ban violated Article III.
4. For a contrary view, see Cone (2001).
5. See, for example, Weiler (2000) and Robbins (2003).

REFERENCES

Chrysotile Institute (CI) (2004), 'Chrysotile not included in the Rotterdam Convention', Press Release, Montreal, Quebec, CI, 20 Oct. (website accessed during January 2005).

Cone, S. (2001), 'The asbestos case and dispute settlement in the World Trade Organization: the uneasy relationship between panels and the Appellate Body', *Michigan Journal of International Law*, **23**(1), 103–42.

Dobbin, M, (2001), 'Canada is a world-class trade bully', *National Post*, 12 November, FP 13.

Dougherty, K. (2000), 'Ottawa will appeal WTO asbestos ruling', *The Gazette*, 19 September, D5.

Fédération des Travailleurs et Travailleuses du Québec (FTQ) (1996), 'Quebec unions denounce France's asbestos ban', Press Release, Quebec, FTQ, 5 July, 5. (The press release was translated by the Asbestos Institute and accessed from its website during January 2005.)

Food and Agriculture Organization (FAO) (2004), 'Rotterdam Convention enters into force', Rome/Geneva: FAO Newsroom, 24 Feb. (website accessed during January 2005).

Gazette (The) (2001), 'Ban upheld: France can bar imports of asbestos on health grounds, WTO rules', 13 March, D15.

Global Environment & Technology Foundation (GETF) (2003), 'Asbestos strategies, lessons learned about management and use of asbestos', GETF, Annandale, Virginia, 16 May.

Goldstein, B. and R. Carruth (2004), 'The precautionary principle and/or risk assessment in World Trade Organization decisions: a possible role for risk perception', *Risk Analysis*, **24**(2), 491–9.

Horn, H. and J. Weiler (2004), 'EC – asbestos, European Communities – measures affecting asbestos and asbestos-containing products', *World Trade Review*, **3**(1), 129–51.

Howse, Robert and Elisabeth Tuerk (2001), 'The WTO impact on internal regulations – a case study of the Canada–EC asbestos dispute', in Grainne De Burca and Joanne Scott (eds), *The EU and the WTO, Legal and Constitutional Issues*, Oxford, UK and Portland, OR: Hart Publishing, pp. 283–328.

Kanth, D. (2000), 'WTO divided over move to settle trade disputes', *Business Times*, 24 November, 24.

Kazan-Allen, L. (2002), 'Chile bans asbestos', International Ban Asbestos Secretariat, London (website accessed during January 2005).

Kazan-Allen, L. (2005), 'National asbestos bans', International Ban Asbestos Secretariat, London, revised 4 Jan. (website accessed during January).

Knight, D. (2000), 'Trade-health: WTO ruling reveals toxic logic, warn groups', *Global Information Network, Interpress Service*, 19 September.

Mealey's Litigation Report (2000), 'Asbestos', **15**(16), 22 September.

Natural Resources Canada (2003), 'Chrysotile', *Canada Minerals Yearbook*, 1997, 1998, 1999, 2000, 2001, 2002, Natural Resources Canada, Ottawa (website accessed during March 2005).

Robbins, J. (2003), 'False friends, amicus curiae and procedural discretion in WTO appeals under the hot-rolled lead/asbestos doctrine', *Harvard International Law Journal*, **44**(1), 317–29.

Schiller, B. (2000), 'WTO rejects Canada's case on asbestos', *Toronto Star*, 19 September, E3.

Weiler, J. (2000), 'The rule of lawyers and the ethos of diplomats: reflections on the internal and external legitimacy of WTO dispute settlement', The Jean Monnet Seminar and Workshop on the European Union, NAFTA and the WTO, Advanced Issues in Law and Policy (Working Paper 9/100), Harvard Law School, Cambridge.

Wikipedia (2006), 'Tonne–conversion of units', *Wikipedia Free Encyclopedia* (website accessed during May 2006).

Wirth, D. (2002), 'EC – measures affecting asbestos and asbestos containing products', *American Journal of International Law*, 96(2), 435–39.

WTO (1994), *General Agreement on Tariffs and Trade* (GATT), Geneva: WTO.

WTO (2000a), *EC – Measures Affecting Asbestos and Products Containing Asbestos, Report of the Panel* (WT/DS135/R), Geneva: WTO, 18 September.

WTO (2000b), *EC – Measures Affecting Asbestos and Products Containing Asbestos, Communication from the Appellate Body* (WT/DS135/9), Geneva: WTO, 8 November.

WTO (2001a), *Minutes of General Council Meeting, 22 November 2000* (WT/GC/M/60), Geneva: WTO, 23 January.

WTO (2001b), *EC – Measures Affecting Asbestos and Products Containing Asbestos, Report of the Appellate Body* (WT/DS135/AB/R), Geneva: WTO, 12 March.

WTO (2005a), *US – Continued Suspension of Obligations in the EC Hormones Dispute, Request for the Establishment of a Panel* (WT/DS320/6), Geneva: WTO, 14 January.

WTO (2005b), *Canada – Continued Suspension of Obligations in the EC Hormones Dispute, Request for the Establishment of a Panel* (WT/DS321/6), Geneva: WTO, 14 January.

WTO (2005c), *The Future of the WTO, Addressing Institutional Challenges in the New Millennium, Report by the Consultative Board to the Director-General Supachai Panitchpakdi*, Geneva: WTO.

Xinhua News Agency (2001), 'EU welcomes WTO's support for French ban on asbestos', 14 March, 1.

6. Salmon, apples and agricultural products

Chapter 6 explores WTO dispute resolution rulings on three food safety measures: an Australian ban on imports of fresh, frozen and chilled salmon and Japanese import restrictions on apples and on agricultural products. Like the hormones case, each of these disputes hinged on the scientific justification and risk assessment requirements accompanying food safety standards. But the three disputes differed from the hormones dispute in a crucial respect. The salmon ban and the import restrictions on apples and agricultural products appeared to be designed primarily to promote domestic producers rather than public health. Because most of the food safety complaints that reach the WTO involve similar measures, the three disputes illustrate the important role that the Sanitary and Phytosanitary (SPS) Agreement's risk assessment (Article 5.1) and scientific justification (Article 2.2) requirements play in distinguishing between protectionist and legitimate sanitary regulations.

In the apples and agricultural products disputes, Japan became the first WTO member to invoke provisions in the SPS Agreement that incorporated the precautionary principle (Article 5.7). Although the attempts were unsuccessful, they shed light on how the precautionary principle might be invoked more successfully in the future. The three disputes dealt a blow to efforts to harmonize food safety standards as the SPS Agreement's harmonization provisions (Articles 3.1–3.3) did not figure in the disputes and the rulings supported WTO members' right to determine their levels of sanitary protection. The three disputes demonstrated the effectiveness of panel consultations with scientific experts but raised troubling questions about the willingness of WTO members to comply with adverse rulings. The chapter concludes by exploring the implications of Australia's and Japan's actions at the compliance phase for the credibility of the dispute resolution process.

6.1   SALMON

In 1975, Australia imposed a ban on imports of members of the salmonidae fish family including salmon, trout, charr, grayling and whitefish (hereafter salmon). Under regulations issued by quarantine officials during the 1980s, exceptions were made for canned and heat-treated salmon (smoked salmon). Imports of fresh, frozen and chilled salmon were prohibited. In December 1996, the Australian Quarantine and Inspection Service rejected Canada's request to rescind the ban.[1] According to the agency's 1996 Salmon Import Risk Analysis, the ban was necessary to protect local salmon aquaculture and recreational fisheries from some 24 diseases present in North American salmon. Shortly thereafter, Canada concluded that consultations with Australia would not resolve the matter and requested that a WTO panel investigate it (WTO, 1998b).

Canada charged that that there was no scientific evidence to support the ban. Evisceration (the removal of the intestines) was sufficient to address potential disease threats associated with trade in dead fish. Eviscerated salmon marketed for human consumption had never been identified as a source of disease in aquaculture or fisheries. Australian fish stocks faced far greater risks from imports of live ornamental fish or fish imported for bait or fish feed. However, Australia did not ban such imports. In fact, its 1996 risk assessment had not even investigated those threats. The risk assessment was deficient in other respects. It addressed only wild, ocean-caught Pacific Canadian salmon but Canada exported four other types of salmon as well.[2] And it provided no explanation for reversing the conclusions of the May 1995 draft report, which recommended that the ban be lifted. Canada concluded that the ban was designed to protect the domestic salmon industry from competition rather than domestic fish from disease threats (WTO, 1998b).

Australia acknowledged that there was no evidence that salmon imports had introduced disease into local fish populations but maintained that the high biological and economic consequences resulting from such an introduction necessitated an import ban. Australia added that the absence of evidence of disease introduction was not equivalent to evidence that disease introduction would not occur. In the presence of uncertainty, it was sufficient to identify potential disease risks (WTO, 1998b).

Since the dispute centered on whether the salmon ban was consistent with the SPS Agreement's scientific evidence (Article 2.2) and risk assessment (Article 5.1) requirements, the panel decided to consult scientific experts. After seeking nominations from the parties and the

Office International des Epizootics (OIE), the international regulatory authority for animals,[3] the panel selected four experts: Dr David E. Burmaster, Alceon Corporation, United States; Dr Christopher J. Rodgers, Fish Disease Consultant, Spain; Dr James Winton, US Fish and Wildlife Service, United States; and Dr Marion Wooldridge, Central Veterinary Laboratory, United Kingdom. In a process duplicated by the panels in the agricultural products and apples disputes, the panel circulated questions to the experts who provided written responses that were made available to the parties. Later, the panel met jointly with the experts and the parties to clarify their views on the issues in dispute (WTO, 1998b).

The experts identified several deficiencies in Australia's risk assessment. Dr Wooldridge observed that the 1995 draft report had investigated the probability that salmon imports would introduce disease but the 1996 final report merely discussed the possibility of disease introduction. Dr Burmaster added that a proper risk assessment must assess probability. Dr Rodgers explained that direct contact between imported and local fish posed the greatest disease risk. Contact of this sort was most likely to occur when live fish were imported to stock local waters and when bait and other fish were used as feed for farm-raised fish (aquaculture). Dr Winton remarked that he knew of no instances where eviscerated fish imported for human consumption had introduced disease into fisheries. Because evisceration was highly effective in reducing transmission risk, the Office International des Epizootics (OIE) Fish Disease Commission (on which he served) regarded it as unnecessary to subject eviscerated fish to trade restrictions (WTO, 1998b).

The panel began its analysis by examining whether the 1996 risk assessment met the requirements for a proper risk assessment under Article 5.1. The panel was able to make a conclusive finding on only the first element: the assessment had identified diseases posing risks to local fish stocks and associated biological and economic consequences. The risk assessment examined 'some elements of both probability and possibility' of disease introduction (WTO, 1998b, para. 8.83) and to 'some extent' analyzed risk reduction under various measures that might be applied (WTO, 1998b, para. 8.91). The panel was reluctant to give its seal of approval to these aspects of the assessment and decided to 'assume – without making a finding' that the risk assessment satisfied the final two elements of a proper risk assessment (WTO, 1998b paras 8.83 and 8.91). With this equivocal position on the propriety of the risk assessment, the panel signaled its dissatisfaction with the risk assessment's relationship to the ban.

In the next part of its analysis, the panel ruled that the ban was not based on the risk assessment as required by Article 5.1. While this conclusion was not surprising, the panel's explanation was. The ban and the heat treatment requirements were 'two sides of a single coin' (WTO, 1998b, para. 8.95). However, the 1996 risk assessment failed to make a 'substantive assessment' of the efficacy of heat treatment (WTO, 1998b, para. 8.98). Indeed, it indicated that there was uncertainty surrounding the susceptibility of some pathogens to heat. Noting that the Appellate Body in the hormones dispute ruled that risk assessments must 'reasonably support' the measures imposed (WTO, 1998a, para. 208, cited in WTO, 1998b, para. 8.99), the panel found that there was no 'rational basis' for the heat treatment requirement and, consequently, the ban (WTO, 1998b, para. 8.100). The ban was inconsistent with the SPS Agreement's risk assessment requirement (Article 5.1) and, consequently, its scientific justification mandate (Article 2.2). Without support from the risk assessment, there was insufficient scientific evidence to warrant the ban (WTO, 1998b).

Turning to Article 5.5, the panel investigated Canada's complaint that it was inconsistent to ban imports of fresh, frozen or chilled salmon and to impose fewer restrictions on imports of bait and ornamental fish. Citing the experts' testimony and two studies prepared by Australia's Bureau of Resource Sciences, the panel found that these distinctions in sanitary protection were arbitrary and unjustifiable because the other fish posed disease risks at least as great as those posed by salmon. In the final part of its analysis under Article 5.5, the panel concluded that the ban was a disguised restriction on trade. The panel cited several reasons, including the far more restrictive regulation of salmon as compared to other fish imports, the failure to control the movement of certain domestic fish products posing disease threats, and the lack of justification for the decision to reverse the 1995 draft report's recommendation to lift the ban. After finding that the ban violated Article 5.5, the panel ruled that the ban also violated Article 2.3's more general prohibition against measures constituting disguised restrictions on trade (WTO, 1998b).

The panel also ruled that the ban violated Article 5.6's prohibition against measures that were more trade-restrictive than necessary. Again, the panel anchored its analysis to the lack of justification for the heat treatment requirement. In order to find a violation under Article 5.6, it was necessary to establish that at least one of the other policy options examined in Australia's risk assessment was reasonably available, significantly less trade-restrictive than heat treatment and met

Australia's level of protection. The first two requirements were dispensed with easily. As the risk assessment discussed four processing options, the panel gathered that they represented routine practices. Since only heat treatment changed the nature of the salmon, the other four options were significantly less trade-restrictive. To determine whether any of the measures met Australia's appropriate level of protection, the panel ruled that its desired level of protection could be deduced from the measures applied currently (WTO, 1998b). Although Australia held that heat treatment provided a higher level of protection than the other measures, the panel asserted that, owing to the uncertainty surrounding its effectiveness, heat treatment did not provide protection 'as high or conservative as Australia submits' (WTO, 1998b, para. 8.178). It went on to conclude that one of the other four options met Australia's level of protection because it provided protection equivalent to that afforded by heat treatment (WTO, 1998b).

The Appellate Body rejected most of the panel's reasoning under Article 5.1. The measure at issue was the import ban not the heat treatment requirement. By definition, fresh, frozen and chilled salmon were not subject to heat treatment. Since the panel analyzed the wrong measure, the Appellate Body reversed its conclusions under Article 5.1. In the interests of resolving the dispute, the Appellate Body examined whether the import ban was supported by the risk assessment. In the course of its review, the Appellate Body concluded that Australia had not performed a proper risk assessment within the meaning of Article 5.1. Australia had not satisfied two of the required elements (WTO, 1998c). It was not sufficient to make 'some evaluation' of the probability of disease introduction (WTO, 1998c, para. 124). Similarly, it was not permissible to make 'some evaluation' of the probability of disease introduction under various measures that might be applied (WTO, 1998c, para. 134). Since Australia had failed to conduct a proper risk assessment, the Appellate Body ruled that the import ban was not based on a risk assessment as required under Article 5.1. For the same reason, the ban was incompatible with Article 2.2's requirement that sanitary measures be maintained with sufficient scientific evidence (WTO, 1998c).

Likewise, the Appellate Body rejected the central elements of the panel's analysis under Article 5.6. Again, the panel erroneously examined heat treatment. It should have investigated whether the import ban on fresh, frozen and chilled salmon was more trade-restrictive than necessary. The Appellate Body attempted to perform the analysis that the panel failed to perform but it was unable to determine whether any alternative measures met Australia's level of protection. The import ban implied a zero-risk level but throughout the dispute Australia maintained that it desired to reduce risk to low but non-zero levels. Despite the panel's assertions to the contrary, Australia's level of protection could not be implied from the measures imposed. WTO members were entitled to determine the level of their sanitary protection without the interference of panels and the Appellate Body. Stymied, the Appellate Body could do no more than reverse the panel's finding of a violation under Article 5.6. It could not determine whether the ban was more trade restrictive than necessary. The panel had failed to make the necessary factual findings because of its erroneous decision to focus on heat treatment (WTO, 1998c).

In addition, the Appellate Body faulted the panel for limiting its analysis under Articles 5.5 and 2.3 to the ocean-caught Pacific salmon addressed by the risk assessment. Because the panel's failure to examine other Canadian salmon provided only a 'partial resolution' of the dispute, the Appellate Body completed the missing analysis and concluded that the import ban was inconsistent with Articles 5.5 and 2.3 with respect to the other Canadian salmon subject to the ban as well as ocean-caught Pacific salmon (WTO, 1998c, para. 223).

When the Dispute Settlement Body adopted the panel rulings as modified by the Appellate Body, Australia indicated its intention to comply. Subsequently, it sought a 15-month implementation period, the maximum amount of time permitted under the dispute settlement rules. When Canada advocated a briefer implementation period, the matter went to arbitration. During the arbitration proceedings, Australia argued that a lengthy implementation period was necessary because it would need to conduct a risk assessment in order to determine how to bring its regulations into conformance with the rulings. Citing the arbitration report in the hormones case, the arbitrator observed that governments were expected to comply with the dispute resolution rulings as quickly as practicable. It would be unreasonable to delay the process to allow time to conduct a risk assessment that might well be designed to support the offending ban. Moreover, Australia could implement the recommendations relatively easily, as no legislative approval was necessary. The arbitrator rejected Australia's arguments and decided that eight months constituted a reasonable period of time for compliance (WTO, 1999b).

When the implementation period expired, the ban remained in effect. Two weeks later, Australia instituted new quarantine and inspection requirements that replaced the ban. Fresh, frozen and chilled salmon imports were permitted provided that they were consumer-ready; that is, small portions of eviscerated fish intended for household consumption (including skinned fillets of any size, skin-on fillets of less than 450 grams and headless fish of less than 450 grams). Headless, gutted and gilled salmon of greater weight could be imported for additional processing at approved facilities in Australia. The latter requirement was necessary because waste disposal from processing facilities posed the greatest disease threat to Australian fish stocks. The revised regulations continued to place greater restrictions on imported salmon than on imports of ornamental and bait fish (WTO, 2000).

Canada maintained that the new requirements continued to deny Canadian salmon full access to the Australian market and challenged Australia's compliance measures. The panel reconvened to investigate the matter and sought the assistance of the scientific experts previously consulted. As only Dr Wooldridge was available, she was joined by two new experts; Dr Gideon Brückner, Department of Food Safety and Veterinary Public Health, South Africa; and Dr Alasdair McVicar, Aberdeen Marine Laboratory, United Kingdom. Dr Wooldridge continued to question the adequacy of Australia's risk assessment and the inconsistent treatment of salmon and other fish imports, but Drs Brückner and McVicar viewed the risk assessment as acceptable. Unlike its predecessor, the 1999 risk assessment addressed the probability of disease introduction and the likelihood of the same under various measures that might be applied. The varying quarantine and inspection procedures for salmon and other fish were appropriate because they achieved a similar level of sanitary protection. Some of the diseases believed to affect live ornamental fish had been observed primarily in experimental conditions. It was unclear whether they occurred under natural conditions. Salmon, live ornamental and other fish hosted some of the same diseases but, because they experienced different strains of these diseases, the consequences of disease introduction were likely to vary. Finally, diseases were more likely to be transmitted within than across species. Thus diseases present in salmon posed greater risks to salmon than the presence of the same diseases in other fish (WTO, 2000).

However, Drs Brückner and McVicar disputed the consumer-ready requirements. Dr McVicar explained that the removal of skin was unnecessary; washing would suffice to address disease risks. Dr Brückner stated that there was no scientific basis to require consumer-ready imports and to restrict the processing of non-consumer-ready fish to Australian facilities. These requirements could be considered to be more trade-restrictive than necessary (WTO, 2000).

Australia could not dispute the experts' rejection of the consumer-ready requirements because they had not been investigated in the 1999 risk assessment. As a result, the panel concluded that the consumer-ready requirements were incompatible with Article 5.1's risk assessment obligations and, by extension, Article 2.2's scientific justification obligations. The panel also ruled that the consumer-ready requirements were more trade-restrictive than necessary under Article 5.6. The panel identified several less restrictive measures that could achieve Australia's sanitary objectives, including sector-specific packaging and permit requirements. The panel added that such requirements might be altogether unnecessary if Australia were to adopt Canada's recommendation to require processing facilities to treat and control their waste. The panel rejected Canada's challenge to the revised regulations under Articles 5.5 and 2.3. According to the experts, the remaining distinctions in treatment among salmon, bait fish and ornamental fish reflected varying risks and consequences of disease introduction. Since these distinctions were neither arbitrary nor unjustifiable, it was not necessary to examine whether they constituted disguised restrictions on trade (WTO, 2000).

In May 2000, two months after the compliance panel rulings were issued, Canada and Australia reached an agreement providing for the importation of fresh, frozen and chilled salmon. The agreement restricted imports to headless, eviscerated salmon but struck the consumer-ready requirements. In accordance with the compliance panel's recommendation, the agreement set varying requirements depending on whether the products were intended for the retail or commercial sector (Bilateral Agreement between Canada and Australia, 2000).

6.2   AGRICULTURAL PRODUCTS

In order to prevent the introduction of pests that posed a risk to domestic agriculture, the Japanese Plant Protection Law of 1950 authorized the Ministry of Agriculture Forestry and Fisheries to impose import bans on agricultural products subject to infestation by certain pests including the codling moth. The ban applied to eight US agricultural products: apples, apricots, cherries, nectarines, pears, plums, quince and walnuts. Under guidelines developed in 1987, imports of these products could circum-

vent the ban provided that they satisfied rigorous quarantine and fumigation requirements that applied to each variety of the eight products. In
order to bypass the ban, exporting nations were required to demonstrate
that fumigation with methyl bromide achieved 100 percent mortality
during three types of tests. The basic test determined the dose necessary
to produce 100 percent mortality at the most resistant stage of the
codling moth's life cycle, using a small number of insects in various
developmental phases. Next, the efficacy of this dose was tested in a
large-scale test of 30 000 insects (at the most resistant stage) performed
over three trials of 10 000 insects each. In the final test, Japanese officials performed an on-site confirmatory test of 10 000 insects. Once
the tests were completed successfully, Japanese officials were required
to hold a public hearing to solicit comments from farmers and other
stakeholders before approving the products for import (WTO, 1998d).

Under Japan's varietal testing requirement, the testing regime applied
to *each variety* of each product seeking access to the Japanese market.
While the US accepted the necessity of eradicating the threat of codling
moth infestation, it contended that there was no scientific basis for the
varietal testing requirement. Treatment that was effective for one variety
of a product (Macintosh) would be effective for others (Granny Smith,
Gala and so on). Product testing was the norm in international trade and
provided a less trade-restrictive alternative to varietal testing to prevent
the introduction of the codling moth into Japan (1998d).

Although the US had been seeking access to the Japanese market
since the 1960s, it had experienced limited success because of varietal
testing and other requirements. Apple and nectarine exports to Japan
accounted for just 0.14 percent and 0.26 percent of total US apple and
nectarine exports, respectively (WTO, 1998d). Japanese regulators had
approved two varieties of apples (Red and Golden Delicious) but
Japanese consumers preferred other varieties, so, in effect, the market
remained closed (Hieger, 1999). The situation was better for walnuts and
cherries as Japan accounted for 19 percent and 62 percent of US exports
of those products, respectively. Nevertheless, the varietal testing
requirement curtailed US exports of walnuts and cherries by reducing
the number of varieties available in the Japanese market (WTO, 1998d).

According to the US, nations had a right to impose measures to
protect plant health and life but the 'varietal testing requirement was
exactly the kind of unnecessary and unjustified measure that the SPS
Agreement was intended to prohibit' (WTO, 1998d, para. 4.19). In the
course of responding to the varietal testing requirement, the US had

tested seven varieties of apples, nine varieties of cherries, ten varieties of nectarines and four varieties of walnuts. No differences in treatment effectiveness across varieties had been observed. Every on-site confirmatory test had achieved 100 percent mortality using the same treatment level for all varieties of a given product. Moreover, these results were consistent with those reported by other nations seeking to export agricultural products to Japan. No nation had been required to make varietal modifications in its codling moth fumigation treatments in order to eradicate the pest. In short, the effectiveness of product-level fumigation treatment had been 'conclusively established' (WTO, 1998d, para. 4.24).

Japan countered that the US had not demonstrated that product testing would be effective for all varieties. Other data suggested the possibility of differing varietal responses to fumigation treatment. In the absence of evidence to the contrary, Japan was entitled to maintain varietal testing as a provisional measure until additional information was available. No other treatment regime met Japan's level of protection, which was commensurate with the infestation risk under an import ban (zero-risk) (WTO, 1998d).

The panel's examination of the dispute centered on Article 2.2 of the SPS Agreement, which required that regulations addressing animal, human and plant health be 'based on scientific principles' and 'not be maintained without sufficient scientific evidence' unless exceptions for provisional measures applied (WTO, 1994). Owing to the nature of the matters in dispute, the panel decided to consult scientific experts. After consulting the parties and soliciting nominations from them as well as the International Plant Protection Convention (IPPC), the panel selected three experts: Dr Neil Heather, Entomologist, University of Queensland, Australia; Dr Patrick Ducom, Fumigation Expert, Lormont, France; and Mr Robert Taylor, Fumigation Specialist, Natural Resources Institute, United Kingdom (WTO, 1998d).

The experts confirmed that most governments employed product testing. Varietal testing was restricted to Japan and New Zealand. Dr Heather noted that quality standards for commercially traded fruit were such that they were 'essentially free' of codling moth infestation even in the absence of quarantine and fumigation (WTO, 1998d, para. 6.52). The experts dismissed the evidence presented by Japan, pointing to the possibility of varietal differences. The experts noted that the results had not held in large-scale tests suggesting that maturity, environment and factors other than varietal difference accounted for the differences observed in the small-scale studies cited by Japan. The experts were not able to rule out the existence of varietal differences but they agreed that it had yet to be demonstrated that they existed and were of sufficient magnitude to affect treatment efficacy. Dr Heather concluded that methyl bromide fumigation was a 'very robust treatment' as demonstrated by the success of each of the large-scale and confirmatory tests performed by the US (WTO, 1998d, para. 10.263).

On the basis of the experts' testimony and the evidence presented by the parties, the panel concluded that the varietal testing requirement was not maintained with sufficient scientific evidence as required by Article 2.2 of the SPS Agreement. The panel limited its findings to apples, cherries, nectarines and walnuts because no evidence had been presented regarding apricots, pears, plums and quince. Drawing on the reasoning employed by the Appellate Body in the hormones dispute, the panel explained that there was no 'rational or objective relationship' between the varietal testing procedure and available scientific evidence (WTO, 1998d, para. 8.42). The panel emphasized that the experts characterized varietal differences as theoretically possible but unsubstantiated by existing research (WTO, 1998d).

These hypothetical risks did not justify the varietal testing requirement as a provisional measure because Japan had not fulfilled all of the obligations accompanying the imposition of precautionary measures under Article 5.7 of the SPS. Governments were permitted to take action on a provisional basis in situations where there was insufficient scientific evidence to support the measures imposed, provided that they sought additional information within a reasonable period of time. However, Japan had not undertaken even one study that examined whether varietal differences *caused* treatment efficacy to vary over the 20 years during which the varietal testing requirement had been applied to the specific products involved in the dispute (WTO, 1998d).

Under Article 5.6, a measure was considered more trade-restrictive than necessary if another significantly less restrictive measure could achieve Japan's appropriate level of protection and was economically and technically feasible. In the course of arguments before the panel, the US proposed product testing as an alternative measure. However, the panel ruled that product testing could not meet Japan's appropriate level of protection. The panel noted that the experts said it was possible that product testing would not result in effective treatment of all varieties. Thus, in the absence of large-scale testing of each variety, Japan could not be assured of achieving its appropriate level of protection: 100 percent mortality, the equivalent of an import ban (WTO, 1998d).

In an unusual move, the panel went on to propose its own alternative measure, sorption testing. In its analysis, the panel relied heavily on the experts' testimony. According to the experts, if varietal differences existed, they would arise primarily from variation in sorption, the amount of methyl bromide absorbed by agricultural products during the fumigation process. Surprisingly, sorption testing had not been undertaken to address varietal differences. Since it focused only on each product's or variety's absorption of methyl bromide, it was easier to perform than the existing tests because no insects were needed. The test process would be speedier yet equally effective. If additional varieties demonstrated sorption levels within the range observed for varieties previously approved, no additional testing would be necessary. Where anomalous levels were observed, additional testing would be required, but most likely it would be less burdensome than existing procedures. The panel reasoned that sorption testing was technically feasible, met Japan's level of protection and was significantly less trade restrictive than varietal testing. As a result, sorption testing constituted a less trade-restrictive alternative to varietal testing. The panel also explored whether monitoring gas concentration levels during the fumigation process could provide a less trade restrictive alternative to varietal testing, but it was unable to determine whether that approach was economically or technically feasible according to the evidence presented in the dispute (WTO, 1998d).[4]

Japan and the US appealed various aspects of the panel rulings. The Appellate Body upheld the panel on all of the rulings discussed above, with the exception of those under Article 5.6. The Appellate Body reversed the panel's finding that varietal testing was more trade-restrictive than necessary because the panel had failed to abide by the rules on burden of proof. The US was obliged to make a prima facie case that sorption testing represented a less trade-restrictive alternative to varietal testing. Since the US had not even addressed sorption testing in its arguments, it had not established the requisite prima facie case. The Appellate Body reversed the panel on one other matter. The panel stated that it was unnecessary to examine claims under 5.1 regarding the adequacy of Japan's risk assessment process because of its conclusion that varietal testing was maintained without sufficient scientific evidence under Article 2.2. The Appellate Body ruled that the panel exercised false judicial economy because the rulings under Article 2.2 did not apply to apricots, pears, plums and quince. The Appellate Body went on to find that varietal testing of apricots, pears, plums and quince was inconsistent with Article 5.1 because Japan's risk assessment had not addressed the efficacy of varietal testing or any other measure in combating the codling moth in those four products (WTO, 1999a).

The Appellate Body issued its rulings in February 1999. In early March, Japan approved the admission of five additional varieties of US apples (Braeburn, Fuji, Gala, Granny Smith and Jona Gold) (*Seattle Times*, 1999). Since confirmatory tests had been completed nearly two years earlier, it was unclear whether the timing was coincidental or indicated Japan's intention to comply in a speedy fashion. US exporters predicted that it would take some time for Japan to accept the decision and this proved correct (Hieger, 1999). When the reasonable period of time for compliance expired in December 1999, Japan rescinded the varietal testing requirement but the US and Japan were not able to agree on a framework for an alternative testing regime until August 2001. As outlined in the framework, Japan decided to forgo specific methodologies and instead agreed to negotiate with governments on a case-by-case basis over appropriate methods that might include, but were not limited to, the measurement of gas concentrations (WTO, 2001a). Two months later, Japan announced that a gas concentration quarantine methodology would be employed to test the efficacy of methyl bromide treatment on additional varieties of the eight US agricultural products that figured in the dispute (WTO, 2001b). As of the end of 2005, the revised testing process appeared to be as burdensome as its predecessor. As in the past, only sizable quantities of cherries and walnuts were exported from the US to Japan. US exports of cherries and walnuts amounted together to $126 million in 2005. Combined exports of apples, apricots, pears and quince declined to less than $79 000 in 2005 after reaching $1.2 million in 2000. Over the same period, combined peach and nectarine exports fell by 62 percent, while plum exports (including prunes) decreased by 42 percent. Data for nectarines and plums were not available independently of peaches and prunes, respectively (USDA, 2006).

6.3   APPLES

The apples dispute between the US and Japan also involved The Plant Protection Law of 1950, which identified the fire blight bacterium as one of 15 quarantine pests subject to control by Japanese authorities. As with the codling moth, apples and other plants known to host fire blight were subject to an import ban. Native to North America, fire blight was introduced to several other countries or regions, including New Zealand,

Europe and the Mideast, during the twentieth century. A pernicious disease, fire blight arrested the development of infected fruit, causing them to shrivel and die. Infected fruit bore an ooze or inoculum which posed a transmission risk via wind, insects and possibly birds. Although fire blight had been detected in Japan during the early 1990s, the country appeared to have eradicated the disease (WTO, 2003a).

The US claimed that apples of commercial quality were not capable of transmitting fire blight and sought to export apples to Japan, beginning in 1982. For over a decade, the US and Japan were unable to reach agreement on a quarantine process that would produce a level of protection for Japanese agriculture and forestry that was equivalent to an import ban (zero-risk). In the meantime, New Zealand successfully negotiated an agreement with Japan permitting the importation of apples, provided that a number of fire blight protective measures were undertaken during cultivation, storage and shipping. In 1994, Japan issued regulations that imposed the same extensive set of requirements on US apple imports.[5] Apples were to be produced in orchards that were certified as blight-free by the USDA, surrounded by 500-meter buffer zones and inspected three times annually. Harvested apples, packing crates and packing facilities were to be disinfected with chlorine. Apples designated for the Japanese market were to be separated post-harvest from others. US authorities were required to certify the apples as blight-free and chlorine-treated. Japanese officials were required to confirm the US certification and inspection processes (WTO, 2003a).

In May 2002, the US requested that the WTO establish a panel to address its complaint against the fire blight restrictions. As with the varietal testing requirement, the US objected that there was no scientific evidence to support the fire blight protective regime. Fire blight was readily detectable through routine inspection procedures as it affected blossoms and immature fruit, arresting their development. Since only mature, symptomless apples were harvested and traded commercially, US apples exported to Japan did not pose a disease threat. US apple exports totaled 10.5 million tons over 35 years and had never been linked to fire blight. In fact, there was no evidence that apples introduced fire blight anywhere in the world despite being traded internationally for more than a century. Japan's restrictions were unnecessary and extreme. Among the 66 nations identified as fire blight-free, at least 58 imposed no import restrictions related to fire blight (WTO, 2003a).

Japan argued that the safety of mature, symptomless apples had not been established. Fire blight might be undetected yet present internally (endophytic) as well as externally (epiphytic) in apples traded commercially. Even where fire blight was detectable through inspection procedures, contaminated apples might accidentally be included in apple shipments because of errors made in harvest and handling processes. While the probability of introducing fire blight into Japan was low, the risk was nevertheless real. Wind, insects and birds might carry the pathogen to domestic plants via discarded infected fruit. The absence of evidence showing that the disease had been disseminated in that manner did not demonstrate the absence of risk. Japan emphasized that it sought to retain its blight-free status and necessarily required protection equivalent to an import ban. As a result, Japan had taken a comprehensive approach to fire blight regulation that included measures addressing apples at each stage of their development from blossom to shipment (WTO, 2003a).

As in the salmon and agricultural product disputes, the central questions facing the panel were whether sufficient scientific evidence and the risk assessment process supported the measures at issue as required by the SPS Agreement's Articles 2.2 and 5.1, respectively. After consulting the parties and soliciting nominations from them as well as the International Plant Protection Convention (IPPC), the panel consulted four scientific experts: Dr Klaus Geider, Professor of Molecular Genetics and Phytopathology, University of Heidelberg, Germany; Dr Chris Hale, Science Capability Leader, Insect Group (Plant Health and Fire Blight), HortResearch, New Zealand; Dr Chris Hayward, Consultant on Bacterial Plant Diseases, Australia; and Dr Ian Smith, Director-General, European and Mediterranean Plant Protection Organization, France (WTO, 2003a).

According to the experts, immature fruit were susceptible to fire blight and ceased to develop to maturity once infected. Mature fruit, including apples, were not susceptible to the disease. Although Japan contended that the results of one study demonstrated that fire blight could be present within mature, healthy-looking apples, the experts disagreed, noting several flaws in the study, including lack of clarity surrounding the maturity of the apples examined. According to Dr Hale, supplemental information received from the study's authors clarified their results and established that they were consistent with those reported elsewhere in the literature. A few studies, including one conducted by Dr Hale, indicated that fire blight could be present externally on mature apples. However, the presence of fire blight on the surface of an apple posed a negligible transmission risk since the pathogen was unlikely to survive harvest, storage and shipping. Even if it did, there was a still smaller probability that it would be transferred to a host capable of transmitting the disease (WTO, 2003a). The experts could not rule out the possibility that infected, immature apples could pass undetected through harvest, inspection, storage and shipping, but the risk was 'small' or 'debatable' (WTO, 2003a, para. 8.161). In any case, discarded infected fruit had never been shown to serve as a pathway for the disease even under experimental conditions in which infected apples were placed in orchards. Dr Geider concluded that the dissemination of fire blight through commercially traded apples could not be 'scientifically totally excluded' but it was 'extremely unlikely either that it had occurred or could occur' (WTO, 2003a, para. 6.37). The other experts agreed citing imports of infected nursery plants as the most likely vehicle for transmission of the disease to blight-free areas (WTO, 2003a).

Relying heavily on the experts' testimony, the panel concluded that neither mature, symptomless apples nor infected, immature apples were likely to serve as pathways for the disease. As a result, there was insufficient evidence to support Japan's claim that imported apples could transmit fire blight. The panel characterized the fire blight regime as disproportionate to the transmission risk and highlighted two elements that were not supported by the evidence presented: (1) the 500-meter buffer zone; and (2) the tri-annual inspection requirement (WTO, 2003a).

The panel also concluded that Japan had violated Article 5.1's risk assessment requirements. Japan had identified fire blight as a disease posing a threat to domestic plant life but it had failed to assess the probability that fire blight would be introduced into Japan via apples and the likely effectiveness of measures that might be applied to eliminate that risk. In addition, the fire blight restrictions were incompatible with Article 5.7's requirements for precautionary measures. Precautionary measures were justified on a provisional basis in situations where insufficient scientific evidence was available to support the measures imposed. In the case of fire blight, abundant evidence indicated that the risk of transmission from apples was negligible (WTO, 2003a).

As in the salmon and agricultural products disputes, the parties appealed several aspects of the panel rulings. Unlike the outcome in the other two disputes, the Appellate Body upheld each of the apples panel's rulings (WTO, 2003b). However, the panel's ability to get the legal issues right and the Appellate Body's strong support for the panel rulings did not translate into a speedy resolution of the case. As in the salmon and agricultural products cases, compliance was problematic. On 30 June 2004, the day that the reasonable period of time for compliance expired, Japan issued fire blight restrictions that reproduced the previous ones in all but three aspects. The 500-meter buffer zone was converted to ten meters. The inspection requirement was reduced from three to one per year and packing crates were no longer subject to the disinfection requirement. The US objected on the grounds that there was no scientific evidence that apples of any kind could transmit fire blight to blight-free orchards. Japan responded that it had gathered new scientific evidence indicating that mature apples could pose an infection risk. The original panel was appointed to address the matter. As in the salmon dispute, the panel essentially reheard the dispute in the course of the compliance proceedings (WTO, 2005a).

During the implementation period, Japan commissioned four studies addressing gaps in the scientific evidence that it presented to the original panel. According to Japan, one study demonstrated that mature, symptomless apples could carry fire blight latently. Another indicated that fire blight could survive in fruit under certain storage conditions. A third suggested that a transmission pathway from discarded infected fruit to other fruit could be completed by flies. Relying on the results of these three studies, the fourth calculated the probability of completing the transmission pathway from infected fruit to other fruit (WTO, 2005a).

The panel assembled the same group of scientific experts to review the evidence from the four studies. According to the experts, the results of two of the studies did not support Japan's claims. The latency study had been unable to demonstrate that mature, symptomless apples could develop fire blight and the pathway study had failed to establish that flies could transmit fire blight from infected fruit to other fruit. While the storage study's conclusions were consistent with its results, they were not applicable to commercial conditions because of the extreme artificiality of the test conditions employed. The probability study was suspect because it relied on the three disputed studies while ignoring others in the literature suggesting that neither mature, symptomless apples nor discarded infected ones could transmit the disease to other fruit (WTO, 2005a).

The panel concluded that the studies did not provide sufficient scientific evidence to support Japan's assertions that mature, symptomless apples could harbor fire blight latently or that discarded infected apples could serve as a pathway to introduce fire blight to Japan. Explaining that it desired to resolve the dispute fully, the panel went on to examine each of the elements of the fire blight regime. Applying Article 2.2's sufficient scientific evidence requirement to each, the panel rejected all but two. The only regulations compatible with the scientific justification requirement were those mandating that US officials certify the blight-free status of apples exported to Japan and those requiring that Japanese officials confirm the US certification procedures (WTO, 2005a).

The compliance report dealt a stunning and comprehensive blow to Japan's fire blight regime. The only surviving measures, certification of apples as blight-free and related confirmation measures, represented standard commercial practices. Although Japan expressed disappointment with the compliance rulings, it quickly reached an agreement with the US to remove the quarantine and inspection requirements struck by the compliance panel (WTO, 2005b, 2005c). This response was unexpected, given Japan's tardy response to the agricultural products rulings and the breadth of the blow to the fire blight restrictions. From Japan's perspective, the panel's decision to strike the requirement limiting imports to apples harvested from blight-free orchards was probably the most problematic. The blight-free orchard requirement was the most restrictive element of the regime and the only one prompting disagreement among the experts. Drs Hale and Hayward were persuaded that the requirement was unnecessary in light of studies demonstrating that blight-free apples had been harvested from blight-infected trees. Although Drs Geider and Smith did not dispute that evidence, they suggested that the blight-free requirement might be a reasonable measure anyway (WTO, 2005a). On its face, the compliance panel's decision appeared to relate to the weighing of scientific evidence, a matter over which panels had discretion. Moreover, the evidence supported the decision made by the panel. However, had Japan appealed, there was a possibility that the Appellate Body would have been troubled since the panel did not afford Japan the discretion recommended by Drs Geider and Smith on the most significant aspect of its sanitary regime.

6.4 RISK ASSESSMENT, SCIENTIFIC EVIDENCE AND THE PRECAUTIONARY PRINCIPLE

The salmon, apples and agricultural products disputes have contributed to the controversy surrounding the WTO. For many, the results of the decisions spoke for themselves. Since each of the decisions went against the country imposing a sanitary measure, it was apparent that sanitary protection was being compromised by the WTO's prioritization of trade over other social goals (Public Citizen, 2004). For others, the decisions suggested that the SPS Agreement's scientific evidence and risk assessment requirements were burdensome and possibly unattainable (Guzman, 2004; Sykes, 2002). On the contrary, the analysis undertaken in this chapter demonstrates that the scientific justification requirements play a crucial and necessary role in distinguishing between legitimate sanitary measures and protectionist ones imposed under the guise of promoting health and safety.

In all three disputes, the health risks posed were dubious. Australia claimed that dead salmon posed a risk to local fish stocks and Japan claimed that healthy, mature apples posed a risk to domestic orchards even though there was no evidence that either product had ever introduced the diseases in question anywhere in the world. In order to support the possibility of transmission from those unlikely sources, they concocted transmission pathways that could be completed in only improbable circumstances (WTO, 1998b, 2003a). Hypothetical risks also figured in the agricultural products dispute. Japan speculated that there were varietal differences in the effectiveness of fumigation treatment although there was no evidence from the large-scale tests performed that such differences existed (WTO, 1998d).

Citing these hypothetical risks, Japan became the first WTO member to invoke the SPS Agreement's Article 5.7 for provisional measures undertaken on a precautionary basis. While both attempts failed, they shed light on ways other governments might employ the precautionary principle and provisional measures more successfully in the future. First, provisional measures were not exempt from the risk assessment process applicable to other measures. Second, provisional measures were appropriate for situations where the risk assessment process yielded insufficient evidence to support the measure imposed (WTO, 2003a). This could occur in situations where 'little, or no, reliable evidence was available' or where available studies yielded inconclusive results (WTO, 2003a, para. 8.219). Neither situation applied to fire blight since there was a great deal of evidence suggesting that mature apples posed no more than a negligible risk. Third, governments must base their precautionary measures on available pertinent information. The available pertinent information did not support the restrictions imposed by Japan.

Fourth, within a reasonable period of time, governments must comply with Article 5.7's requirements to seek additional information to support the measures imposed. The varietal testing requirement could not be deemed provisional because for over 20 years Japan failed to conduct a single study examining whether varietal differences *caused* treatment efficacy to vary (WTO, 1998d, 2003a).

The risk assessment and scientific evidence supporting each of the measures at issue were deficient. In the salmon dispute, Australia merely identified the diseases posing a threat and their anticipated consequences. Australia failed to address the probability that the diseases would be introduced and the efficacy of various measures in preventing disease introduction (WTO, 1998c). In the agricultural products dispute, the available evidence did not support the existence of varietal differences in treatment effectiveness (WTO, 1998d). Similarly, in the apples dispute, Japan presented no evidence that substantiated its claims regarding fire blight transmission mechanisms (2003a, 2005a).

In the salmon dispute, Australia's inability to justify more permissive treatment of live ornamental and bait fish despite health risks equal to or greater than those associated with salmon appeared to provide a clear example of inconsistent distinctions in the level of sanitary protection – distinctions that the panel and Appellate Body concluded disguised a protectionist measure as one promoting fish safety (WTO, 1998b, 1998c). However, these rulings too reflected failures in Australia's risk assessment procedures. During the compliance phase, Canada complained that Australia continued to grant more liberal treatment to live ornamental and bait fish than to salmon, but the panel found that Australia was able to support differential treatment because of differing disease risks and consequences that were addressed by its 1999 risk assessment (WTO, 2000). Had Australia performed a proper risk assessment in 1996, most likely it would have been able to avert the original panel's characterization of the ban as a disguised restriction on trade.

6.5   RISK LEVELS AND INTERNATIONAL STANDARDS

Despite striking the sanitary regulations in dispute, the rulings affirmed that governments have the right to determine their own levels of sanitary protection. In the salmon dispute, the panel stated that members could not set a zero-risk level because doing so would validate any import ban imposed (WTO, 1998b). Although that finding had not been appealed, the Appellate Body made a special point of addressing it, noting that members were permitted to set any level of sanitary protection, including zero-risk. Subsequently, the Appellate Body reversed the panel's conclusion that the salmon ban was more trade-restrictive than necessary because the panel substituted its judgment for Australia's regarding the level of sanitary protection sought (WTO, 1998c). In the agricultural products dispute, the panel ruled that product testing could not meet Japan's level of sanitary protection owing to the possible existence of varietal differences (WTO, 1998d). Subsequently, the panel's conclusion that another measure (sorption testing) did meet Japan's appropriate level of protection was struck by the Appellate Body on procedural grounds (WTO, 1999a). In the apples dispute, the compliance panel ruled that limiting imports to mature, symptomless apples met Japan's level of sanitary protection (WTO, 2005a). Unlike the agricultural products panel, the apples panel was not willing to factor hypothetical risks into its analysis of the appropriate level of protection. While its decision was more consistent with the SPS Agreement's scientific evidence requirements, it was questionable whether it satisfied Japan's desire to seek protection equivalent to an import ban. On the other hand, if the fire blight restrictions struck by the panel provided no genuine sanitary protection, it would appear that Japan's actual level of protection was undiminished. Similarly, the salmon and agricultural product rulings preserved the existing level of sanitary protection since less trade-restrictive alternatives were available to address the negligible risks posed (Victor, 2000).

International food standards were scarcely a factor in the three disputes despite the SPS Agreement's harmonization provisions requiring governments to base their sanitary regulations on international standards. While Canada invoked the harmonization provisions in its challenge to Australia's salmon ban, neither the panel nor the Appellate Body issued a ruling affecting those provisions (WTO, 1998b, 1998c). The harmonization provisions were not cited by the US in its complaints against Japan's varietal testing and fire blight restrictions (WTO, 1998d, 2003a). The insignificance of the harmonization provisions in these disputes, along with the appellate rulings in the hormones case affirming governments' right to set their own food safety standards, should serve to defuse concerns that international food safety standards will compromise more rigorous national ones. Indeed, some concluded that the rulings set back efforts to harmonize food safety standards and contrasted with the gas and shrimp–turtle rulings, which provided strong support for international environmental standards (Cottier, 2001).

However, international standard setting bodies were consulted in the three disputes. The salmon panel requested nominations for scientific experts from the Office International des Epizootics (OIE) and a member of the OIE's Fish Disease Commission served as one of the scientific experts advising the panel (WTO, 1998b). The agricultural products and apples panels sought nominations for experts from the International Plant Protection Convention (IPPC) (WTO, 1998d, 2003a). The OIE's risk assessment guidelines figured in the salmon dispute, as did its Fish Disease Commission's food safety standards (WTO, 1998b). In the agricultural products and apples disputes, Japan claimed to abide by the IPPC's risk assessment guidelines (WTO, 1998d, 2003a).

During the compliance phase of the salmon dispute, two of the experts remarked that Australia's 1999 risk assessment met the OIE guidelines. In a strange twist, Dr Wooldridge, who had participated in the most recent effort to revise the OIE risk assessment guidelines, disagreed. As Dr Wooldridge noted, the risk assessment process was a complex one that could lead to outcomes that were open to varying interpretations (WTO, 2000). The panels in all three disputes shared this view and deferred to the governments imposing the measures in dispute to the extent possible within the dispute resolution rules. The original salmon panel was unwilling to rule against the obviously deficient 1996 risk assessment conducted by Australia (WTO, 1998b). The compliance panel in the salmon dispute approved the risk assessment process but found that it did not support the consumer-ready requirements (WTO, 2000). The agricultural products and apples panels found that, as there was insufficient evidence to support the measures at issue, they were not based on a risk assessment (WTO, 1998d, 2003a).

6.6　PANELS' HANDLING OF LEGAL AND SCIENTIFIC MATTERS

As in the other disputes explored in this volume, the panels made several significant errors. However, the performance of the panels improved with the passage of time. The most serious and perplexing errors were made in the salmon dispute. At the outset, the panel observed that the measure in dispute was the salmon ban and limited its terms of reference to the fresh, frozen and chilled salmon subject to ban. Over the course of the proceedings, the panel shifted its focus to the exemption for heat-treated salmon even though cooked salmon were not subject to the ban. The salmon panel limited all but its risk assessment rulings to wild, ocean-caught Pacific salmon even though four other types of Canadian salmon figured in the dispute (WTO, 1998c). Similarly, the agricultural products panel erroneously limited some of its findings to four of the eight agricultural products in dispute (WTO, 1999a). Both the salmon and agricultural product panels engaged in tortuous assessments of the existence of less trade-restrictive trade measures that raised more questions than they answered. By contrast, the Appellate Body upheld the apples panel on each matter appealed (WTO, 2003b). The apples panel benefited from the precedents established in the previous disputes as was apparent by its frequent references to rulings in the hormones, salmon and agricultural products disputes.

The legitimacy of the dispute settlement process has been challenged on the grounds that the panels and Appellate Body lacked the expertise to address scientific matters (Guzman, 2004; Harlow, 2004). But the three disputes suggested that these concerns were excessive. Consultation with scientific experts proved adequate to address the scientific aspects of the issues in dispute. Frequently, the parties presented conflicting evidence, but, with the assistance of the experts, the panels were able to sort through their competing claims and to clarify the issues in dispute. The panels' ability to focus the experts' attention on the central issues at stake and to deploy the experts' views effectively in their analyses of the matters in dispute was commendable and marked a striking contrast to their tendency to err on matters of law. Australia and Japan held contrary views and challenged the panel's weighing of the evidence in the three disputes. The Appellate Body rejected their appeals, explaining that panels were charged with making an objective assessment of the facts (WTO, 1998c, 1999a, 2003b). They were not required to share the disputants' interpretation of the scientific evidence presented (WTO, 1998c).

6.7 COMPLIANCE AND THE CREDIBILITY OF THE DISPUTE RESOLUTION PROCESS

Compliance proved problematic in each of the three disputes. Instead of complying with the rulings or choosing to face trade penalties, Australia used the implementation period to perform the risk assessment that it failed to do when crafting the original policy. Subsequently, the entire case was heard again with nearly the identical result: the consumer-ready requirements were no more compatible with Australia's risk assessment obligations under the SPS Agreement than the salmon ban (WTO, 2000). In the agricultural products case, Japan rescinded the offending quarantine regulations but two additional years elapsed before the US and Japan were able to announce a framework for a new quarantine process that fell well short of resolving the issues triggering the dispute (WTO, 2001a, 2001b). Like Australia in the salmon dispute, Japan used the implementation period in the apples dispute to gather new evidence to support its sanitary regulations. Continuing the parallel, the entire case was revisited to no effect. Instead, the compliance panel issued a more resounding rejection of the fire blight restrictions (WTO, 2005a).

Since there is a losing side in each dispute, for the dispute resolution process to be effective it is obvious that governments cannot simply abide by decisions that favor them. Further, in light of the diversity of the organization's membership, it is essential that the process give members latitude in the means by which they choose to comply and adequate time to implement necessary changes. WTO rulings attempt to balance these principles by requesting that members bring offending regulations into conformance with treaty obligations rather than ordering specific implementation steps. But Australia's and Japan's actions suggested that there were two problems with this approach. First, it assumed good faith on the part of losing governments. Second, it assumed that the rulings left no ambiguity about the nature of the implementation steps to be taken.[6]

Australia's and Japan's dilatory actions in the compliance phase of the salmon and agricultural products disputes unnecessarily prolonged the dispute resolution process, reducing its effectiveness for the other disputants and diminishing its credibility. The panel rulings in the apples dispute bear on the second issue. During the implementation phase, Japan addressed three of the ten fire blight regulations at issue in the dispute, two of which had been faulted by the panel in its rulings. However, the panel intended the decision to be read as a more comprehensive condemnation of the fire blight regime. Its compliance rulings struck all but two of the nine remaining restrictions at issue although no new evidence was presented invalidating the offending restrictions (WTO, 2005a). Instead, realizing that it failed to provide a sufficiently detailed set of rulings in its original report, the panel redeployed the evidence presented previously, making sure to address each of the restrictions constituting the fire blight regime. The specificity of the compliance recommendations left no doubt about the nature and extent of the fire blight regulations' incompatibility with WTO rules and charted a straightforward route to compliance. It remained to be seen whether the clarity of the recommendations speeds Japan's compliance. As illustrated by the agricultural products dispute, the announcement of an intention to comply might lead to compliance of only a superficial sort. Suggestions to improve compliance are discussed in Chapter 9.

NOTES

1. Australian authorities also rejected a request to lift the ban from the US. The US and Australia were able to resolve their dispute through consultations that concluded several months after the resolution of the dispute between Canada and Australia (Australia – Measures Affecting the Importation of Salmonids (WT/DS21)) (WTO, 2006).
2. Other Canadian salmon exports included wild, freshwater-caught Pacific salmon, Pacific salmon cultured in seawater on the Pacific coast, Atlantic salmon cultured in seawater on the Pacific coast and Atlantic salmon cultured in seawater on the Atlantic coast.
3. The Office International des Epizootics (OIE) is also known as the World Organization for Animal Health.
4. The panel also concluded that Japan had not met its notification obligation under Article 7 and Annex B of the SPS Agreement.
5. The regulations were amended in 1997 but remained substantially the same.
6. The EU raised this issue in its third party submission to the apples compliance panel (WTO, 2005a).

REFERENCES

Bilateral Agreement Between Canada and Australia (2000), as reflected in Letters Exchanged between the Canadian and Australian Ambassadors to the WTO, International Trade Canada (ITC), Ottawa, 16 May (website accessed during July 2005).

Cottier, Thomas (2001), 'Risk management experience in WTO dispute settlement', in David Robertson and Aynsley Kellow (eds), *Globalization and the Environment, Risk Assessment and the WTO*, Cheltenham, UK and Northampton, MA, USA: Edward Elgar, pp. 41–62.

Guzman, A. (2004), 'Food fears: health & safety at the WTO', *Virginia Journal of International Law*, **45**(1), 1–39.

Harlow, S. (2004), 'Science-based trade disputes: a new challenge in harmonizing evidentiary systems of law and science', *Risk Analysis*, **24**(2), 443–7.

Hieger, J. (1999), 'State fruit growers hail trade ruling on Japan', *Yakima Herald-Republic*, 23 February, A1.

Public Citizen (2004), 'Backgrounder: US threats against Europe's gmo policy and the WTO SPS Agreement', Public Citizen, Washington, DC (distributed at WTO Public Symposium, Geneva, Switzerland, May).

Seattle Times (The) (1999), 'Japan to let in more apples, state group applauds decision on apples', 10 March, C1.

Sykes, A. (2002), 'Exploring the need for international harmonization: domestic regulation, sovereignty, and scientific evidence requirements: a pessimistic view', *Chicago Journal of International Law*, **3**(2), 353–67.

USDA (US Department of Agriculture) (2006), 'US trade exports – FATUS export aggregations', USDA, Washington, DC, Foreign Agricultural Service, FASOnline (website accessed during February).

Victor, D. (2000), 'The Sanitary and Phytosanitary Agreement of the World Trade Organization: an assessment after five years', *New York University School of Law Journal of International Law and Politics*, **32**(4), 865–937.

WTO (1994), *Agreement on the Application of Sanitary and Phytosanitary Measures* (SPS), Geneva: WTO.

WTO (1998a), *EC – Measures Concerning Meat and Meat Products (Hormones), Report of the Appellate Body* (WT/DS26/AB/R and WT/DS48/AB/R), Geneva: WTO, 16 January.

WTO (1998b), *Australia – Measures Affecting the Importation of Salmon, Report of the Panel* (WT/DS18/R), Geneva: WTO, 12 June.

WTO (1998c), *Australia – Measures Affecting the Importation of Salmon, Report of the Appellate Body* (WT/DS18/AB/R), Geneva: WTO, 20 October.

WTO (1998d), *Japan – Measures Affecting Agricultural Products, Report of the Panel* (WTO/DS76/R), Geneva: WTO, 27 October.

WTO (1999a), *Japan – Measures Affecting Agricultural Products, Report of the Appellate Body* (WT/DS76/AB/R), Geneva: WTO, 22 February.

WTO (1999b), *Australia – Measures Affecting the Importation of Salmon, Report of the Arbitrator* (WT/DS18/9), Geneva: WTO, 23 February.

WTO (2000), *Australia – Measures Affecting the Importation of Salmon, Recourse to Article 21.5 by Canada, Report of the Panel* (WT/DS18/RW), Geneva: WTO, 18 February.

WTO (2001a), *Japan – Measures Affecting Agricultural Products, Communication from Japan and the United States* (WT/DS76/12), Geneva: WTO, 30 August.

WTO (2001b), *Amendment of the Plant Quarantine Measures Regarding the Dispute – Japan – Measures Affecting Agricultural Products, Committee on Sanitary and Phytosanitary Measures Notification* (G/SPS/N/JPN/75), Geneva: WTO, 1 November.

WTO (2003a), *Japan – Measures Affecting the Importation of Apples, Report of the Panel* (WT/DS245/R), Geneva: WTO, 15 July.

WTO (2003b), *Japan – Measures Affecting the Importation of Apples, Report of the Appellate Body* (WT/DS245/AB/R), Geneva: WTO, 26 November.

WTO (2005a), *Japan – Measures Affecting the Importation of Apples, Recourse to 21.5 of the DSU by the United States, Report of the Panel* (WT/DS245/RW), Geneva: WTO, 23 June.

WTO (2005b), *Japan – Measures Affecting the Importation of Apples, Statement by Japan* (WT/DS245/19), Geneva: WTO, 22 July.

WTO (2005c), *Japan – Measures Affecting the Importation of Apples, Notification of Mutually Agreed Solution* (WT/DS245/21), Geneva: WTO, 2 September.

WTO (2006), *The Disputes*, Geneva: WTO (website accessed during February).

7. Generic drugs

Chapter 7 examines the dispute between Canada and the EU over regulations that promoted the development of generic drugs. At the time, Canadian law permitted generic drug manufacturers to use patented products to perform investigative work related to regulatory approval requirements and to stockpile production prior to a patent's expiration. The EU alleged that the regulatory review and stockpiling exceptions violated the Agreement on Trade-Related Aspects of Intellectual Property Rights (TRIPS), which granted patent holders the exclusive right to produce and sell their products (Article 28.1). Canada maintained that the regulatory review and stockpiling exceptions were necessary to insure that Canadians had access to affordable medicine. Although the WTO panel approved Canada's regulatory review exception, the rulings received little support in the public health community because the panel's narrow interpretation of the agreement constrained governments seeking to justify other restrictions on patent rights. Concern was greatest in the developing world, where a variety of patent restrictions were likely to be necessary to combat AIDS, tuberculosis, malaria and other diseases. In response to the rulings and related developments, developing nations launched a campaign to insure that their obligations under TRIPS would not impede their public health strategies. Because the generic drug rulings contributed to the campaign and were ultimately overshadowed by it, the chapter closes with a discussion of the TRIPS and Public Health initiative, the most significant development at the WTO with respect to patent protection and public health.

7.1 PHARMACEUTICAL REGULATION AND PATENT LAW

Canada's efforts to promote the generic drug industry began in 1923 with the passage of compulsory licensing legislation. Compulsory licenses were designed to promote competition, decrease drug prices and increase consumers' access to pharmaceuticals by permitting generic drug manufacturers to produce patented drugs during the patent term. In exchange for the right to compete with patent owners, generic manufacturers were required to provide compensation in the form of royalty payments. In an effort to boost domestic production, the law required generic manufacturers to use domestically produced active ingredients in drugs manufactured under compulsory licenses. The local production requirement proved to be a significant impediment because of the small size of the Canadian pharmaceutical market (WTO, 2000a). Over the next four and one-half decades, generic manufacturers applied for just 49 compulsory licenses; only 22 were approved by Canadian authorities (Lexchin, 1997). In 1969, the law was changed to permit generic manufacturers to use imported active ingredients in drugs produced under compulsory licenses. The change provided a major stimulus to the generic industry: 613 compulsory licenses were approved during the period 1969–92 (Reichman and Hsenzahl, 2002).

Historically, patent law was largely a domestic matter. Although the Paris Convention on the Protection of Industrial Property obliged Canada and other signatories to extend national treatment to foreigners filing patent applications, it set no standards for patent protection. Governments were permitted to determine their own rules for patent terms, compulsory licenses and other practices. Standards varied widely with a significant portion of the developing world failing to provide patent protection of any kind (WTO, 2000a).

By the 1980s, the US, the EU and other industrialized nations made enhancing protection for patents and other forms of intellectual property a priority in both regional and multilateral trade negotiations. In anticipation of new obligations under the North American Free Trade Agreement (NAFTA) and the WTO's Agreement on Trade-Related Aspects of Intellectual Property Rights (TRIPS), Canada made several changes to its patent law. Under legislation adopted in 1987, the patent term was extended to 20 years beginning in 1989. Patents issued previously retained their 17-year terms. Canada also prohibited the issuance of compulsory licenses during the first seven to ten years of a patent term, depending on whether active ingredients were manufactured domestically. The measure was a stopgap as the NAFTA and TRIPS agreements were expected to restrict compulsory licenses even further (WTO, 2000a).

In 1992, amid controversy, Canada introduced further amendments to its Patent Act that repealed the compulsory licensing system. New compulsory licenses ceased to be issued as of December 1991; licenses issued previously remained in effect (WTO, 2000a). Backed by research-based firms, the measures had a sizable impact on the industry. By 1995, R&D expenditures averaged 11.8 percent of sales, up from 6.1 percent in 1988. With returns to shareholders' equity averaging 29.6 percent over the same period, the industry was among the most profitable in Canada (Lexchin, 1997).

In order to reduce the impact of the elimination of the compulsory licensing system, the legislation contained two amendments designed to insure that generic sales commenced immediately upon patent expiration. The regulatory review exception or early working exception permitted 'any person to make, construct, use or sell' patented products during the patent term provided that their activities were 'reasonably related to the development and submission of information' required by regulators in Canada or other countries (Canada, 1992, Section 55.2 (1), cited in WTO, 2000a, p. 2). The stockpiling exception allowed persons qualifying for the regulatory review exception to produce and store products intended for sale after patent expiration. Regulations adopted in 1993 limited stockpiling to the six months preceding patent expiration. The amendments applied to all patented products; the implementing regulations were restricted to medicine (WTO, 2000a).

Under Canadian law, regulators were obliged to review new drugs to assess their safety and efficacy. Both patented and generic drugs were subject to regulatory review. For generic drugs, the development and regulatory review processes averaged from three to six and a half years. Product development occurred over two to four years and regulatory review averaged one to two and a half years. In the final product development phase, the generic manufacturer was required to perform tests demonstrating that the generic drug contained the same amount of active ingredients as the patented drug, was in a comparable form and was biologically equivalent. The testing process averaged one to three years for generic manufacturers but was lengthier for manufacturers of patented drugs. As developers of new active ingredients, they were required to use extensive pre-clinical and clinical testing to establish the safety and efficacy of their products. After filing an application for a patent, an innovator was likely to spend from eight to 12 years developing the drug into a marketable form and completing the regulatory review process. On average, original manufacturers enjoyed exclusive marketing rights for a similar period of eight to 12 years because the 20-year patent term began at the application date (WTO, 2000a).

7.2   THE WTO DISPUTE

The EU challenged the regulatory review and stockpiling exceptions on the grounds that they infringed patent rights established during the Uruguay Round in TRIPS (Agreement on Trade-Related Aspects of Intellectual Property Rights). In December of 1997, the EU requested that Canada begin consultations on the matter. The following November, the EU concluded that the dispute could not be resolved through consultations and requested a panel investigation. Formation of the panel was delayed by the parties' inability to agree on its composition. Ultimately, the WTO's Director-General established the panel, which met the parties in June and July 1999 and issued its report in March 2000 (WTO, 2000a).

There was considerable interest in the dispute among WTO members. After TRIPS went into effect, Italian and Japanese courts upheld regulatory review exceptions for manufacturers developing generic drugs. A German court ruled that tests undertaken to establish the safety of generic drugs were compatible with the nation's experimental use exemption. Similarly, Portuguese authorities concluded that the nation's experimental use exemption applied to activities associated with the development of generic drugs. Four signatories to TRIPS (Argentina, Australia, Hungary and Israel) had amended their patent laws to permit regulatory review exceptions. Eleven nations, including five developing nations, joined the proceedings as third party participants: Australia, Brazil, Colombia, Cuba, India, Israel, Japan, Poland, Switzerland, Thailand and the US. Only Switzerland objected to the regulatory review exception. The US and Japan joined Switzerland in opposing the stockpiling exception. The other eight third party participants shared Canada's view that both exceptions were permissible under TRIPS (WTO, 2000a).

The EU charged that the regulatory review and stockpiling exceptions violated Articles 28.1 and 27.1 of TRIPS. Article 28.1 granted patent owners the right to prohibit the unauthorized production, use, sale or importation of their products. The EU complained that the regulatory review exception permitted generic manufacturers and their suppliers to engage in all four activities and that the stockpiling exception permitted patented materials to be used, manufactured and stored during the final six months of the patent term. European pharmaceutical companies estimated that the exceptions reduced their sales by C$100 million annually (WTO, 2000a).

The EU contended that both exceptions ran afoul of Article 27.1's prohibition against discrimination by field of technology because they applied exclusively to the pharmaceutical industry. In addition, the stockpiling exception violated Article 33 by reducing the patent term from 20 years to 19 years and six months. The EU acknowledged that Article 30 permitted governments to authorize certain exceptions to the patent rights conferred in Article 28.1 but claimed that the regulatory review and stockpiling provisions did not satisfy Article 30's requirements. Further, since regulations qualifying for exceptions under Article 30 were held to Article 27.1's non-discrimination provisions, Canada could not justify the regulatory review and stockpiling amendments under Article 30 (WTO, 2000a).

Canada conceded that the regulatory review and stockpiling provisions were incompatible with Article 28.1, but argued that both qualified as exceptions under Article 30 and were permissible on that basis. The regulatory review and stockpiling exceptions insured that competition between generic and patent-owning manufacturers could ensue immediately upon patent expiration. Competition was essential to reducing prices and increasing access while containing healthcare expenditures. Drug expenditures had increased from C\$1.1 billion in 1975 to C\$8.6 billion in 1992–93, creating painful tradeoffs within the healthcare system. As patented drug costs spiraled out of control, the system depended increasingly on generic drugs, which accounted for 40 percent of all prescriptions in Canada in 1997 but just 15 percent of total drug expenditures. Canada observed that the generic drug industry played a similar role in the EU where several bodies including the European Parliament, Council of the European Union and EC Commission had called for a regulatory review exception to ensure that generic drugs were available immediately upon patent expiration (WTO, 2000a).

Canada maintained that Article 27.1's non-discrimination provisions did not apply to measures qualifying as exceptions under Article 30. Moreover, the regulatory review and stockpiling exceptions were compatible with Article 27.1 because the legislation creating the exceptions did not limit their use to the pharmaceutical sector. With respect to Article 33, stockpiling did not reduce the patent term because no sales were permitted to final consumers prior to patent expiration (WTO, 2000a).

Canada added that the regulatory review exception applied to activities undertaken to comply with foreign approval requirements to insure that the needs of developing nations that relied on drug imports were addressed. Failure to exempt those activities would delay access to essential drugs in the developing world and impose costly and unnecessary testing burdens on developing nations. Canada cited several World Health Organization (WHO) reports documenting drug shortages and capacity constraints that hampered efforts to respond to the AIDS, TB and malaria pandemics plaguing the developing world (WTO, 2000a).

7.3 PANEL RULINGS

In its opening remarks, the panel noted that the key legal issues in dispute related to the parties' different interpretations of Articles 30, 27.1 and 33 (WTO, 2000a). However, the panel's findings addressed only Articles 30 and 27.1, as does the discussion that follows. The panel approved the regulatory review exemption but rejected the stockpiling exemption. It is difficult to quarrel with the panel's principal conclusions. A variant of the widely accepted experimental use exemption, the regulatory review exception ensured that the introduction of generic drugs would not be delayed by regulatory approval requirements that would otherwise extend patents several years beyond their 20-year terms. By contrast, there was scant justification for stockpiling which, in effect, reduced the patent term by six months since generic manufacturers were permitted to produce and store new drugs during the six months prior to expiration.

Unfortunately, the reasoning employed by the panel was problematic and created confusion about the ability of governments to seek exceptions under Article 30 and to make use of compulsory licensing provisions under Article 31, even though the latter provisions were not at issue in the dispute. Ignoring rulings by the Appellate Body in the hormones case that gave exceptions equal standing with general obligations, the panel took an excessively narrow view of Article 30's scope and purpose (Howse, 2000).

Article 30 set three conditions for regulations qualifying as exceptions: (1) 'limited exceptions' to patent rights were permitted, provided that (2) they did not 'unreasonably conflict' with the 'normal exploitation' of a patent, and (3) they did not 'unreasonably prejudice the legitimate interests of the patent owner, taking account of the legitimate interests of third parties' (WTO, 1994).

The panel failed to produce a viable framework to analyze Article 30's 'limited' requirement and reached the contradictory conclusion that regulatory review qualified as a limited exception but stockpiling did not (Howse, 2000). The panel observed that an unlimited quantity of products could be stockpiled over six months, a 'commercially significant period of time' (WTO, 2000a, p. 156). By contrast, investigative work occurring under the regulatory review exemption was bounded by regulatory requirements, which prohibited commercial activities until expiration. The panel's logic was unpersuasive. Producers and regulators viewed the regulatory review exception as the more significant of the two measures (Canada, 2000; *Canada NewsWire*, 2000) because it speeded the introduction of generic drugs by three to six and a half years. The panel acknowledged the latter point but held that economic considerations were addressed by Article 30's other two requirements (WTO, 2000a).

The panel's analysis of Article's 30 'normal exploitation' requirement focused on the EU's argument that market exclusivity typically extended for a brief period beyond the expiration of a patent because competitors were prohibited from making and using patented products during the patent term. The panel reasoned that the regulatory review exemption did not conflict with normal patent exploitation during that period since most patented products were not subject to regulatory approval. Thus most owners could not anticipate that market exclusivity would be extended because of regulatory processes that delayed the introduction of competing products (WTO, 2000a).

The panel's examination of Article 30's 'legitimate interest' requirement also focused on an additional period of market exclusivity. The EU claimed that patent owners had a legitimate interest in an extended period of market exclusivity because the regulatory process consumed a substantial part of the patent term. The panel observed that the WTO membership was divided on the issue. Some nations granted patent owners affected by regulatory delays patent extensions; others did not. Additionally, among those permitting patent extensions, all but the EU and Switzerland had eliminated the possibility of a period of extended market exclusivity by putting regulatory review exceptions in place. Under these circumstances, patent owners' interest in an extended period of exploitation was 'neither so compelling nor so widely recognized' as to qualify as a legitimate interest (WTO, 2000a, p. 168). This ruling invented criteria that had no basis in the agreement and imposed requirements that further restricted Article 30's scope. There was a more straightforward option available to the panel. It could have concluded that patent owners had a legitimate interest in an additional period of market exclusivity but that interest was not unreasonably prejudiced in light of the legitimate interests of consumers, regulators and other third parties (Howse, 2000).

Reasoning of that sort would have been compatible with the balance of interests addressed in the TRIPS Agreement. Although the agreement was designed to promote intellectual property rights, WTO members sought to balance those interests against others, as was apparent from the opening paragraph of the agreement. The preamble declared that intellectual property rights were being established to 'reduce distortions and impediments to international trade' but it also obliged members to insure that those rights 'do not themselves become barriers to legitimate trade' (WTO, 1994). Article 7 stipulated that the development and dissemination of technology should benefit producers and consumers 'in a manner conducive to social and economic welfare, and to a balance of rights and obligations' (WTO, 1994). Article 8.1 entitled members to 'adopt measures necessary to protect public health and nutrition' provided that their programs were consistent with the agreement (WTO, 1994). In order to put these principles and objectives into effect, Article 30 gave members broad authority to enact patent legislation that balanced competing social interests.

The panel never explicitly acknowledged that consumers, regulators and society at large had legitimate interests at stake in the dispute. The omission was striking because Canada's defense of the exceptions rested chiefly on their role in promoting its public health strategy. The narrow and technical nature of the panel's ruling left the impression that other parties' interests were subordinate to those of patent owners even though the panel never made a statement to that effect.

The panel's restrictive interpretation of Article 30 led it to misconstrue the relationship between Articles 30 and 27.1. While the panel held that Article 30 was subject to Article 27.1, the only sensible interpretation worked in reverse: Article 27.1 was subject to Article 30. In other words, exceptions justified under Article 30 were exempt not only from Article 28.1's prohibition against patent infringement but also from Article 27.1's prohibition against discrimination by field of technology. The panel concluded otherwise, noting that the agreement did not contain language exempting Article 30 from Article 27.1 (WTO, 2000a). In doing so, the panel lost sight of Article 30's purpose, which was to establish the conditions for measures qualifying as exceptions. In the absence of language imposing Article 27.1 on Article 30, its provisions did not come into play.

The panel also observed that the agreement did not contain language expressly subjecting Article 31 to Article 27.1, but Canada and the EU agreed that Article 27.1 applied to Article 31's compulsory licensing provisions. Indeed, Article 27.1's prohibition against discrimination by field of technology was intended to prevent governments from using compulsory licenses to promote competition in sectors dominated by foreign firms such as pharmaceuticals and agrochemicals while forgoing the practice in fields dominated by domestic producers. In addition, Article 31 contained a footnote explaining that it addressed unauthorized use not covered by Article 30. The panel concluded that the close relationship between Articles 30 and 31 justified a joint interpretation with respect to Article 27.1 (WTO, 2000a).

The panel's reasoning was flawed. Article 27.1's applicability to Article 31 was irrelevant. Articles 30 and 31 did not share the same function or the same relationship to other treaty provisions (Abbott, 2002). Article 30 established the grounds upon which members could seek exceptions to their obligations. Article 31 established the rules governing the issuance of compulsory licenses. Further, another article implied that Article 31 was subject to Article 27.1's anti-discrimination provisions. Article 70.6 exempted compulsory licenses issued prior to the agreement's effective date from Article 27.1. By implication, compulsory licenses issued after the agreement went into effect were subject to Article 27.1 (Abbott, 2002). However, as we will see in the discussion that follows, Article 27.1 was never raised as an obstacle to reforming Article 31's compulsory licensing provisions specifically for pharmaceutical products in the multi-year TRIPS and Public Health campaign waged by developing countries. In any case, neither Article 70.6 nor any other provision imposed Article 27.1 on Article 30.

To find a regulatory review compatible with Article 27.1, the panel was forced into contortions. The panel declared that 'no systematic information' had been presented on regulatory review's sectoral impact despite Canada's admission that it had been applied only in the pharmaceutical sector (WTO, 2000a, p.173). In the absence of such evidence, the panel decided to examine whether there were any 'practical considerations' that restricted regulatory review to the pharmaceutical sector (WTO, 2000a, p.173). Evidently, the legislation's implementing regulations, which were limited to patented medicines, did not qualify as practical considerations. These regulations alone provided a 'practical reason' why the regulatory review exception had not and would not affect patent holders in other fields (WTO, 2000a, p. 173). The public debate on the measure, which centered exclusively on the pharmaceutical sector, was yet another indicator that the regulatory review exception had a discriminatory purpose and effect (WTO, 2000a). The panel's analysis of Article 27.1 was unsatisfactory but not entirely so. The panel's twisted logic managed to preserve the regulatory review exception's compatibility with TRIPS.

7.4 AFTERMATH

Canadian officials greeted the rulings with enthusiasm despite the blow to stockpiling explaining that the benefits arising from that exception were 'minimal' as compared to those derived from the regulatory review exception (Canada, 2000, p. 2). The Canadian generic drug manufacturers association hailed the decision as 'excellent news' observing that it permitted generic manufacturers 'to give Canadians the choice and savings they deserve' (*Canada Newswire*, 2000, p. 1). Canada declined to appeal the rulings, as did the EU, although they disagreed on the amount of time necessary to implement the rulings. An arbitrator decided that six months was sufficient and set a deadline of October 2000 (WTO, 2000b). Canada repealed the stockpiling exception in June 2001, about eight months after the deadline elapsed (Canada, 2001).

The parties' decision not to appeal the rulings was unusual as WTO members tended to appeal adverse panel rulings as a matter of course. Appeals were filed in seven of the nine disputes explored in this volume. As in the other disputes, there appeared to be significant flaws in the panel's reasoning, so the parties' acceptance of the generic drug rulings cannot be attributed to an impeccable panel record. In this instance, the most likely explanation is the most obvious one: both parties were satisfied with a decision that struck stockpiling but affirmed the regulatory review exception. For Canadian regulators, protecting early working of patented ingredients under the regulatory review exemption was most critical. For the Europeans, eliminating stockpiling was the principal goal. Although the EU insisted that its member states did not have a regulatory review exception, judicial action at the state level and legislative action at the union level suggested that a European consensus was developing in favor of one.

However, developing nations complained that the panel's narrow interpretation of the TRIPS Agreement would restrict their ability to employ compulsory licenses and other measures that limited patent rights (WTO, 2001a, 2001b, 2001c). These matters were not reviewed by the Appellate Body because WTO rules permitted only disputants to file appeals. Had these aspects of the rulings been appealed, it is unlikely that they would have survived the Appellate Body's scrutiny because of their inconsistency with the gasoline, shrimp–turtle, hormones and asbestos rulings. In each of those disputes, both the panel and appellate rulings addressed the multiple stakeholders and objectives that influenced government policy. In the gasoline dispute (Chapter 2), both the panel and Appellate Body closed their reports by affirming members' right to set their own environmental policies. In the shrimp–turtle dispute (Chapter 3), the panel and Appellate Body based a significant portion of their rulings on the disputants' commitments under multilateral environmental treaties. In the hormones dispute (Chapter 4), the panel and Appellate Body acknowledged the health goals pursued by the EU but faulted its risk assessment process. In the asbestos dispute (Chapter 5), the panel and appellate rulings affirmed governments' right to restrict trade to promote public health. Although these panels recognized other social objectives, they tended to give greater weight to trade goals. But the Appellate Body emphasized that governments had a 'right and duty' to pursue both types of objectives and cited various provisions in the WTO agreements that empowered governments to do so (WTO, 1998, para. 177). By contrast, the generic drugs panel examined the interests at stake in the dispute in a narrow, legal manner that stressed the limitations placed on governments in their pursuit of health and other non-trade objectives.[1]

7.5   TRIPS AND PUBLIC HEALTH

The panel's decision created uncertainty about the extent to which governments could pursue public health objectives through the promotion of generic drugs. The stakes were especially high for developing nations as a result of the devastating impact of AIDS and other life-threatening diseases. With the enactment of TRIPS in 1995, many developing countries agreed to honor patents and other forms of intellectual property for the first time. In order to facilitate the transition, developing nations were granted five-year grace periods (Articles 65.1 and 65.2). Least-developed nations and nations that had not honored patents in the past were granted transitional periods of 11 and ten years, respectively (Articles 66.1 and 65.4).[2] Special rules applied to pharmaceuticals and agricultural chemicals requiring governments to establish patent application systems (known as mail box systems) and to provide for exclusive marketing rights during the transitional period (Articles 70.8, 70.9) (WTO, 1994).

Developing countries became increasingly uneasy about their obligations under TRIPS as developed nations, especially the US, used the dispute resolution system and other fora to enforce and strengthen patent protection.[3] The US and EU prevailed in two separate disputes with India regarding patent protection for pharmaceuticals and agricultural chemicals.[4] As a developing nation that did not previously provide patent protection, India was not obliged to honor patents until the beginning of 2005. However, India had not complied with its obligations to establish a patent application system and to provide for exclusive marketing rights during the transitional period (WTO, 2005d).

The US was involved in five other pharmaceutical patent disputes with developing nations. The US challenged Pakistan's pharmaceutical and agricultural chemical patent regime on the same grounds as in the dispute with India.[5] The US filed two separate complaints against Argentina that cited a slew of patent violations including failures to protect test data, extend patentability to certain subjects, and adequately restrict the issuance of compulsory licenses.[6] The US objected to Brazilian legislation that subjected patents that were not worked locally (no local production) to compulsory licensing.[7] In response, Brazil challenged provisions of US law requiring local working under certain circumstances.[8] Brazil did not pursue its complaint once it was able to reach a mutually agreed solution with the US in the other dispute (WTO, 2005d). Although the US also reached mutually agreed solutions with Pakistan and Argentina, some criticized the US for extracting commitments from Argentina that exceeded its obligations under TRIPS (Shanker, 2004). Concern grew as the US used bilateral and regional trade agreements to pursue 'TRIPS-plus' patent rules (Abbott, 2005; Correa, 2004; Shashikant, 2005) and threatened to sanction eight developing countries (Argentina, Brazil, Dominican Republic, Egypt, India, South Africa, Thailand and Vietnam) and Israel for alleged violations of trade rules affecting pharmaceutical patents (Oxfam, 2001).

In March 2001, the pharmaceutical industry joined the fray. At a time when the United Nations (UN), the World Health Organization (WHO) and non-governmental organizations (NGOs) including Oxfam and Médecins sans Frontières (Doctors Without Borders) were undertaking major initiatives to address the impact of HIV/AIDS, malaria, tuberculosis and other infectious diseases in Africa and elsewhere in the developing world, 41 pharmaceutical manufacturers launched a court challenge to a South African law that permitted officials to issue compulsory licenses on public health grounds (Matthews, 2004). The next month, Zimbabwe on behalf of the African Group (the WTO's 41 African members) requested that the WTO's TRIPS Council hold a special session to clarify the relationship between intellectual property rights and public health (WTO, 2001a). Developing nations led by Brazil supported the African Group's appeal. Their statement, 'TRIPS and Public Health', emphasized that there was sufficient flexibility within the TRIPS Agreement to permit governments to protect public health. Nevertheless, it was necessary to develop a 'common understanding' of those flexibilities to insure that intellectual property rights did not interfere with access to affordable drugs (WTO, 2001b, p. 5).

The TRIPS Council met in a special session in June of 2001 to take up these concerns. Several members criticized the generic drugs rulings. India stated that Article 30 was not subject to Article 27.1, explaining it was 'not legally correct to allow an exception to a rule to be trumped by the rule itself' (WTO, 2001c, p. 25). Thailand declared that Article 27.1's non-discrimination provisions did not apply to compulsory licenses satisfying Article 31's requirements. Venezuela and Kenya objected to interpretations of TRIPS that threatened poor people's access to medicine by limiting compulsory licenses (WTO, 2001c). Brazil called for a declaration providing 'clear guidance' to insure that the dispute resolution system was not used to enforce 'restrictive', 'unbalanced' and 'incorrect' interpretations of TRIPS (WTO, 2001c, p. 9). On the other hand, Canada, the US and Egypt praised the generic drug rulings, observing that the panel's approval of the regulatory review exception aided governments seeking to promote generic drugs (WTO, 2001c).

As the meeting progressed, attention focused increasingly on the restrictions affecting compulsory licenses in Article 31 of the TRIPS Agreement. Developing nations objected to Article 31(b), which required governments to seek authorized use of patented products on reasonable commercial terms prior to issuing compulsory licenses. Although Article 31(b) contained exemptions for 'public noncommercial use', a 'national emergency' and other situations of 'extreme urgency' (WTO, 1994), it was unclear whether those exemptions applied to the health crises facing developing nations (WTO, 2001c). Article 31(f) created concerns because it required compulsory licenses to be issued 'predominantly' to supply the domestic market (WTO, 1994). Developing nations argued that the provision must be interpreted in a liberal fashion or changed to insure that nations with insufficient manufacturing capacity could employ compulsory licenses. Developed countries sought to reassure developing nations that Article 31(b) would not hamper their efforts to respond to the AIDS crisis as it qualified as a national emergency despite its ongoing character. There was less agreement on Article 31(f) but the EU, Norway and Japan agreed that domestic supply restrictions should be addressed without committing to a specific mechanism (WTO, 2001c).

Pressure mounted to respond to the TRIPS and Public Health initiative as the November 2001 Ministerial meeting approached. The previous Ministerial held in Seattle in 1999 collapsed in part because developing nations were not satisfied with the results of the Uruguay Round. While they had fulfilled their commitments to honor intellectual property and open the service sector to foreign competition, developed nations had not removed trade barriers affecting agricultural products and textiles & apparel. In response to this criticism, the WTO was preparing to use the 2001 Ministerial meeting to launch the Doha Development Round, a round of trade negotiations dedicated to issues of concern to developing nations (Kelly, 2005).

Determined to avoid a Seattle-like débâcle, WTO members responded to developing nations' campaign with the Doha Declaration on the TRIPS Agreement and Public Health. The declaration stated that members had a right to use the flexibilities in the agreement 'to the full' and that TRIPS 'does not and should not' prevent governments from protecting the health of their citizens (WTO, 2001d, para. 4). It extended the transition period for pharmaceutical patents by ten years (from 2006 to 2016) for least-developed countries. Two provisions addressed Article 31(b). The first asserted that members had the right to issue compulsory licenses and to determine the terms upon which they were issued. The second authorized members to define national emergencies and other urgent situations while establishing the general understanding that HIV/AIDS, tuberculosis, malaria and other epidemics qualified as national emergencies or situations of extreme urgency. Members were unable to agree on how to address the domestic supply restriction (WTO, 2001d). The declaration acknowledged that members with limited or no manufacturing capacity 'could face difficulties in making effective use of compulsory licensing' and bound members to find an 'expeditious' solution by the end of 2002 (WTO, 2001d, para. 6).

The 2002 deadline was missed as finding a solution was contentious. Initially, the African Group and the US proposed a moratorium on disputes involving Article 31(f). However, they backed away from that proposal once it became clear that it was vulnerable to a legal challenge. Thereafter, the US proposed waiving Article 31(f) for developing nations with insufficient manufacturing capacity. The EU proposed amending Article 31(f) to allow compulsory licenses to be issued for pharmaceutical exports to nations experiencing health crises provided that measures were undertaken to prevent abuse and diversion to other markets. As an alternative to amending Article 31(f), the EU proposed that WTO members agree to grant exceptions under Article 30 to nations issuing compulsory licenses for pharmaceutical imports necessary to address health crises. As with the waiver, an authoritative interpretation of this sort could be declared by consensus or a three-quarters vote of the membership. Because amendments required a two-thirds vote of the membership and ratification by a like number of national legislative bodies, the case for the waiver and interpretation rested in part on the ease with which they could be adopted. Soon developing nations and NGOs began to advocate on behalf of an authoritative interpretation of Article 30. The EU increasingly favored an amendment, fearing that a foreign supply exemption was too broad to qualify as a limited exception under Article 30 (Matthews, 2004).[9]

Substantive disagreements on disease and product coverage as well as eligible participants also divided the membership. The US argued that the use of compulsory licenses to supply foreign markets should be limited to drugs necessary to treat the three major pandemics affecting the developing world: HIV/AIDS, malaria and tuberculosis. The EU and developing nations favored broad disease coverage and opposed restricting the program to the three diseases. With respect to products, the US proposed limiting coverage to drugs while the EU and developing nations argued that diagnostic kits should be included as well. On eligibility, developing nations proposed that participation be open to all members as both importers and exporters. The EU joined the US in desiring to restrict importing to least-developed and low-income developing nations despite criticism that such a definition excluded 72 countries without sufficient manufacturing capacity. The US sought to restrict exporting to developing nations on the grounds that permitting the participation of developed countries would impede the development of the pharmaceutical sector in the developing world. Others maintained that excluding developed countries as exporters would have the harmful short-run effect of reducing the number of suppliers of inexpensive generic drugs (Matthews, 2004).

The stalemate was broken in August 2003, when the US dropped its opposition to broad disease and product coverage in exchange for a set of procedural and anti-diversion safeguards affecting importing and exporting members. Importers were required to specify the names and quantities of products to be imported, to take steps to avoid trade diversion and to insure that compulsory licenses were issued. Importing nations other than least-developed countries were required to establish that they had insufficient or no manufacturing capacity. Twenty-three developed countries pledged not to participate as importers (Australia, Austria, Belgium, Canada, Denmark, Finland, France, Germany, Greece, Iceland, Ireland, Italy, Japan, Luxembourg, Netherlands, New Zealand, Norway, Portugal, Spain, Sweden, Switzerland, United Kingdom and United States). Exporting nations were to export only the amount required by importing nations and the full amount of the production authorized by compulsory license. Suppliers were to use special packaging, labeling, coloring and shaping to distinguish their products and to maintain a website detailing shipment size, destination and distinguishing features. In instances where compulsory licenses were issued in both exporting and importing nations, the importing nation's royalty payment would be waived to avoid double remuneration. The decision established mid-June 2004 as the deadline for converting the waiver into an amendment (WTO, 2003b).

Despite these stringent conditions, developed countries remained concerned that the waiver was open to abuse. To address these concerns, the Chair of the General Council issued a statement representing the members' understanding of the decision (WTO, 2003a). The Chair's statement stipulated that the waiver be used 'in good faith to protect public health' and not to advance commercial or industrial development (WTO, 2003a, para. 2). It reiterated the importance of anti-diversion efforts, recommended that members employ state-of-the-art anti-diversion practices and provided examples of measures employed by the major pharmaceutical companies. The Chair's statement limited the participation of ten prospective EU members (Czech Republic, Cyprus, Estonia, Hungary, Latvia, Lithuania, Malta, Poland, Slovak Republic and Slovenia) and 11 other members (Hong Kong, Israel, Korea, Kuwait, Macao, Mexico, Qatar, Singapore, Taiwan, Turkey and United Arab Emirates) as importers to national emergencies and other situations of extreme urgency. The prospective EU members agreed to opt out fully as importers upon their accession to the EU (WTO, 2003a).

The Chair's statement was a stumbling block in the amendment negotiations. While developing countries such as Malaysia, the Philippines, Argentina and Brazil distinguished between the decision and the Chair's statement, developed countries tended to view them as equally important. Australia, Canada, Switzerland and the US sought to incorporate the Chair's statement into the text of the amendment. Developing and developed countries also disagreed on the nature of the amendment process with developed countries including Australia, Canada, EU, Japan, Switzerland and the US holding that it was merely a technical exercise designed to convert the decision into an amendment without substantive changes (WTO, 2005a, 2005b, 2005c). When the African Group submitted a new proposal in December 2004, developed nations rejected it on the grounds that it jeopardized the consensus reached in 2003. The EU issued a stinging critique: the proposal broadened product coverage, weakened anti-diversion, notice and transparency provisions, and changed the purpose of the amendment from responding to health crises to creating local manufacturing capacity (WTO, 2005b). Brazil, Argentina, Malaysia and the Philippines supported the African Group's proposal. India, Korea, Hong Kong and Taiwan opposed changing the conditions detailed in the waiver. Israel and Turkey were willing to consider the African Group's proposal as long as their 'opt-outs' remained voluntary and partial (WTO, 2005a, 2005b, 2005c).

After missing the initial deadline set for mid-2004, members vowed to reach an agreement by mid-2005, well before the December Ministerial meeting in Hong Kong. As with previous deadlines, it lapsed without an agreement being reached. Throughout the fall, negotiations continued, principally between the African Group and the US, but other countries were involved as well, including the EU, Brazil, India, Hong Kong, Korea and Israel (ICTSD, 2005). The parties proved determined to go to the meeting with an agreement. In early December, the logjam was broken when the African Group accepted the waiver text including the cumbersome notice, transparency and anti-diversion requirements and the US compromised on the Chair's statement. In an unusual and carefully orchestrated process, the TRIPS Council agreed without debate to send the amendment to the General Council for approval along with the Chair's statement. On 6 December just days before the Ministerial meeting was to begin, the General Council adopted the amendment in the form of a protocol, which would go into effect upon ratification by two-thirds of member governments. As at the TRIPS Council, there was no debate on the amendment. Instead, the 11 countries partially opting out of the system pledged to limit their use of the waiver to national emergencies and other situations of extreme urgency. Afterwards, the Chair of the General Council read the Chair's statement that accompanied the 30 August 2003 decision and gaveled the amendment through (ICTSD, 2005; WTO, 2005f).[10]

The amendment preserved the substance of the waiver but packaged it into three parts. An additional article (Article 31 bis) permitted exports of pharmaceutical products under compulsory licenses to countries with insufficient manufacturing capacity. An annex contained the notice, transparency and anti-diversion requirements affecting importers and exporters. An appendix to the annex addressed the determination of insufficient manufacturing capacity. The protocol gave members until December 2007 to act on the amendment. In the interim, the waiver applied (WTO, 2005g).

Some 50 NGOs, including Oxfam, Doctors Without Borders and the Third World Network, charged that the US and EU were attempting to divert attention away from the lack of progress on agriculture and other issues of concern to developing nations in the Doha Round. They characterized the waiver process as 'burdensome and unworkable' and protested that the effort to produce a permanent solution had produced an ineffectual one (NGO Statement, 2005, p. 1). In order to put the waiver into effect, exporting as well as importing governments were required to make changes in their national laws. Between September 2003 and December 2005, only Norway, Canada and India had made the legal changes necessary to participate as exporters. Only four other nations were close to completing the process (EU and Korea) or had announced intentions to participate as exporters (China and Switzerland) (WTO, 2005c, 2005f, 2006). Even where countries enacted implementing legislation, participation was not assured as generic manufacturers were likely to be dissuaded by the production, reporting and anti-diversion requirements. According to Doctors Without Borders, the 'drug-by-drug, country-by-country' compulsory licensing requirement was fundamentally at odds with the dimensions of the health crises facing developing nations and the economies of scale that drove the pharmaceutical industry (Doctors Without Borders, 2005, p. 1).

In addition, national authorities had the power to impose requirements beyond those in the waiver itself. For example, Canada's 'good faith' clause permitted patent owners to challenge export licenses on the grounds that they served commercial rather than humanitarian purposes (where prices were greater than or equal to 25 percent of those on patented products) (WTO, 2005e). The Canadian legislation also restricted export licenses to a two-year term (with one-time renewal) and limited eligibility to certain drugs (Ripley, 2004). The Canadian Generic Pharmaceutical Association (CGPA) complained that the legislation favored original manufacturers and predicted that its members would not participate in the program (CGPA, 2004; Milne, 2004).

That developed nations were willing to accept the amendment was not surprising, but what about developing nations? Why did they not hold out for the African Group's proposal? Several possibilities come to mind. First, a deal, even a flawed one, was better than no deal. With some developing nations joining developed nations in opposing substantive changes to the waiver, a decision to push for more ran the risk of jeopardizing the entire arrangement at a time when governments were beginning to act on the flexibilities clarified in the waiver and the Doha declaration. During 2004, Malaysia issued a public-use order that authorized a local firm to import three HIV/AIDS drugs from an Indian generic manufacturer. Zimbabwe declared a national emergency and issued compulsory licenses permitting three firms to produce or import HIV/AIDS drugs. Indonesia passed a decree authorizing local production of two patented antiretrovirals (ARVs) (Shashikant, 2005).

Second, the waiver achieved the developing countries' major objective: the removal of the domestic supply restriction affecting compulsory licenses for a broad set of diseases and products (drugs and diagnostic kits necessary to respond to national emergencies and other urgent situations). Third, the notice, transparency and anti-diversion requirements were onerous but had scarcely been tested. Pragmatism required lifting opposition to what amounted to potential problems. Although it might be difficult to change these procedural requirements, it certainly would be far more difficult to change the substantive requirements affecting disease and product coverage.

Fourth, the importance of the waiver declined in the short term as a result of other developments. With the extension of the transitional period for pharmaceutical patents, least-developed nations were not obliged to honor patents until 2016. In an attempt to counter bad publicity and the threat of local competition, the major multinational firms began to sell patented medicines to developing nations at steeply discounted prices and participated in a variety of other 'access initiatives' in partnerships with developing nations and international organizations (PhRMA, 2004). Charitable and multilateral organizations including the Gates Foundation, the Global Fund to Fight AIDS, Tuberculosis and Malaria, UNAIDS and the World Health Organization (WHO) made substantial commitments to improve access to medicine in the developing world, as did the Bush Administration through its $15 billion Emergency Plan for AIDS Relief in Africa and the Caribbean (*Lancet*, 2005; Paulson, 2005; Ramsay, 2002). Initially stymied by domestic production requirements, the Bush program moved closer to fruition in 2005 with the FDA's approval of South African production of a generic version of an AIDS drug under patent in the US (*Medical Letter on the CDC & FDA*, 2005).

National efforts were also improving as over 30 developing nations followed the WHO's lead and adopted Brazil's successful program as a model. Relying on government procurement, generic production and discounted patented medicines, Brazil reduced mortality dramatically by distributing HIV/AIDS drugs free of charge to all in need. The model was taking hold as plans were underway to begin local manufacturing in Ethiopia, Namibia and Uganda (Cohen and Lybecker, 2005). In light of these developments, it was time to declare victory and prepare for the next battle: access to new and more expensive drugs as resistance to older drugs inevitably occurred (Doctors Without Borders, 2006). This battle would provide the true measure of the Doha declaration and the waiver agreement.

NOTES

1. Williams (2001) took the contrary position that the panel's narrow, legalistic approach was consistent with previous WTO jurisprudence and reflected the membership's desire for a predictable, rules-based dispute resolution process.
2. The UN's least-developed designation applied to 32 WTO members: Angola, Bangladesh, Benin, Burkina Faso, Burundi, Cambodia, Central African Republic, Chad, Democratic Republic of Congo, Djibouti, Gambia, Guinea, Guinea Bissau, Haiti, Lesotho, Madagascar, Malawi, Maldives, Mali, Mauritania, Mozambique, Myanmar, Nepal, Niger, Rwanda, Senegal, Sierra Leone, Solomon Islands, Tanzania, Togo, Uganda and Zambia.
3. For a discussion of the beneficial role that the dispute resolution process may play in clarifying the relationship between intellectual property rights and public health, see Curti (2001).
4. India – Patent Protection for Pharmaceutical and Agricultural Chemical Products (WT/DS50) and India – Patent Protection for Pharmaceutical and Agricultural Chemical Products (WT/DS79).
5. Pakistan – Patent Protection for Pharmaceutical and Agricultural Chemical Products (WT/DS36).

6. Argentina – Patent Protection for Pharmaceuticals and Test Data Protection for Agricultural Chemicals (WT/DS171) and Argentina – Certain Measures on the Protection of Patents and Test Data (WT/DS196).
7. Brazil – Measures Affecting Patent Protection (WT/DS199).
8. United States – US Patents Code (WT/DS224).
9. See Haag (2002) for a good discussion of the difficulty of reconciling the generic drug panel's narrow interpretation of Article 30's limited requirement with an authoritative interpretation of Article 30 creating a broad exemption to address foreign supply under compulsory licenses.
10. The Chair's statement was identical to that accompanying the August 2003 decision except for the first paragraph, which indicated that the agreement did not affect the applicability of non-violation complaints under GATT Article XXIII 1(b) and 1(c) to TRIPS, a matter on which members held varying views.

REFERENCES

Abbott, F. (2002), 'Compulsory licensing for public health needs: the TRIPS agenda at the WTO after the Doha declaration on public health', Quaker United Nations Office, Geneva, Occasional Paper 9, February.

Abbott, F. (2005), 'The WTO medicines decision: world pharmaceutical trade and the protection of public health', *American Journal of International Law*, **99**(2), 317–58.

Canada (1992), *Patent Act of 1992*, cited in WTO (2000a), p. 2.

Canada (2000), 'Canada welcomes WTO ruling on EU challenge of Canada's pharmaceutical patent regime', *News Release*, Department of Foreign Affairs and International Trade, Ottawa, 17 March.

Canada (2001), *An Act to Amend the Patent Act* (Bill S-17), Assented to on 14 June, cited in Daniel Gifford (2004), 'Government policy towards innovation in the United States, Canada and the European Union as manifested in patent, copyright, and competition laws', *Southern Methodist University Law Review*, **57**(4), 1339–83, footnote 41.

Canada NewsWire (2000), 'Pharmacy bills stay high thanks to WTO ruling on patent extensions, Canadians delayed access to lower cost generic drugs', 7 March.

CGPA (Canadian Generic Pharmaceutical Association) (2004), 'Bill C-9, An Act to Amend the Patent Act and the Food and Drugs Act, comments from Canada's generic pharmaceutical industry', CGPA, Toronto, February.

Cohen J. and K. Lybecker (2005), 'AIDS policy and pharmaceutical patents, Brazil's strategy to safeguard public health', *The World Economy*, **28**(2), 211–30.

Correa, C. (2004), 'Bilateralism in intellectual property: defeating the WTO systems for access to medicine', *Case Western Reserve Journal of International Law*, **36**(1), 79–94.

Curti, A. (2001), 'The dispute settlement understanding: an unlikely weapon in the fight against AIDS', *American Journal of Law and Medicine*, **27**(4), 469–86.

Doctors Without Borders (2005), 'Amendment to WTO TRIPS Agreement makes access to affordable medicines even more bleak', Doctors Without Borders / Medecins Sans Frontieres (*MSF Article*), Geneva, 6 December (website access during December 2005).

Doctors Without Borders (2006), 'Five years after Doha, drug prices are on the rise', Doctors Without Borders / Medecins Sans Frontieres, Geneva (*Press Release*), 14 November.

Haag, T. (2002), 'TRIPS since Doha: how far will the WTO go toward modifying the terms for compulsory licensing?', *Journal of the Patent and Trademark Society*, **84**(12), 945–81.

Howse, R. (2000), 'The Canadian generic medicine panel, a dangerous precedent in dangerous times', *Journal of World Intellectual Property*, **3**(4), 493–507.

ICTSD (International Centre for Trade and Sustainable Development) (2005), 'Members strike deal on TRIPS and Public Health, civil society unimpressed', *Bridges Weekly Trade News Digest*, **9**(42), 7 December, 2–5.

Kelly, T. (2005), 'Why are developing countries still negotiating, the WTO's Successes at the Doha Round?', *Challenge*, **48**(3), 109–24.

Lancet (The) (2005), 'Maintaining anti-AIDS commitment post "3 by 5" ', 26 November–2 December, 1828.

Lexchin, J. (1997), 'After compulsory licensing: coming issues in Canadian pharmaceutical policy and politics', *Health Policy*, **40**(1), 69–80.

Matthews, D. (2004), 'WTO decision on implementation of paragraph 6 of the Doha declaration on the TRIPS Agreement and Public Health: a solution to access to medicines problem?', *Journal of International Economic Law*, **7**(1), 73–107.

Medical Letter on the CDC & FDA (2005), 'HIV/AIDS treatment, production on generic AIDS drug could begin in March', 20 February, 66.

Milne, C. (2004), 'AIDS drug bill still flawed, MSF says', *Medical Post*, 4 May, 4.

NGO Statement (on TRIPS and Public Health) (2005), 'WTO members should reject bad deal on medicines', 3 December (www.cptech.org/ip/wto/p6/12032005.html).

Oxfam (2001), 'Patent injustice: how world trade rules threaten the health of poor people', Oxford: Oxfam.

Paulson, T. (2005), 'Gates gives millions for malaria vaccine, Microsoft chairman makes eliminating disease top priority', *Seattle Post–Intelligencer*, 31 October, A1.

PhRMA (Pharmaceutical Research and Manufacturers of America) (2004), 'Global partnerships, the humanitarian programs of the pharmaceutical industry in developing nations', PhRMA, Washington, DC, November.

Ramsay, R. (2002), 'Global fund makes historic first round of payments', *The Lancet*, 4 May, 1581.

Reichman, J. and C. Hsenzahl (2002), 'Non-voluntary licensing of patented inventions: history, TRIPS, and the Canadian and United States practice', *Bridges Monthly Review*, **6**(7), 3.

Ripley, D. (2004), 'Balancing act: Canada shares its patented pharmaceuticals with the world while balancing the needs of public health and private rights: a close inspection of the Jean Chrétien Pledge to Africa Act', *Canadian Chemical News*, **56**(9), 15–17.

Shanker, D. (2004), 'Argentina–US mutually agreed solution, economic crisis in Argentina and failure of the WTO dispute settlement system', *Journal of Law and Technology*, **44**(4), 565–615.

Shashikant, S. (2005), 'More countries use compulsory license, but new problems emerge', Third World Network, Geneva, 19 May.

Williams, D. (2001), 'Developing TRIPS jurisprudence, the first six years and beyond', *Journal of World Intellectual Property*, **4**(2), 176–209.

WTO (1994), *Agreement on Trade-Related Aspects of Intellectual Property Rights* (TRIPS), Geneva: WTO.

WTO (1998), *EC – Measures Concerning Meat and Meat Products (Hormones), Report of the Appellate Body* (WT/DS26/AB/R and WT/DS48/AB/R), Geneva: WTO, 16 January.

WTO (2000a), *Canada – Patent Protection of Pharmaceutical Products, Report of the Panel* (WT/DS114/R), Geneva: WTO, 17 March.

WTO (2000b), *Canada – Patent Protection of Pharmaceutical Products, Arbitration Report* (WT/DS114/13), Geneva: WTO, 18 August.

WTO (2001a), *TRIPS Council Minutes of Meeting, 2–5 April 2001* (IP/C/M/30), Geneva: WTO, 1 June.

WTO (2001b), *TRIPS and Public Health* (IP/C/W/296), Geneva: WTO, 29 June.

WTO (2001c), *Special Discussion on Intellectual Property and Access to Medicines* (IP/C/M/31), Geneva: WTO, 10 July.

WTO (2001d), *Doha Declaration on the TRIPS Agreement and Public Health* (WT/MIN(01)/DEC/2), Geneva: WTO, 20 November.

WTO (2003a), *The General Council Chairperson's Statement* (WTO News, 2003 News Items), Geneva: WTO, 30 August.

WTO (2003b), *Implementation of Paragraph 6 of the Doha Declaration on the TRIPS Agreement and Public Health, Decision of 30 August 2003* (WT/L/540), Geneva: WTO, 2 September.

WTO (2005a), *TRIPS Council Minutes of Meeting, 1–2 December 2004* (IP/C/M/46), Geneva: WTO, 11 January.

WTO (2005b), *TRIPS Council, Minutes of Meeting, 8–9 and 31 March 2005* (IP/C/M/47), Geneva: WTO, 3 June.

WTO (2005c), *TRIPS Council, Minutes of Meeting, 14–15 June 2005* (IP/C/M/48), Geneva: WTO, 15 September.

WTO (2005d), *The Disputes*, Geneva: WTO (website accessed during November).

WTO (2005e) *TRIPS Council, The TRIPS Agreement and Public Health, Communication from Canada* (IP/C/W/464), Geneva: WTO, 14 November.

WTO (2005f), *Members OK Amendment to Make Health Flexibility Permanent* (WTO: 2005 Press Releases (Press 426)), Geneva: WTO, 6 December.

WTO (2005g), *TRIPS Council, Implementation of Paragraph 11 of the General Council Decision of 30 August 2003 on the Implementation of Paragraph 6 of the Doha Declaration on the TRIPS Agreement and Public Health, Proposal for a Decision on an Amendment to the TRIPS Agreement* (IP/C/41), Geneva: WTO, 6 December.

WTO (2006), *TRIPS Council, Minutes of Meeting, 25–26 and 28 October, 29 November and 6 December 2005* (IP/C/M/49), Geneva: WTO, 31 January.

8. GMOs

In 2003, Argentina, Canada and the US challenged the EU's biotech food policy alleging that the EU had imposed a de facto moratorium on the approval of new products containing genetically modified organisms (GMOs) beginning in 1998. Earlier that year, the EU approved new composition, labeling and traceability standards for GMOs and other novel foods. The new standards were expected to end the moratorium but their effect on the dispute was unclear because they did not go into effect until April 2004 – after the establishment of the GMOs panel and well before the anticipated release of the rulings in this complex case involving delays in the processing of 27 individual product applications and six state-level GM bans as well as the general moratorium.

The panel emphasized the narrow scope of its examination, explaining that it had not investigated the safety of biotech products, the likeness of biotech and conventional products, the EU's right to establish pre-marketing approval procedures or the consistency of those procedures with WTO obligations (WTO, 2006). It was true that the long-awaited dispute left much unresolved, but not as much as the panel's comment suggested. The dispute revealed a great deal about the safety of biotech products and the efficacy of the EU's risk assessment procedures. Most important, while there was consensus within the mainstream scientific community that genetically modified (GM) food was as safe as conventional food, there was less agreement about the nature and magnitude of real and potential environmental risks. These environmental risks provided a basis to support five of the six bans under the Sanitary and Phytosantitary (SPS) Agreement's Article 5.7, which permitted temporary, precautionary measures in cases of insufficient scientific evidence. But the panel ignored key elements of the experts' testimony and concluded that the EU's risk assessment did not support the state-level bans. What could have been a pathbreaking decision, the first to approve precautionary measures invoked under Article 5.7, may instead become known as the one in which a panel's mishandling of scientific testimony diminished members' rights.

8.1 GMOs UNDER CULTIVATION

The large-scale cultivation of GMOs began in 1996 and experienced explosive growth over the next decade. By 2005, 8.5 million farmers in 21 countries were devoting 222 million acres of farmland to the production of biotech crops. These 21 countries included 13 developing and transitional economies (Argentina, Brazil, China, Colombia, Honduras, India, Iran, Mexico, Paraguay, Philippines, Romania, South Africa and Uruguay) and eight developed nations including five in the EU (Australia, Canada, Czech Republic, France, Germany, Portugal, Spain and US). Production was highly concentrated in five nations, which accounted for 94 percent of global production: US (55 percent), Argentina (19 percent), Brazil (10 percent), Canada (6 percent) and China (4 percent). Between 2004 and 2005, production grew rapidly in the developing world especially in Brazil and India, where the number of hectares devoted to GM crops nearly doubled and tripled, respectively. Interestingly, GM corn cultivation was introduced in the Czech Republic in 2005 and resumed in France and Portugal after four to five year hiatuses (ISAAA, 2006).

In 2005, herbicide-tolerant genetically modified (GMHT) crops remained the most prevalent, accounting for 71 percent of all biotech production. Insect-resistant GM crops remained in second place with an 18 percent share, but were facing increasing competition from those with stacked genes (two or three traits), which held an 11 percent share (ISAAA, 2006). As of 2004, GM crops accounted for a significant share of production in four markets: soybeans (56 percent), cotton (28 percent), canola (19 percent) and corn (14 percent) (Zarrilli, 2005). GM rice was cultivated on a commercial scale for the first time in 2005. Its introduction was likely to accelerate biotech production in the developing world where rice was the major subsistence crop and food source (ISAAA, 2006).

8.2 GMOs: A RISK TO PUBLIC HEALTH AND THE ENVIRONMENT?

The rapid introduction and expansion of GMOs provoked controversy, especially in Europe, where a majority of consumers viewed biotech food as unsafe (Geitner, 2004a). Critics contended that GMOs posed serious risks to human and animal health, including toxicity, allergenicity and antibiotic resistance (Gene Watch et al., 2004; Public Citizen, 2004). Environmentalists feared that GMOs would have irreversible effects on farmland biodiversity and the broader ecosystem and highlighted risks to non-target organisms, conventional crops, wild relatives and weeds via cross-pollination and seed dispersal (Brendel, 2002; Egziabher, 2003; GRAIN, 2004).

The panel consulted six experts on these matters: Dr David Andow, Department of Entomology, University of Minnesota, United States; Dr Marilia Regini Nutti, Brazilian Agricultural Research Corporation (EMBRAPA), Brazil; Dr Allison Snow, Department of Evolution, Ecology and Organismal Biology, Ohio State University, United States; Dr Geoff Squire, Scottish Crop Research Institute, United Kingdom; Dr Marion Healy, Food Standards Australia New Zealand (FSANZ), Australia and Dr John Snape, Crop Genetics, John Innes Centre, United Kingdom. According to the experts, national and international bodies had studied GM food extensively, promoted the adoption of international risk assessment standards for GM food (the Codex Alimentarius Commission's Principles for the Risk Analysis of Foods Derived from Modern Biotechnology) and concluded that food containing GMOs posed no greater health risks than conventional food. Analyses of meat, milk and eggs produced from animals consuming GM feed demonstrated that they were equivalent to those produced from animals consuming conventional feed (WTO, 2006). Dr Nutti testified that 'numerous experiments' had examined antibiotic resistance marker genes present in GMOs; none had reported a transfer of antibiotic resistance genes from GM food to animals or humans (WTO, 2006, Annex H, para. 58). Further, such transfers were unlikely to occur as the conditions required were incompatible with the digestive process. Dr Andow added that there were no reports in the literature of negative impacts on plants and animals and that 'any undetected adverse effects would likely be several orders of magnitude smaller than naturally occurring phenomena' (WTO, 2006, Annex H, para. 175). Dr Healy registered an important caveat: the safety of existing GM foods did not imply the safety of future products as their compositions were likely to vary owing to the use of different transformation technologies (WTO, 2006).

Historically, the impacts of new crops on the environment had not received the same level of scrutiny as food risks. But, as GM crops began to be grown on a large-scale and questions were raised about their effect on agricultural ecosystems and the broader environment, research efforts had intensified and identified three major concerns: effects on non-target organisms, the development of resistance in weeds and the coexistence of GM and conventional crops. Potential adverse impacts on non-target organisms were linked to insect-resistant 'Bt' crops[1] like corn and cotton that contained toxins derived from bacteria (Bt toxins) that were designed to kill insects that preyed on these crops. Bt toxins worked continuously throughout the growing season against internal and external pests, thereby providing more effective protection than pesticides, which dissipated soon after application and attacked only external pests. Since pest control in conventional cotton and some types of corn required heavy and frequent spraying, Bt crops might have a favorable impact on agricultural workers and non-target organisms by promoting reduction in pesticide use.[2] But relatively few studies had examined the impact of Bt toxins on non-target organisms including insects, birds and other organisms that feed on target organisms or encounter Bt toxins in pollen or soil. Although any adverse impacts were likely to be small and reversible, the small number of studies, their mixed results and methodological flaws led the experts to recommend additional research in the form of large-scale, multi-year field experiments (WTO, 2006).

Like conventional herbicide-tolerant crops, herbicide-tolerant GMs (GMHT) crops resisted herbicides, allowing farmers to eradicate weeds without destroying their crops. The herbicides used with HT crops created two kinds of environmental risks. First, repeated herbicide use was virtually certain to increase weed resistance problems unless appropriate risk management strategies were implemented. Second, frequent herbicide use threatened agricultural ecosystems because weeds constituted a major food source for a large number of other organisms. According to the experts, neither risk differed qualitatively or quantitatively for GM versus non-GM herbicide-tolerant crops. In both cases, risk rose with scale and frequency of herbicide use (WTO, 2006).

Like conventional crops, GM crops exhibited gene flow, the transfer of insect resistance, herbicide resistance and other traits to other crops, wild relatives and weeds via the dispersal of pollen and seeds. The transfer of these traits was a natural part of the life cycle. As discussed above, Bt toxins and herbicide resistance may pose risks to non-target organisms and exacerbate weed resistance problems but there was no evidence that gene transfer from GMOs promoted the development of hybrids whose uncontrolled growth endangered wild relatives and other plants growing in the wild. The experts dismissed the specter of irreversible or cataclysmic impacts on farmland biodiversity and lamented that distorted media coverage had led the public to grossly exaggerate environmental risks (WTO, 2006).

However, several of the experts raised concerns about the coexistence of GM and non-GM crops. The possibility of cross-pollination was greatest for GM canola. New studies indicated that accidental release of canola seed could produce long-lived plants and that pollen from GM canola plants could be dispersed over large distances (at least three kilometers). Nevertheless, they emphasized that the coexistence problem was primarily an economic problem for farmers rather than an environmental one. Under the new standards that went into effect in the EU in 2004, GM-free status was limited to food meeting a stringent 0.9 percent GM content threshold. Producers were also required to document and retain records on the movement of food and ingredients through each stage of the distribution channel. In order to meet the GM-free threshold, conventional crops would have to be segregated from GM crops within and across farms. In the absence of community or regional decision making, farmers would have to determine their planting patterns in collaboration with their neighbors (WTO, 2006).

8.3   EU GMO REGULATORY FRAMEWORK

There were sharp disagreements between states and ministries within the EU about the desirability of GMOs and the appropriate regulatory framework. Trade and industry ministries tended to favor expanding biotech production while environmental ministers tended to favor taking a more cautious approach (Southey, 1997). Among states, attitudes and policy tended to be most hostile in Austria, Greece and Luxembourg and most favorable in the Netherlands and Finland. The more restrictive regulations adopted in the former countries proved more influential and had a 'ratcheting up' effect on EU policy (Bernauer and Caduff, 2003, p. 7).

Under legislation adopted in 1990 (EC Directive 90/220) and amended in 2001 (EC Directive 2001/18), the EU established regulations affecting the release of products containing GMOs to the environment. Biotech food was regulated under procedures adopted in 1997 (EC Regulations 258/97) affecting novel foods and ingredients. The regulations created a multi-tiered process that distributed responsibilities among member states and EU scientific panels, regulatory and political bodies. In the first step, firms seeking to market products containing GMOs in the EU were required to file an application in a single member state. Member states were to conduct a risk assessment and issue an opinion within 90 days. Applications receiving the support of a member state were forwarded to the other member states for review and comment. Where no objections were raised, the product was approved for use throughout the EU. Applications eliciting objections were forwarded to a scientific panel for review. Applications receiving favorable reviews from the EU's scientists were forwarded to the Regulatory Committee whose members (one from each state) were to propose and vote upon a draft measure. Decisions receiving the support of a supermajority (known as qualified majority) of Regulatory Committee members were approved (or rejected) for sale, processing or cultivation throughout the EU. Applications that failed to receive support from a qualified majority of Regulatory Committee members were to be forwarded to the Council of Ministers (one vote from each state) for approval or rejection within 90 days. When no action was taken within the 90-day period, the European Commission was obliged to adopt the decision despite the absence of a qualified majority within the Regulatory Committee and the Council of Ministers (European Commission, 2003; WTO, 2006).

Between 1992 and 1997, 14 GM products were authorized under Directive 90/220 for varying purposes including cultivation, processing, food and feed. By the end of 1998, an additional 14 products had been approved, including eight GM foods under the expedited review process for novel foods that were substantially equivalent to conventional foods. The authorizations affected five crops (canola, chicory, corn, cotton and soybeans) and related processed foods including flour, tofu, baked goods, snack foods and soft drinks as well as a vaccine (European Commission, 2004).

8.4   THE MORATORIUM

In 1998, the divisions among the EU member states about the direction of GM regulation produced a stalemate. No additional products were approved for cultivation, import and processing under the regulations affecting the release of GMOs to the environment (Directive 90/220 and its successor Directive 2001/18) until 2004. By July 2004, 24 applications were pending: half were originally filed under Directive 90/220 and, thus, pre-dated the entry into force of Directive 2001/18 in 2002. For part of the period, new GM food continued to be authorized under the expedited process for substantially equivalent novel foods (Regulation 258/97). Six GM foods were authorized on that basis between 1999 and 2002; none were authorized between 2002 and the entry into force of the new content, labeling and traceability standards in April 2004 (European Commission, 2004).

Argentina, Canada and the US maintained that the EU imposed a de facto moratorium on the approval of new products containing GMOs as of October 1998. The EU contended that no decision had been made to suspend its approval process, but a host of documents issued by the EU referred to a moratorium or general suspension, as did numerous statements by EU trade, environment, health and other officials. The panel decided that 'systematic opposition' began in June 1999 when Denmark, Greece, France, Italy and Luxembourg (Group of Five or G-5) declared that they would 'take steps' to suspend GMO approvals until labeling and traceability standards were implemented (WTO, 2006, para. 7.1258). Prior to the declaration, the Regulatory Committee continued to put applications to a vote but failed to do so subsequently when the G-5 functioned as a 'blocking minority' (WTO, 2006, para. 7.606). The Regulatory Committee also failed to forward applications to the Council of Ministers for action after June 1999 and the Council of Ministers did not act on any applications after that date. The panel concluded that the EU had suspended its approval process without issuing a formal decision. A de facto moratorium existed between June 1999 and August 2003, the date that the panel was established (WTO, 2006).

8.5   UNDUE DELAY

The complainants did not challenge the EU's right to establish an approval process or object to its specific procedures. They objected to the moratorium because it interfered with the operation of existing procedures. They also protested the EU's failure to complete those procedures with respect to 27 specific product applications. Since the general and product-specific approval suspensions did not alter existing procedures or establish new ones, the panel concluded that they were not the types of measures subject to the SPS Agreement's scientific justification (Article 2.2), risk assessment (Article 5.1), distinctions in sanitary protection (Articles 2.3 and 5.5), levels of trade restriction (Article 5.6) and publication and notification (Article 7 and Annex B) provisions (WTO, 2006). But the SPS Agreement's Article 8 and Annex C(1)(a) were applicable (WTO, 2006). Article 8 compelled WTO members to abide by Annex C in the application of inspection and approval procedures. Annex C(1)(a) prohibited 'undue delay' in the 'fulfilment of sanitary or phytosanitary measures' (WTO, 1994a).

The panel observed that not all delays were undue. The key issue was whether or not any delays that occurred were justifiable. In order to reach a conclusion on this matter, the panel examined the movement of each of the 27 product-specific applications through the approval process and concluded that 23 of the 27 applications experienced undue delays within the meaning of Annex C(1)(a). The multi-tiered process provided numerous opportunities for delay and most of the applications experienced multiple 'unjustifiably long' delays (WTO, 2006, para. 7.2011). Frequently, member states did not observe the 90-day deadline for acting on original applications. Applications sent to the scientific committees and other member states languished for months or years as reviews proceeded slowly or were prolonged by repeated and unnecessary requests for additional information. Applications forwarded to the Regulatory Committee stalled there. Neither the Regulatory Committee nor the Council of Ministers acted on a single application between June 1999 and August 2003. Essentially, the EU did not conform to its approval process. The resulting delays were unjustifiable and, thus, undue, as were those associated with the general suspension of product approvals arising from the moratorium (WTO, 2006).

8.6   STATE BANS

Six EU member states (Austria, France, Germany, Greece, Italy and Luxembourg) enacted bans affecting seven GMOs approved for use and sale in the EU prior to 1998. These 'safeguard' actions were permissible under the EU's environmental release (90/220 and 2001/18) and novel foods (258/97) regulations in cases where governments were able to present new information demonstrating health or environmental risks. Argentina, Canada and the US maintained that the six nations had been unable to adduce any new information to support the bans. They noted that the EU's scientific committees had examined the information presented by the six nations and confirmed their original favorable assessments. Consequently, the bans were incompatible with the SPS Agreement's risk assessment (Article 5.1) and scientific justification requirements (Article 2.2).

The panel agreed, emphasizing that none of the additional studies presented by the six nations qualified as a risk assessment under the SPS Agreement's Article 5.1. While several studies identified possible adverse environmental impacts on target and non-target species, none evaluated the likelihood of the occurrence of those impacts. As a result, the new assessments did not satisfy the criteria for risk assessments established by the Appellate Body in the salmon dispute (Chapter 6). The only risk assessments which satisfied that criteria were the original ones completed by the member states and EU scientific committees. Since those assessments concluded that it was safe to market the products in the EU, the panel rejected the EU's attempt to invoke rulings in the hormones case (Chapter 4) permitting precautionary measures in cases of divergent scientific opinion and life-threatening health risks. The risk assessments neither expressed divergent views about the safety of GMOs nor posited potential life-threatening risks. Further, since the original assessments qualified as risk assessments under Article 5.1, there was sufficient evidence to evaluate the health and environmental risks raised by the six states. Hence the bans were incompatible with Article 5.7, which applied only in situations where there was insufficient scientific evidence to perform valid risk assessments (WTO, 2006).

The panel observed that a risk assessment could support different types of regulations but the measures imposed must satisfy the rational relationship test articulated by the Appellate Body in the hormones dispute. Since the original risk assessments indicated that GMOs were as safe as conventional products, they could not rationally support statewide bans. Moreover, the EU had not identified limitations of the original assessments that were addressed by the states' new assessments nor had the six governments explained 'how and why' their assessments differed from the original ones (WTO, 2006, para. 7.3062).

Up to this point, the panel's reasoning struck a reasonable balance among the competing objectives addressed in the SPS Agreement. However, the panel took an overly restrictive view of the scope for action against potential risks. Invoking the Appellate Body's hormones rulings, the panel appeared to exclude preventative measures against serious but not life-threatening risks, exactly the kind of risks of concern to the six states and more generally to the environmental community (WTO, 2006). Elsewhere the Appellate Body provided support for governments seeking to address such risks. In the hormones dispute, the Appellate Body stated that governments had a 'right and duty' to protect the health of their citizens (WTO, 1998a, para. 177). In gasoline, the Appellate Body explicitly rejected the notion of requiring governments to demonstrate the efficacy of their environmental measures, explaining that their impacts might not be apparent for years (WTO, 1996). In shrimp–turtle, the Appellate Body upheld an import ban on shrimp that were harvested in a manner that endangered sea turtles (WTO, 1998b). It is difficult to square these more expansive rulings with those limiting preventative measures to life-threatening situations.

Moreover, the SPS Agreement's Article 5.7 did not limit preventative measures to life-threatening situations. As the Appellate Body explained in the agricultural products and apples disputes (Chapter 6), governments seeking to invoke Article 5.7 faced a four-part test (WTO, 1999, 2003). Provisional measures could be adopted 'in cases where relevant scientific evidence is insufficient' provided that governments based them on 'available pertinent information', 'seek to obtain the additional information necessary to make a more objective assessment of risk' and evaluate the measures imposed 'within a reasonable period of time' (WTO, 1994a). Neither Article 5.7 nor the Appellate Body restricted provisional measures to life-threatening risks. Indeed, they did not address the nature of the risks imposed in any way whatsoever. Thus provisional measures that addressed non-fatal risks should be compatible with Article 5.7 as long as they satisfy its four requirements.

The panel erred in its application of the first leg of this test to the state-level bans. As the Appellate Body further explained in the apples dispute, scientific evidence was 'insufficient' where it was unavailable, unreliable or inconclusive (WTO, 2003). The panel ruled that there was sufficient evidence to perform the original risk assessments, which did not support the member state bans. This conclusion was appropriate for Italy, which maintained that its ban was necessary to address food safety risks that were not supported by the available evidence. But the experts' testimony validated the environmental concerns raised by the five other states. Their testimony suggested that, *when the five bans were imposed*, they were compatible with the four-part test under Article 5.7. Further, despite subsequent developments in science and risk management, the continued imposition of the bans could be justified given remaining uncertainties.

Three of the six experts consulted by the panel addressed environmental risks. Testimony from Dr Andow was most significant. Dr Andow testified that, when France imposed its ban on MS1/RF1 canola in 1998, there was insufficient evidence to address several issues, including pollen dispersal under large-scale cultivation, the evolution of HT resistances in weeds, impacts on non-target species and coexistence with non-GM crops (WTO, 2006). Dr Snow agreed that further study was necessary to address France's concerns about gene dispersal and appropriate crop management strategies, explaining that the EU's scientific committee had 'underestimated the extent of gene flow that is to be expected' to canola plants and weeds (WTO, 2006, Annex H, para. 790 (ii)). Dr Squire added that there was 'insufficient knowledge' in 1998 to address cross-pollination between GM and non-GM crops under large-scale cultivation (WTO, 2006, Annex H, para. 795).

The three experts also addressed the French and Greek bans on Topas 19/2 canola. Because Topas 19/2 was approved for import and processing, Drs Snow and Squire dismissed France's and Greece's concerns that it posed a risk to conventional crops and weeds. However, Dr Andow testified that the risk to conventional crops via accidental release and small-scale cultivation had not been studied when the bans were imposed in 1998. Also, since Topas 19/2's molecular structure had not been fully analyzed, it was possible that unidentified transgene products posed unanticipated environmental risks. Dr Andow concluded that there was insufficient evidence for a risk assessment of Topas 19/2 with respect to the coexistence and molecular characterization issues when the bans went into effect (WTO, 2006).

Austria, Germany and Luxembourg asserted that their bans on Bt-176 corn were justified because of risks to non-target organisms. Dr Andow harshly criticized the EU's Scientific Committee on Plants' (SCP) risk assessment of Bt-176, explaining that the committee ignored some environmental risks, did not weigh conflicting evidence appropriately and reached some wrong conclusions. As early as 1996, the EPA had determined that resistance risks in non-target organisms qualified as environmental risks. However, the SCP had not mandated risk management measures to address such risks. In addition, new studies submitted to the SCP by the three states indicated that Bt-176 might have adverse impacts on lacewings, swallows and monarch butterflies. Previous studies had identified risks only to monarch butterflies. Dr Andow concluded that there was insufficient evidence to assess risks associated with the cultivation of Bt-176 corn when the three states imposed their bans (WTO, 2006).

Dr Andow also testified that there was insufficient evidence to perform a risk assessment of the two other forms of GM corn banned by Austria: MON 810 and T-25. Like Bt-176, there was insufficient evidence to assess risks to non-target organisms from MON 810. For T-25, there was insufficient evidence to assess weed resistance and risk management practices, essential aspects of the risk assessment but ones ignored by the SCP entirely (WTO, 2006).

Dr Andow concluded that the five states' bans were justified given the state of science and risk management at the time of imposition. Other risk management options were available possibly as early as 1999 (Bt-176) and as late as 2003 (MON 810) but certainly by 2005 thanks to advances in science and risk management. For example, risks to non-target species could be managed by restricting cultivation to designated areas, performing field experiments and developing rigorous monitoring systems. But Dr Andow left open the possibility that those options would not meet the states' acceptable level of risk. Many questions remained unanswered. While some concerns such as gene flow were most likely hypothetical, weed resistance and coexistence constituted real risks (WTO, 2006).

Drs Snow and Squire addressed only the MS1/RF1 and Topas 19/2 bans. Although they declined to comment on whether the bans were justified, Dr Snow remarked that France 'needed more information' on HT resistance risks (WTO, 2006, Annex H, para. 793) and Dr Squire observed that risk management could be used to reduce but not eradicate risk (WTO, 2006).

At the very least, this testimony demonstrated that the bans were imposed and maintained for several years in accordance with Article 5.7. Further, the uncertainties remaining as of 2005 with respect to weed resistance and coexistence and related management practices made a strong case that the imposition of the bans through 2005 was compatible with Article 5.7 despite the availability of less restrictive risk management options. Admittedly, not all of the states submitted evidence documenting those uncertainties, but it was available to the panel via submissions from the EU and the experts. The panel's failure to incorporate this testimony into its rulings deprived the member states of their right to impose provisional measures.

8.7   RECONCILING OBLIGATIONS UNDER WTO AND OTHER INTERNATIONAL AGREEMENTS

The panel also bungled an opportunity to expand on rulings in previous disputes promoting a mutually supportive relationship between obligations under WTO and other international agreements. As in the hormones dispute, the EU argued that the precautionary principle was an established principle of international law as evidenced by its inclusion in various multilateral environmental agreements including the Convention on Biological Diversity (CBD) and the protocol to it, the Cartagena Protocol on Biosafety. The Protocol, which regulated the cross-border trade in living modified organisms (LMOs), was most relevant to the dispute. Its provisions required members to assess the health risks associated with such trade, permitted members to employ a precautionary approach and allowed members to prohibit LMO imports (Cartagena Protocol on Biosafety, 2000).[3] Argentina, Canada and the US argued that the Protocol was not pertinent to the dispute because they were not parties to it. Moreover, the available scientific evidence indicated that GMOs were as safe as conventional food. As a result, the international standard-setting bodies (Codex and the International Plant Protection Convention (IPPC)) had developed risk assessment guidelines for GMOs that were comparable to those for other foods (WTO, 2006).

The panel misconstrued or ignored the precedents established on these matters in the hormones, gasoline and shrimp–turtle disputes. In the hormones dispute (Chapter 4), the Appellate Body declined to take a position on the status of the precautionary principle as a *general principle* of international law, explaining that it lacked 'authoritative formulation' outside of international environmental law (WTO, 1998a, para. 123). Thus the Appellate Body acknowledged the precautionary principle's 'authoritative' status in international environmental law, but the GMOs panel refused to take a position on the precautionary principle, citing the Appellate Body's reluctance to do so in the hormones dispute. In the gasoline dispute (Chapter 2), the Appellate Body ruled that WTO agreements did not stand apart from other international agreements (WTO, 1996). In the shrimp–turtle dispute (Chapter 3), the Appellate Body used various international environmental agreements to interpret the disputants' obligations under the GATT's Article XX despite acknowledging that not all of the governments were parties to the agreements (WTO, 1998b). Nevertheless, the GMOs panel ruled that it was not necessary to take into account the Cartagena Protocol on Biosafety or the Convention on Biological Diversity because not all of the disputants were parties to them (WTO, 2006).

Despite these actions, the panel offered some support to the precautionary principle and MEAs. For example, the panel did not dismiss the EU's position that uncertainties surrounding GMOs' health and environmental impacts warranted suspension of approvals during the period in which it developed and implemented new standards to address those risks. The panel explained that Annex C(1)(a) did not preclude 'a prudent and precautionary approach' (WTO, 2006, para. 7.1523). Further, deferrals might be appropriate provided they were undertaken on a case-by-case basis, but an across-the-board 'holding pattern' rendered the prohibition against undue delay in the completion of approval procedures meaningless (WTO, 2006, para. 7.1527). The panel also rejected the notion of creating a loophole that would allow governments to use the evolving nature of science and the time-consuming nature of the rule development process to evade their obligation to justify their sanitary measures with risk assessments (WTO, 2006).

And while the panel ruled that it was not necessary to consider the Convention on Biological Diversity (CBD), it solicited nominations for scientific experts from the CBD as well as other international organizations, including Codex, the Food and Agriculture Organization (FAO), International Plant Protection Convention (IPPC), Office International des Epizootics (OIE) and World Health Organization (WHO). In addition, the panel asked the experts to evaluate whether the risk assessments conducted by the EU and members states were compatible with international guidelines. These guidelines were discussed throughout their extensive testimony, most notably by Dr Nutti and Dr Andow. Dr Nutti repeatedly cited the Codex food safety risk assessment standards in her analysis. Dr Andow testified that five of the six statewide bans were consistent with Annex III of the Cartagena Protocol on Biosafety, which authorized members to seek additional information, monitor LMOs and undertake other risk management strategies where risk levels were uncertain (WTO, 2006). The panel's questions and the experts' responses picked up where the hormones, gasoline and shrimp–turtle rulings left off. Unfortunately, they were buried in Annex H of the 2376-page panel report, so they will be overshadowed by the more prominent and less favorable panel rulings discussed above. But, most likely, the GMOs rulings will not subvert the precedents established in the gasoline, hormones and shrimp–turtle disputes because, unlike the rulings in those disputes, the GMOs rulings were not reviewed by the Appellate Body.

8.8   UNRESOLVED MATTERS

Several issues were left unresolved. First, did the moratorium end with the entry into force of new composition, labeling and traceability standards in the EU in 2004? The EU did begin to act on applications that had been stalled in its approval pipeline. Two of the products at issue in the dispute (Bt-11 sweet corn and NK603 corn) were approved in 2004 (WTO, 2006). Several more were approved in 2005 and 2006 (Schomberg and Smith, 2006). With these approvals in mind, the panel's Interim Report concluded that the moratorium had ceased to exist and did not request that the EU bring the moratorium into conformance with WTO obligations. But Argentina, Canada and the US objected that such a conclusion could adversely affect their options during the compliance phase (WTO, 2006). Their concerns proved persuasive and the panel declined to take a position on whether the moratorium remained in existence in its final report. Instead, it adopted language proposed by Canada requesting that the EU bring the moratorium into conformance with WTO obligations 'if, and to the extent that, that measure has not already ceased to exist' (WTO, 2006, para. 8.16).

While this language satisfied the complainants, it was not clear that it would materially affect the outcome of the dispute. The moratorium ceased to exist in 2004, when the EU resumed consideration of marketing applications. If the moratorium no longer existed, it could not continue to cause undue delays in the operation of the EU's approval procedures. And since most of the 23 product applications held up by undue delays were subsequently withdrawn by the applicants, the main action during the compliance would involve the statewide bans (WTO, 2006). Two months after the rulings were issued, Austria affirmed its ban and received the support of all but four member states (Czech Republic, United Kingdom, Netherlands and Sweden) (Bounds, 2006a). As of January 2007, five of the six bans remained in effect. Although France, Germany, Greece and Luxembourg had yet to respond to the rulings, it was likely that some or all would choose to retain their bans given the strong support for Austria. Italy lifted its ban in 2004 (WTO, 2006). Thus the GMOs dispute was likely to prove as intractable as the hormones dispute unless compliance action brought the Appellate Body into the case. As discussed above, there was a case for maintaining the five state-level bans under Article 5.7 until the coexistence issue was resolved, but it was a case that the Appellate Body was more likely to make than the panel.

Second, were the composition, labeling and traceability standards introduced in the EU in 2004 compatible with WTO rules? Since these standards went into effect after the formation of the panel, they did not figure in the panel's rulings. Nor did the panel rule on whether the labeling provisions in effect during the dispute were compatible with WTO obligations. However, the panel did opine that labels designed to protect the environment and public health were subject to the SPS, but those promoting informational or nutritional objectives were not (WTO, 2006). This latter conclusion was odd: surely labels promoting good nutrition advanced public health. Once again, the panel unnecessarily constrained governments seeking to regulate health risks.

The panel did not address the applicability of the Technical Barriers to Trade Agreement (TBT). The TBT required governments to impose technical regulations that were no more trade restrictive than necessary 'to fulfill a legitimate objective' and specifically defined several legitimate objectives including the 'prevention of deceptive practices' and the 'protection of human health or safety, animal or plant life or health, or the environment' (WTO, 1994b, Article 2.2). Thus informational labels were subject to the TBT, not the SPS Agreement; labels that promoted health and environmental goals fell within the reach of both agreements. As a practical matter, it will not make much difference whether labels promoting health and environmental objectives are challenged under the SPS Agreement or the TBT. Governments invoking a 'legitimate objective' under the TBT must assess the risks of non-fulfillment taking into account 'available scientific and technical information, related processing technology or intended end-uses of products' (WTO, 1994b, Article 2.2). In the case of GMOs, these are the same issues that would be examined under the SPS Agreement's risk assessment (Article 5.1) and scientific justification (Article 2.2) requirements.

Product labels have yet to be the subject of formal rulings in a food safety dispute at the WTO but the hormones panel's observation that some nations used labels to achieve the objectives sought by the EU implied that labels offered a solution to that dispute (WTO, 1997). To date, the political environment in the EU has prevented authorities from opting for that approach. And it was not clear that it would offer an immediate resolution to the dispute as beef exporters opposed them.

Similarly, GM exporters objected to the EU's GMO labeling and traceability standards as unnecessary and misleading (Becker and Barboza, 2003; European Commission, 2006). But, despite the rapid growth of biotech crops and their introduction to an expanding group of countries, the industry and its supporters were on the defensive. Monsanto withdrew plans to introduce GM wheat after US and Canadian farmers opposed its introduction, citing a dearth of export markets and the likelihood of adverse effects on exports of conventional wheat. Previously, Monsanto stopped developing GM potatoes and vegetables and Bayer halted production of GM corn (Pollack, 2004; Geitner, 2004b). Several African countries rejected GM food aid from the US, fearing that it posed a risk to domestic crops and, consequently, European export markets. Subsequently, the Southern Africa Development Community (SADC) recommended that GM food aid be milled or sterilized before distribution and Uganda authorized GM imports for consumption but not cultivation (Zarrilli, 2005). Egypt and Saudi Arabia banned GM wheat imports and Sri Lanka prohibited all GM food imports (Public Citizen, 2004). And GM bans were adopted or under consideration in several counties in California (Miller, 2004).

In 2000, GM corn that was authorized only for use in feed was found in taco shells and other foods necessitating over 300 product recalls in the US (European Commission, 2003; Gene Watch et al., 2004). In 2005, the EU tightened restrictions on US GM feed imports after Syngenta revealed that it accidentally included unapproved GM varieties in seeds shipped to the US for cultivation (Meller, 2005). In 2006, the EU began testing all shipments of rice from the US after traces of unauthorized GM rice were found in exports to the Netherlands and France. As GM rice was not grown commercially in the US, its presence raised, arguably, the most serious questions about the adequacy of risk management in the US. US rice farmers feared that they would lose access to the European market altogether and initiated a lawsuit against Bayer, the patent owner (Bounds, 2006b).

The ratcheting up effect observed in the EU was beginning to be evident elsewhere as the leading GM importers (Japan, China, Korea and Russia) were adopting mandatory GM labels and setting low content thresholds for 'GM-free' products (Gruère, 2005). Australia and New Zealand also instituted mandatory labeling requirements (Zarrilli, 2005). Even before the EU's new labeling standards went into effect, large retailers reported that they did not use GM ingredients in their products and were reluctant to stock GM products since upwards of 75 percent of European consumers opposed GM foods (Geitner, 2004a). Likewise, Japanese food manufacturers and retailers catered to consumer demand for GM-free food (Gruère, 2005). As of 2005, some 30 members of Codex favored requiring labels on all foods containing GMOs or derived from GM ingredients. A much smaller group, the US, Argentina and five other nations, favored imposing labels on GM food that contained allergens, caused physiological reactions or did not satisfy the substantial equivalence test (Gruère, 2005). Since international organizations tended to work by consensus, the debate on labels was likely to continue for some time, but the direction of change favored the EU. That was noteworthy because Codex standards were granted a presumption of compatibility with WTO obligations under the SPS Agreement's harmonization provisions.

Third, were GMOs 'like' their non-GMO counterparts? Canada and Argentina contended that the moratorium, product-specific delays and bans were incompatible with the GATT's Article III, which required imports to be treated as favorably as 'like' domestic products. As in other disputes, the disputants debated the 'likeness' of GMOs and non-GMOs using the four-part criteria developed under the GATT: properties, end-uses, consumer preferences and tariff classifications. If GMOs were 'like' non-GMOs, the EU was obliged to treat the former as favorably as the latter. If not, it was not obliged to do so. The panel hedged. It exercised judicial economy on Canada's claims under Article III. Although it examined Argentina's claims, it rejected them without making a likeness determination, explaining that it was not 'self-evident' that differential treatment of GMOs and non-GMOs amounted to discrimination by national origin (WTO, 2006, para. 7.2514). While the panel's conclusion was favorable to governments seeking to regulate GMOs, it was not likely to influence future disputes. The panel reversed the standard analysis and examined whether the treatment of GMOs and non-GMOs varied by national origin (Palmer, 2006). Since it did not, it did not make a likeness determination. In gasoline (Chapter 2), asbestos (Chapter 5) and other WTO disputes, the panels and Appellate Body explored differences in national treatment after making a likeness determination.

8.9   PANEL PERFORMANCE AND REFORM

The panel's performance was disappointing and ultimately unacceptable. As discussed above, the most problematic aspects of the panel's report resulted from its decision to ignore crucial scientific testimony and its misreading or misapplication of rulings from the gasoline, hormones and shrimp–turtle disputes in its analysis of precautionary measures invoked under Article 5.7. In each case, the panel took an excessively narrow view of the scope for governments to invoke precautionary measures under Article 5.7. The panel revealed a similar bias in its decision to exclude labels promoting nutritional goals from the health objectives covered by the SPS Agreement. The panel's decision to invert its analysis of the 'likeness' of GMOs and non-GMOs was hard to account for as it was at odds with well-established practice.

The panel's 2376-page report was unnecessarily long and poorly organized. The panel devoted 80 pages to a discussion of the kinds of health and environmental risks covered by the SPS Agreement. Instead of providing a summary of the parties' oral and written arguments, the panel presented multiple sets of oral and written arguments for each party. The panel presented its analysis of delays in the processing of each of the 27 product applications twice: first in its examination of the moratorium and again in its analysis of the applications. Most troubling, important testimony from the experts that supported five of the member state bans did not appear in the main report and was easy to miss as it was relegated to Annex H.

As discussed in Chapter 6, panels made errors in the environmental and health disputes adjudicated previously, but their performances improved over time as more recent panels benefited from precedents established in previous disputes. But the GMOs panel's performance set the clock back and suggested that improvements could not be assured within the current structure. Chapter 9 proposes the creation of a permanent standing panel body to improve panel performance.

NOTES

1. Bt insecticides were also employed, but they were not likely to be harmful to non-target organisms because they decomposed rapidly.
2. See GRAIN (2004) for a contrary view.
3. LMOs included 'GM organisms, GM seeds and raw products from GM crops (used for food or feed)' (Gruère, 2005).

REFERENCES

Becker, E. and D. Barboza (2003), 'Battle over biotechnology intensifies trade war', *The New York Times*, 29 May, C1.

Bernauer, T. and L. Caduff (2003), 'The European Union's food safety trilemma', Center for International Studies, Zurich, Working Paper 3-2003.

Bounds, A. (2006a), 'Austria allowed to keep its ban on gm corn', *Financial Times*, 19 December, 12.

Bounds, A. (2006b), 'EU states order tests on US imports after finding illegal gmos', *Financial Times*, 27 October 7.

Brendel, U. (2002), 'The dangers of genetically engineered plants', Greenpeace, European Unit, *Reports and Briefing Papers* (website accessed during July 2004).

Cartagena Protocol on Biosafety (2000), Montreal: Convention on Biological Diversity.

Egziabher, T. (2003), 'When elephants fight over gmos', *Seedling*, October.

European Commission (2003), 'European Commission regrets US decision to file WTO case on gmos as misguided and unnecessary', EC, Brussels, 13 May, IP/03/681.

European Commission (2004), 'Questions and answers on the regulation of gmos in the EU', *Press Release*, Memo/04/102, 30 April.

European Commission (2006), 'Europe's rules on gmos and the WTO', *Memo*, 7 February.

Geitner, P. (2004a), 'EU adds labels but shuns genetically modified food', *Pittsburgh Post-Gazette*, 17 April, A7.

Geitner, P. (2004b), 'EU ends 6-year biotech moratorium', *Deseret News*, 20 May, A7.

Gene Watch et al. (2004), 'Amicus Curiae Submission in EC – measures affecting the approval and marketing of biotech products', Gene Watch, London (distributed at WTO Public Symposium, Geneva, Switzerland, May).

GRAIN (2004), 'Bt Cotton on Mali's Doorstep, *Seedling*, April.

Gruère, G. (2005), 'An analysis of trade related international regulations of genetically modified food and their effects on developing countries', Washington, DC: International Food Policy Research Institute (IFPRI), EPT Discussion Paper 147.

ISAAA (2006), 'ISAAA Briefs No.34: Executive Summary, Global Status of Biotech/GM Crops in 2005', ISAAA (website accessed January 2007).

Meller, P. (2005), 'Europeans to toughen rules on animal feed from US', *The New York Times*, 13 April, C4.

Miller, S. (2004), 'EU's new rules will shake up market for bioengineered food', *The Wall Street Journal*, 16 April, A1.

Palmer, A. (2006), 'The WTO gmo dispute: implications for developing countries and the need for an appeal', Gene Watch et al., London, November.

Pollack, A. (2004), 'Monsanto shelves plan for modified wheat', *The New York Times*, 11 May, C1.

Public Citizen (2004), 'Backgrounder: US threats against Europe's gmo policy and the WTO SPS Agreement', Public Citizen, Washington, DC (distributed at WTO Public Symposium, Geneva, Switzerland, May).

Schomberg, W. and J. Smith (2006), 'EU won't appeal WTO ruling on gmo moratorium', PLANETARK World Environmental News, 28 November.

Southey, C. (1997), 'Commission tackles genetic issue: Fischler prepares radical plan to label all genetically modified farm products in EU', *Financial Times*, 21 March, 2.

WTO (1994a), *Agreement on the Application of Sanitary and Phytosanitary Measures* (SPS), Geneva: WTO.

WTO (1994b), *Agreement on Technical Barriers to Trade* (TBT), Geneva: WTO.

WTO (1996), *US – Standards for Reformulated and Conventional Gasoline, Report of the Appellate Body* (WT/DS2/AB/R), Geneva: WTO, 29 April.

WTO (1997), *EC – Measures Concerning Meat and Meat Products (Hormones), Complaint by the US, Report of the Panel* (WT/DS26/R/USA), Geneva: WTO, 18 August.

WTO (1998a), *EC – Measures Concerning Meat and Meat Products (Hormones), Report of the Appellate Body* (WT/DS26/AB/R and WT/DS48/AB/R), Geneva: WTO, 16 January.

WTO (1998b), *US – Import Prohibition of Certain Shrimp and Shrimp Products, Report of the Appellate Body* (WT/DS58/AB/R), Geneva: WTO, 12 October.

WTO (1999), *Japan – Measures Affecting Agricultural Products, Report of the Appellate Body* (WT/DS76/AB/R), Geneva: WTO, 22 February.

WTO (2003), *Japan – Measures Affecting the Importation of Apples, Report of the Appellate Body* (WT/DS245/AB/R), Geneva: WTO, 26 November.

WTO (2006), *EC – Measures Affecting the Approval and Marketing of Biotech Products, Report of the Panel* (WT/DS291/R, WT/DS292/R, WT/DS293/R), Geneva: WTO, 29 September.

Zarrilli, S. (2005), 'International trade in gmos and gm products: national and multilateral legal frameworks', New York, UNCTAD, Policy Issues in International Trade and Commodities Study Series 29.

9. Conclusion

9.1 RECONCILING TRADE, THE ENVIRONMENT, PUBLIC HEALTH AND SOVEREIGNTY

Since 1995, the WTO has made rulings in nine disputes involving environmental and public health measures affecting gasoline, shrimp–turtles, hormones, asbestos, salmon, apples, agricultural products, generic drugs and genetically modified organisms (GMOs). These nine disputes address nearly all of the environmental and health controversies surrounding the WTO, yet they have done little to defuse these controversies because all but the asbestos and generic drugs rulings went against the government imposing the regulations in dispute. For critics, these adverse decisions demonstrated that the WTO favored trade at the expense of the environment and public health and posed a threat to sovereignty. But the reasoning employed in the rulings suggests that this criticism is overstated. The rulings allow governments to pursue environmental and health goals provided that they do not discriminate and can provide scientific support for their regulations.

In the gasoline and shrimp–turtle cases, the Appellate Body stated that the environmental regulations imposed by the US were compatible with the GATT's Article XX(g) exception for measures that preserve exhaustible natural resources, but rejected the discriminatory implementation of the regulations. The discrimination was glaring in each case. The US set reformulated gasoline standards that were more stringent for foreign refiners than domestic ones (WTO, 1996b). In the shrimp–turtle case, the US provided more favorable terms to nations in the Americas than the four Asian nations that opposed the TED (turtle excluder device) requirement (WTO, 1998d). In the hormones dispute, the Appellate Body acknowledged that health concerns motivated the EU's ban on hormone-treated beef but concluded that the EU's risk assessment did not support the ban. The EU was not able to present any evidence linking hormones used for growth promotion to health risks (WTO, 1998a).

By contrast, the health risks posed in the salmon, apples and agricultural products disputes were highly questionable: none of the products had ever been tied to a disease outbreak anywhere in the world. Australia cited potential health risks to support the salmon ban but it was difficult to see how salmon imported for human consumption could pose a disease risk to local aquaculture or recreational fisheries. And Australia permitted imports of live bait fish and ornamental fish even though they were more likely to come into contact with local fish populations (WTO, 1998e). Japan failed to perform a risk assessment on four of the eight products at issue in the agricultural products dispute. Its assessment of the other four products failed to demonstrate that there were varietal differences in the efficacy of fumigation treatment (WTO, 1999). Likewise, it was unable to provide any evidence to support its claim that fire blight could be transmitted by commercially traded apples (WTO, 2003b). The dubious nature of these disease risks, along with the lack of scientific support for the sanitary measures implemented, suggested that the latter were designed to protect domestic business interests rather than animal or plant health.

The food safety measures at issue in the hormones, salmon, apples and agricultural products disputes were not able to satisfy the SPS Agreement's risk assessment and scientific justification requirements. Nevertheless, as interpreted by the Appellate Body, the requirements are reasonable. In the salmon dispute, the Appellate explained that the risk assessment process must identify disease risks, evaluate the likelihood of their occurrence and assess the efficacy of various disease reduction measures (WTO, 1998e). However, the Appellate Body rejected the necessity of quantifying the risks posited in the hormones dispute. Also, in the hormones dispute, the Appellate Body ruled that governments were not required to support their measures with a preponderance of evidence but merely with enough evidence to offer reasonable support (WTO, 1998a). In the salmon dispute, the Appellate Body emphasized that governments were entitled to determine their own levels of acceptable risk and ruled that the panel erred by excluding the possibility of a zero risk level (WTO, 1998e). In the apples and agricultural products disputes, the panels and the Appellate Body accepted Japan's decision to set a zero tolerance level for fire blight and codling moth but concluded that there was no evidence that imports of apples and other agricultural products created disease risks for domestic agriculture (WTO, 1999, 2003b).

This evidence-based approach is crucial in light of the proliferation of trade-restrictive food safety measures in recent years (Henson and Loader, 2001). Many of these measures are legitimate. Indeed, food safety concerns are likely to increase with trade liberalization as consumers face products produced under different or unknown regulatory regimes. But the salmon, apples and agricultural products disputes validate developing nations' fears that some of these measures are motivated by protectionist rather than health motives. As a result, it is essential to have a means to distinguish between legitimate health measures and protectionist ones. The risk assessment and scientific justification requirements provide such a mechanism by requiring governments to establish a rational basis for their sanitary policies (Howse, 2000).

Although the precautionary provisions incorporated into the SPS Agreement's Article 5.7 have yet to be invoked successfully, with the exception of the GMOs dispute, the rulings provide more support for the precautionary principle than this outcome suggests. In the hormones dispute, the Appellate Body ruled that governments could take action against potential health risks especially where they posed serious dangers to the public but ruled out action against theoretical risks (WTO, 1998a). In the apples dispute, the Appellate Body ruled that governments could employ precautionary measures on a provisional basis where the available evidence was inconclusive or too limited to be reliable. The problem for Japan was that the available evidence was reliable and conclusive: apple imports did not pose a fire blight risk to local agriculture (WTO, 2003b). In the agricultural products dispute, the Appellate Body linked the provisional nature of precautionary measures authorized under Article 5.7 to the duty to seek additional information to justify them within a reasonable period of time. In over 20 years, Japan never undertook a single study investigating whether varietal differences caused the effectiveness of fumigation treatments to vary in the eight agricultural products at issue in the dispute (WTO, 1999). In sum, governments may take action against real and potential threats but not hypothetical ones. Thus it was disturbing that the GMOs panel ignored expert testimony suggesting that five of the state-level bans could have been imposed on a precautionary basis owing to the insufficiency of scientific evidence (WTO, 2006e). Since the GMOs panel rulings were not appealed, they stand unless the Appellate Body is brought into the case during the compliance phase.

Despite the prominence of the SPS Agreement's harmonization provisions in the debates surrounding the WTO, they were only a factor in the hormones dispute. But even the hormones rulings may be seen as setting back the harmonization effort (Cottier, 2001). The Appellate Body ruled that governments may satisfy the requirement to base their sanitary regulations on international standards (Article 3.1) by adopting regulations that share some but not necessarily all of the elements of the relevant international standards. And the Appellate Body stressed that governments that choose a higher level of safety (Article 3.3) have a sovereign right to set their own standards (WTO, 1998a). In short, the rulings provide support for neither the leveling down nor leveling up hypothesis. Governments may set whatever food safety standards they like provided that the results of a risk assessment support them.

Similarly, the gasoline and shrimp–turtle rulings reveal that governments may set and pursue their own environmental policies provided that they do not implement them in a discriminatory manner. The Appellate Body stressed that the preamble to the WTO Agreement obliged members to adopt policies promoting sustainable development and environmental protection (WTO, 1996b; WTO, 1998d). The shrimp–turtle rulings suggest that these obligations complement those established under multilateral environmental agreements (MEAs). Both the panel and the Appellate Body criticized the US for failing to negotiate sea turtle conservation agreements with the four Asian disputants observing that multilateral conservation efforts were preferred to unilateral actions. They based a substantial part of their analyses on the obligations facing the US and the four Asian nations under CITES and other MEAs protecting sea turtles (WTO, 1998b, 1998d). Most important, the Appellate Body used those obligations to justify the shrimp ban under the GATT's Article XX(g) exception for environmental measures (WTO, 1998d). This element of the rulings could have a significant impact on other governments and MEAs because it suggests that measures to comply with MEAs will be eligible for the Article XX(g) exception (Scott, 2004). At the same time, the Appellate Body upheld the right of the US to impose unilateral environmental measures, explaining that requiring the completion of conservation agreements would hold US efforts hostage to those of its trade partners (WTO, 2001b).

This support for unilateral environmental policies is significant because the shrimp–turtle dispute displays the limitations of MEAs. MEAs are voluntary. Governments cannot be forced to participate. And in most cases, the agreements articulate general principles but do not require specific implementation steps. Consequently, participants may not implement the most effective conservation strategies. These drawbacks are apparent in the Indian Ocean and South-East Asian (IOSEA) sea turtle conservation agreement. As of January 2007, India and Malaysia had not signed on to the agreement (IOSEA, 2007). While the three largest shrimp exporters, Thailand, Viet Nam and Indonesia, were participants, they did not operate TED-certified programs. Several other nations were certified as manual harvesting nations but only China was a significant shrimp exporter. By contrast, 12 nations in the Americas operated TED-certified programs in 2005 (US Department of State, 2005). It is not clear why the Asian nations are more reluctant to mandate TEDs than their counterparts in the Americas but it is likely to have detrimental consequences for sea turtles. Since Thailand and Indonesia operated TED-certified programs as recently as 2001 and 2003, respectively (US Department of State, 2001, 2003), it may be possible to entice them back into the program with financial and technological assistance. Similar efforts should be made to encourage Viet Nam's and India's participation. Together the four nations accounted for nearly 60 percent of US shrimp imports in 2005 (National Marine Fisheries Service, 2006). Consequently, their absence from the program significantly weakens its impact on sea turtle conservation. The emphasis here is on carrots rather than sticks. As the shrimp–turtle rulings recognized, optimal results are achieved when nations develop cooperative solutions to environmental problems but, in the end, the Asian nations have the sovereign right to determine their own environmental policies.

The outcomes in the asbestos and generic drugs disputes differ from those in the other disputes. The asbestos rulings upheld France's asbestos ban and the generic drugs rulings approved Canada's 'early working' exception to patent rights (WTO, 2000, 2001a). The decisions themselves affirmed WTO members' right to restrict trade and patent rights to promote public health but the reasoning employed was less supportive than the overall results. In the asbestos dispute, the Appellate Body overturned the panel's decision to exclude health considerations from the likeness determination but was not able to conclude that asbestos and substitute products were 'not like' in the absence of additional information on the two principal commercial aspects of the relationship, consumer tastes and end-uses (WTO, 2001a). Thus, even as the Appellate Body raised the standing of public health objectives in the WTO, it subordinated them to commercial objectives. This result was especially disappointing in that it occurred after the hormones dispute in which the Appellate Body declared that WTO members had a 'right and duty' to pursue both types of objectives (WTO, 1998a, para. 177). The generic drugs panel's narrow interpretation of the TRIPS Agreement ignored provisions allowing governments to balance patent holders' interests with those of other members of society (Articles 7 and 8) and emasculated provisions permitting exceptions to patent rights (Article 30) and compulsory licenses (Article 31) (WTO, 2000). Along with other factors, the rulings compelled developing nations to launch a campaign to insure that their obligations under TRIPS did not interfere with their public health strategies.

Lengthy but ultimately successful, the campaign was the most significant development affecting patent rights and public health at the WTO. WTO members agreed to waive the domestic supply restriction that prevented countries without sufficient pharmaceutical manufacturing from using compulsory licenses to obtain essential drugs (WTO, 2003a). The obligation to honor pharmaceutical patents was suspended for ten years (from 2006 to 2016) for least-developed nations (WTO, 2001c). The campaign spurred public, private and NGO initiatives that greatly expanded access to medicine in the developing world as well as a de facto moratorium on new disputes involving public health measures in developing nations that restrict patent rights.

However, the waiver agreement contains several flaws that may limit its effectiveness. Developed nations insisted on an onerous set of procedural requirements affecting the production and distribution of drugs issued under compulsory licenses. In order to participate, both importing and exporting nations must change their patent laws. During the first two years that the waiver was in effect, only three exporting nations made the necessary legal changes (Canada, India and Norway). By 2006, the picture looked better as China, the EU and Korea were expected to complete the process (WTO, 2005c, 2006a). But the participation of generic manufacturers remained uncertain as these legal changes did not address the production and distribution restrictions that reduced their incentives to participate. Moreover, the US was notably absent from the list of eligible exporting nations and continued to seek expanded patent rights in other fora. These efforts may decrease the impact of the waiver and other public health initiatives at the WTO.

9.2   AMICUS BRIEFS

Developing nations also displayed their clout in the amicus controversy. Their opposition to the Appellate Body's efforts to expand the scope for amicus submissions in the shrimp–turtle and asbestos disputes forced the Appellate Body to suspend its activities. After they expressed their objections at a special General Council session held to investigate these initiatives, the Appellate Body rejected each of the briefs submitted under an application procedure it developed in the asbestos dispute (WTO, 2001a). In the compliance phase of the shrimp–turtle dispute, the Appellate Body did not reject the briefs submitted but observed that it 'did not find it necessary to take' the briefs 'into account' (WTO, 2001b, para. 78). Initially, panels maintained the practice of accepting briefs that governments incorporated into their submissions while excluding unsolicited briefs. But the GMOs panel adopted the Appellate Body's approach. It accepted unsolicited briefs submitted by environmental NGOs but did not take them into account. Later the GMOs panel expressed disappointment and disapproval because some of the same NGOs obtained unauthorized access to the panel's confidential Interim Report and posted it on their websites (WTO, 2006e).

The briefs stalemate is unfortunate. There is nearly universal agreement in developed nations that the acceptance of amicus briefs enhances the dispute resolution process's legitimacy by providing a mechanism for external actors to present their views (Bacchus, 2004; De La Fayette, 2002; Ragosta, 2000; Wolfe, 2001). And the Consultative Board that examined the WTO's efficacy over its first ten years supported the acceptance of amicus submissions (WTO, 2005a), but its recommendation has yet to have an impact on developing nations, who fear that amicus submissions exacerbate the resource disadvantages they face in the dispute resolution process (Bates, 1999). But they might be unduly pessimistic about the ability of NGOs in the developing world to participate. Seven of the 13 amicus applications submitted in the asbestos dispute were from the developing world from countries as diverse as Colombia, El Salvador, Korea, South Africa, Sri Lanka, Swaziland and Thailand (WTO, 2001a). Only Swaziland was a third-party participant in the dispute. Three of the nations (El Salvador, Swaziland and South Africa) have yet to file a complaint in the dispute resolution process and Sri Lanka has filed only one (WTO, 2007). These data suggest that amicus briefs provide a voice for the diverse constituencies affected by WTO disputes and may be especially valuable for those whose interests would otherwise not be represented: individuals and organizations in developing nations whose governments are *not* active participants in the dispute resolution process.

9.3 EFFICACY OF THE DISPUTE RESOLUTION PROCESS FOR DEVELOPING NATIONS

In the gasoline and shrimp–turtle disputes, developing nations successfully challenged US environmental regulations: Venezuela and Brazil in the former and India, Malaysia, Pakistan and Thailand in the latter. Their success was consistent with results reported by Guzman and Simmons (2005) who found that developing nations waged and won WTO disputes at rates comparable to those of developed nations. However, the same did not hold for least-developed nations. As of January 2007, only one (Bangladesh) had filed a complaint (WTO, 2007). These nations face several constraints that limit their participation in the dispute settlement process. Many do not maintain a delegation at the WTO. Others have small delegations (one or two members) that are absorbed by matters unrelated to disputes. The high cost of conducting a dispute (legal costs average $500 000) also impedes poor nations' access to the dispute resolution process (Bown and Hoekman, 2005).

The WTO has taken several steps to address these capacity limitations. It holds quarterly Geneva Weeks to update members without a permanent presence on important developments during the year (WTO, 2002). The organization holds week-long training sessions for members on the dispute resolution process in Geneva and in several other locations each year (WTO, 2006d). It has developed partnerships with universities and NGOs to offer regional symposia that enhance understanding of the WTO by the broader public in the developing world (Shaffer, 2005). Legal assistance is available on a sliding-fee basis from the Advisory Centre on WTO Law (ACWL) which is funded by member and donor contributions (Bown and Hoekman, 2005).

But more can and should be done. The assistance provided by ACWL is itself limited by capacity constraints. The staff consists of eight lawyers, far too few to provide effective assistance to the WTO's more than 100 developing nation members (ACWL, 2007). The small staff reflects the meager support for the institution from rich nations: the US, Germany, Japan, France and the EU (as a whole) had yet to join as of January 2007 (ACWL, 2007). Since individual members are unwilling to contribute sufficient resources to ACWL, funding could be allocated directly from the WTO's budget. Alternatively, additional WTO staff resources could be deployed to assist developing nations. However, since WTO staff may advise but not advocate on behalf of developing nations, an expanded ACWL staff offers a more effective remedy for developing nations than additional staff assistance from the WTO.[1] Another possibility is to require developed nations that lose disputes to pay the legal costs incurred by developing nation victors (Esserman and Howse, 2003). Both the ACWL and reimbursement proposals suffer from a critical defect: they require the support of developed nations who have shown little inclination to provide it.

Consequently, self-help measures may provide the best option for least-developed nations. For example, the pooling strategy that African nations employed to insure that all of the key Doha Round negotiating issues were monitored could be applied to the dispute resolution process. Nations with small delegations could use a coordinated strategy to track important developments in the dispute resolution process and rotate participation as third parties in disputes of interest to their nations (Mosoti, 2006). They could also create regional advisory centers affiliated with universities and NGOs like the Trade Law Centre for Southern Africa in Stellenbosch, South Africa to provide current research on these issues, to build cadres of local experts and to perform the activities necessary to conduct disputes (developing legal and economic arguments, writing briefs, gathering evidence and providing representation) (Bown and Hoekman, 2005; Mosoti, 2006; Shaffer, 2004). Because establishing regional trade law centers could take some time, in the short term, poor nations could reduce the cost of ACWL and private legal services by pursuing disputes together. Five hundred thousand dollars is likely to be out of reach for most least-developed nations, but $250 000 or $125 000 might be feasible, should two or four nations wage a dispute jointly.

9.4   COMPLIANCE AND LENGTH OF THE DISPUTE RESOLUTION PROCESS

Poor nations face another problem: nations that are vulnerable to retaliation are more likely to liberalize their markets (Bown, 2004). Hence least-developed nations are more likely to comply with adverse rulings than developed nations. Consequently, enhanced capacity to wage and win disputes might not actually open markets in disputes in which poor nations prevail against rich nations. Although this outcome did not occur in the gasoline and shrimp–turtle disputes, it did occur in three prominent agricultural disputes between developing and developed nations: bananas (Ecuador/US–EU), cotton (Brazil–US), sugar (Brazil/Thailand/Australia–EU) (WTO, 2007).[2]

These disputes reflected a broader problem that was apparent in the salmon, apples and agricultural products disputes: it is difficult to secure compliance in agricultural and food safety disputes because producers in the affected industries have inordinate influence on trade policy in developed nations. Compliance also proved illusory in the hormones dispute, but in that case consumers rather than producers dominated policymaking. Consumers' perception of health risk convinced regulators to enact the ban despite opposition (at the outset) from domestic farmers and pharmaceutical companies and to maintain it despite the WTO rulings (Caduff, 2002). Compliance was likely to be problematic in the GMOs dispute for similar reasons.

The dispute resolution rules establish a clear preference for compliance. And, more important, the dispute resolution process cannot be fair or credible unless compliance occurs in part because the existing remedies are inadequate. Typically, the 'winner' suspends concessions affecting exports of political or economic interest to the 'loser.' This response further disrupts trade and has a boomerang effect. Retaliation against the exporters in the 'losing' country harms consumers in the 'winning' country as the imposition of retaliatory tariffs raises the price of imports (Lawrence, 2003). This burden is likely to be especially great for developing nations because of the small size of their economies. These small markets also diminish the threat of retaliation, rendering it less effective for developing nations than for developed nations (WTO, 2005a). Alternatively, the 'loser' compensates the 'winner' by liberalizing trade concessions or providing monetary compensation. Both forms of compensation are preferred to retaliation. Like retaliation, liberalization rebalances commitments unbalanced by the offending measure, but it enhances rather than impedes trade. However, liberalization does not compensate the producers and consumers directly affected by the violation. By contrast, monetary compensation provides a mechanism to make reparations to injured parties. For these reasons, monetary compensation offers the best remedy, especially for developing nations (Fukunaga, 2006).

It would be impractical to mandate monetary compensation because governments that are unwilling to provide it cannot be compelled to do so. But it would be possible to encourage members to commit themselves to monetary compensation as a first option and to use retaliation as a last resort (Esserman and Howse, 2003). Where retaliation is employed, cross-retaliation, the suspension of obligations under agreements other than the GATT, like those affecting services and intellectual property (under GATS and TRIPS), may provide a way for developing countries to retaliate that partially addresses asymmetric market size (Stoler, 2004). Developed nations have put a great deal of effort into opening pharmaceutical and service sectors in the developing world and may be more concerned about diminished access to those sectors than to goods markets. Cross-retaliation does not require a change in the dispute resolution rules, which encourage governments to suspend obligations in the sector affected by the violation but permit suspension in other sectors where 'it is not practicable or effective' to do so in the same sector (WTO, 1994, Article 22.3(c)). It remains to be seen whether this approach is effective. In the bananas dispute, Ecuador was authorized to employ cross-retaliation affecting services and intellectual property but chose not to do so (Lawrence, 2003). In the cotton dispute, Brazil requested authorization to suspend obligations under TRIPS and GATT; arbitration proceedings on the matter have been postponed pending the outcome of the investigation of US compliance measures (WTO, 2005b, 2006c).

Another possibility is to move toward a system that is truly compensatory by providing for retroactive compensation (Gleason and Walther, 2000; Pauwelyn, 2000). The existing system rewards obstructionist governments. The 'sanctions clock' does not begin ticking until the expiration of the reasonable period of time for implementation. Another 30 or 60 days elapses before sanctions can be imposed, depending on whether the amount is determined by agreement among the parties or by an arbitrator (WTO, 1994). As a result, the longer 'losers' delay the process, the longer they postpone facing retaliation or providing compensation. Retroactive compensation promotes compliance by increasing the cost of non-compliance and speeds the process by eliminating the incentives for foot dragging. Both results could also be achieved by tying participation in the dispute resolution process to compliance along the lines proposed by Jara (2006) whereby non-compliers would initially lose the right to participate as third parties in new disputes and would eventually lose the right to initiate new complaints.

The length of the process is also a concern. The resolution of each of the disputes explored in this volume exceeded the time limits established in the dispute resolution rules. As the disputes are complex and frequently involve consultation with scientific experts, it may not be possible to abbreviate panel investigations. But the reasonable period of time provided for implementation could be decreased. As the arbitrator in the hormones dispute observed, the goal should be compliance in the 'shortest period possible' (WTO, 1998c, p. 6). While his decision had a favorable impact on future disputes, implementation periods are still unnecessarily long. Under the North American Free Trade Agreement, 'winners' are permitted to adjust their commitments within 30 days of a dispute resolution ruling where 'losers' fail to comply. Far longer periods were set in the salmon (eight months), agriculture products (nine months) and shrimp–turtle (13 months) disputes (Gleason and Walther, 2000). What can be done? The dispute resolution rules authorize arbitrators to determine the implementation period when disputants cannot agree on a timeframe (WTO, 1994). Arbitrators should use their authority to make the reasonable period of time for implementation reasonable (say, three to six months).

It is important to note that the disputes explored in this volume have been more intractable than most. Overall, the dispute resolution system has been highly successful (McGivern, 2006). Many disputes do not require panel investigations as solutions are found (35 percent) or complaints are withdrawn (21 percent) during the consultation phase of the process (Davey, 2005). And the implementation rate is high in disputes requiring panel investigations. Between 1995 and 2005, panels issued rulings in 105 disputes. 'Winners' filed complaints challenging 'losers'' compliance measures in 28 of these disputes. 'Winners' were authorized to obtain compensation or suspend concessions for non-compliance in just eight of the 105 disputes (Leitner and Lester, 2006).

9.5 PANEL AND APPELLATE PERFORMANCE

The panels made significant errors in all but the apples dispute. Often, the errors were on fundamental matters. In the salmon dispute, the panel focused on heat-treated salmon even though they were not subject to the ban. The salmon panel also limited its rulings to certain Canadian salmon while ignoring others that fell under the ban (WTO, 1998e). Similarly, the agricultural products panel's rulings ignored four of the eight products in dispute (WTO, 1999). The asbestos panel's decision to exclude health considerations from its likeness determination contributed to its erroneous decision that asbestos and its substitutes were like products (WTO, 2001a). The Appellate Body was able to reverse these errors and to resolve the major issues in dispute. But in other instances, there was insufficient information in the panel's report for the Appellate Body to complete the required analysis. As a result, some issues were not addressed fully, including those related to the Agreement on Technical Barriers to Trade (TBT) in the salmon dispute (WTO, 2001a).

Several errors had more far-reaching consequences. The generic drugs panel's (WTO, 2000) narrow interpretation of the TRIPS Agreement created uncertainty about the ability of developing nations to obtain generic drugs under compulsory licenses and contributed to their decision to launch a campaign to clarify the flexibilities provided for public health measures in TRIPS. The gasoline and shrimp–turtle panels' rulings (WTO, 1996a, 1998b) created the impression that trade-restrictive environmental measures were incompatible with WTO obligations and contributed to the environmental community's opposition to the WTO. The GMOs panel's mishandling of some of the experts' testimony and its failure to support the imposition of the state-level bans on a precautionary basis are likely to reinforce environmentalists' objections to the WTO.

These errors increase the burden on the Appellate Body, lengthen the dispute resolution process, diminish its credibility and fuel the controversies surrounding the WTO. The basic problem is that panels are formed on an ad hoc basis from a roster of potential panelists maintained by the WTO Secretariat (Ehlermann, 2003; Wolfe, 2001). The diplomats, law professors and others who serve on the panels have other day-to-day responsibilities that take precedence over their panel duties. These responsibilities reduce the amount of time that panel members can devote to disputes and reduce the opportunities for panelists to meet. The latter problem is magnified in situations where panelists are not based in Geneva (Chang, 2003). Telephone and electronic communication are inadequate substitutes for actual meeting time because of the complexity and novelty of the issues in dispute. Other duties also reduce the number of panels on which panelists can serve, creating a pool of panelists with relatively little experience in WTO jurisprudence. Since the WTO staff who assist panels have other responsibilities, staffing arrangements compound these problems.

Fortunately, we do not have to look far for a more successful model, the Appellate Body. Composed of seven permanent members and assisted by a staff that serves it exclusively, the Appellate Body has produced a high level of jurisprudence (Bourgeois, 2003; Howse and Esserman, 2006; Van den Bossche, 2006). The Appellate Body's strong performance has engendered broad support for the creation of a standing panel body to replace the ad hoc panel system (Bacchus, 2004; Bourgeois, 2003; Chang, 2003; Ehlermann, 2003; McRae, 2004; Wolfe, 2001).[3] Given the heavy caseload, 20 to 30 permanent panel members would be required to rotate service on cases in teams of three.[4] As these permanent panel members develop expertise on the matters in dispute, panel errors should decrease, reducing the burden on the Appellate Body and enhancing the standing of the WTO in the international community. The creation of a standing panel should also speed the panel process as full-time panelists would have more time to devote to it than volunteer panel members.

The Appellate Body has not escaped criticism. Some charge that the Appellate Body's willingness to issue rulings based on vague or contradictory treaty provisions amounts to judicial activism that impinges on member prerogatives. In a democratic, rules-based organization, members, not judges, are supposed to establish the rules (Barfield, 2001). Some suggest that this activism creates a problem of institutional balance (Bartels, 2004). Their concern is that the dispute system threatens to eclipse the WTO's rulemaking bodies, which have been paralyzed by sharp disagreements among member governments. For example, divisions between the US and EU and between developing and developed countries over eco-labels, multilateral environmental agreements (MEAs) and other environmental measures immobilized the Committee on Trade and Environment (CTE) as early as 1996 (Shaffer, 2001). The same countries' inability to come to agreement on agricultural subsidies and tariffs led to the collapse of the Doha Round negotiations in 2003 and again in 2006. Others complain that the Appellate Body has exceeded its authority in an attempt to address concerns of interest to the environmental community and other external constituencies (Appleton, 1999). Critics urge the Appellate Body to exercise restraint, emphasizing that its role is to interpret rather than to create law (Barfield, 2001).

This criticism is misplaced. The Appellate Body has made significant contributions to WTO and international law by adhering closely to treaty text. The Appellate Body has stressed it is customary to interpret treaty provisions using the ordinary meaning of the words employed. This approach firmly rooted its reasoning in international law (Vienna Convention on the Law of Treaties) and provided a way to evaluate its decisions, both of which enhanced the legitimacy of its rulings (Ehlermann, 2003; Howse and Esserman, 2006; Van den Bossche, 2006). Similarly, the Appellate Body's decision to address the environmental and health concerns of interest to NGOs and the broader public in several disputes, including asbestos, gasoline, hormones and shrimp–turtle, and to do so in a way that emphasized linkages between trade law and other international law and the compatibility of trade and non-trade goals added to its credibility and that of the WTO as a whole (Howse and Esserman, 2006; Van den Bossche, 2006). When the Appellate Body was established, Lowenfeld (1994, p. 485) opined that its fate could rest on the 'skill and prestige' of its first members. Twelve years later, it appears that this was an understatement: the Appellate Body's skill and prestige has done no less than create an effective and respected dispute resolution system. It is true that the WTO's rule-making bodies have not enjoyed a similar level of success but the solution lies in improving their workings, not in impairing the Appellate Body's.[5,6]

9.6   CONSULTATIONS WITH SCIENTIFIC EXPERTS

In all but two of the disputes explored in this volume, the panels chose to consult scientific experts. In the hormones and asbestos disputes, the EU argued that panels were required to consult expert review groups and to solicit collective reports from them. However, the Appellate Body concluded that the dispute resolution rules authorized panels to seek the views of individual experts as well as expert review groups (WTO, 1998a, 2001a). Thus far, panels have opted to consult individual experts because individual consultations are speedier (Stewart and Karpel, 2000), allow for a greater 'range of opinions' (WTO, 1997, para. 8.7) and, consequently, afford panels greater latitude in interpreting the advice received.

As the dispute resolution rules said little about the structure and form of these consultations, panels established their own procedures. Typically, panels selected four or five experts after soliciting nominations from the parties and relevant international organizations. After the experts were selected, the panels formulated questions for them to address, based on the parties' submissions. Once the experts' individual responses were received, they were forwarded to the disputants for review. Subsequently, the panels discussed the responses in a joint meeting with the experts and parties and incorporated the experts' testimony into their reports. Some deemed these consultations inadequate. Their principal concern was that panel members lacked the expertise to sort through the conflicting scientific evidence presented by the parties, even with the assistance of experts (Guzman, 2004; Harlow, 2004). Others suggested that consultations with expert review groups were likely to be superior to individual consultations, especially in situations where the science on the matters in dispute was unsettled (Carruth and Goldstein, 2004; Pauwelyn, 2002).

With the exception of the GMOs panel, panelists performed far better on scientific matters than they did on legal matters. Otherwise, despite a few minor errors in the hormones case, the panels demonstrated a remarkable ability to focus the experts' attention on the key matters in dispute and to use their testimony to adjudicate the disputants' conflicting claims. Panel consultations with scientific experts are likely to be even more effective under a permanent panel system as full-time panel members develop expertise in the consultation process.

9.7   TRANSPARENCY AND PUBLIC PARTICIPATION

In response to criticism that its proceedings are not transparent, the WTO has made a wealth of information available on its website. Those interested in the dispute resolution process have ready access to treaty texts and a variety of documents related to each dispute including requests for consultations, and panel, appellate and arbitration reports. All documents are posted in three languages (English, French and Spanish). A tutorial introduces new users to the dispute resolution process and dispute summaries provide helpful overviews of each dispute. Other postings provide non-technical explanations of the dispute resolution system, WTO agreements, the organization's structure and numerous trade tropics (WTO, 2006b). Access to documents has become more timely with the reduction of the derestriction period for restricted materials to six to 12 weeks from eight to nine months (WTO, 2002).

Nevertheless, the WTO should take additional steps to improve the transparency of the dispute resolution process. There is virtually no new information available on the organization's website about the status of a dispute between the request for consultations and the issuance of the panel's report (which occurs some weeks after its release to allow time for translation). Some disputants (for example the US) make their submissions available to the public, but most do not. The WTO should act to eliminate this news blackout by posting disputants' submissions as they become available and posting transcripts of the oral hearings with disputants (Stewart and Burr, 1998). The panel and appellate reports are invaluable to policymakers, scholars and others who have the time and expertise to read them, but their length (400 to 500 pages for the asbestos and shrimp–turtle reports and more than 2000 pages for the GMOs panel report), complexity and terminology limit their usefulness to the broader public. The dispute summaries provide only a partial solution to this problem because they focus primarily on panel and appellate findings. The summaries should be expanded to include sections addressing each of the major components of the dispute resolution process: disputants' arguments, expert testimony, analysis and rulings.

Most important, panel and appellate hearings should be opened to the public. Barring public attendance at and observation of these hearings is not compatible with their judicial character and the wide interest in their outcomes (Bacchus, 2004; Barfield, 2001; Ehlermann, 2003; Ragosta, 2000; Wolfe, 2001). Worse, it fuels suspicion and criticism of those outcomes (Bacchus, 2004). As with amicus submissions, opposition from developing nations has prevented progress on this issue other than experimentation with televised proceedings that began in the retaliatory phase of the hormones dispute. This opposition is misguided. Allowing the public to attend panel hearings or observe televised proceedings does not disadvantage any of the governments participating in them. Indeed, lack of public access detracts from the process and diminishes its results for all participants.

The WTO has also attempted to improve its relationship with NGOs. The WTO holds NGO briefings several times a year in Geneva and other locations around to the world. NGOs host sessions on the full gamut of issues on the WTO's agenda at the WTO's annual public forum. Hundreds of NGOs send representatives to the WTO's biennial Ministerial conferences. The WTO posts NGO position papers on its website, offers an on-line chat space for NGOs and private citizens, and offers webcasts of meetings for the same groups (WTO, 2005a). These activities are valuable but they fall short in one critical way. Unlike the United Nations, the WTO has not been willing to grant NGOs observer status on its committees, councils and other bodies (Charnovitz, 2004). The WTO's Consultative Board dismissed the concept on the grounds that it provided no advantage over attendance at Ministerial conferences, could favor established NGOs over newer organizations and would be difficult to administer (WTO, 2005a). The UN experience indicates that the newcomer and administrative issues are not insuperable obstacles. For example, an annual rotation system could mitigate both concerns.

Moreover, it is clear that observer status implies a different relationship than ad hoc attendance at conferences. Observers would regularly attend a much wider array of meetings (General Council, Dispute Settlement Body, TRIPS Council and so on) and do so on a continuing basis, thereby deepening their knowledge of WTO operations and familiarity with officials. As a result, the presence of observers should improve the WTO's relationships with NGOs as well as increase the transparency of its proceedings. The admittance of observers does not conflict with the intergovernmental character of the organization. Observers do not set the organization's agenda, vote or file complaints. Those activities are reserved for member governments.

9.8 CONCLUDING REMARKS

The WTO's disposition of environmental and health disputes suggests that criticism of the organization has been overblown. The disputes demonstrate that nations retain sovereignty over environmental and health policy and that the WTO is able to reconcile trade, the environment and public health. But several caveats are in order. The small number of disputes (only nine with rulings to date) must be taken into account. The seven-member Appellate Body has been more supportive of environmental and health policy than the panels. To date, changes in the composition of the Appellate Body have not affected this support but there is no guarantee that this will remain true in the future. The dispute resolution system is imperfect. Its limitations led developing nations to seek remedies in other bodies in the amicus controversy and the TRIPS and public health campaign (Iida, 2004). Reforms are necessary to improve compliance, enhance transparency and public participation and reduce the cost of participation by poor nations, yet reforms are not likely to be forthcoming because divisions within the membership preclude reaching a consensus on those matters. And paralysis in the WTO's rulemaking bodies could spill over to the dispute resolution system. For example, a suspension of the Doha Round negotiations could prompt developing nations to challenge developed nations' agricultural policies in the dispute resolution process. If developed nations resist compliance as they have in similar disputes (bananas, cotton, sugar), the gridlock affecting the WTO's rulemaking bodies will have been transferred to the dispute resolution system (ICTSD, 2006).

NOTES

1. Article 27.2 of the Dispute Settlement Understanding (DSU) authorizes WTO staff to provide legal assistance to developing nations participating in the dispute resolution process, but it requires the WTO Secretariat to remain impartial.
2. EC – Regime for the Importation, Sale, and Distribution of Bananas (WT/DS27), US – Subsidies on Upland Cotton (WT/DS267), EC – Export Subsidies on Sugar (WT/DS265, WT/DS266, WT/DS283).
3. Cartland (2003) takes the contrary view that the deficiencies of the ad hoc panel system have been exaggerated.
4. There is wide support for a permanent panel body, but less agreement on its form. See Chang (2003) for a discussion of various options.
5. To break the gridlock affecting the WTO's legislative bodies, it might be necessary to replace consensus-based decision making with the voting procedures included in the WTO Agreement during the Uruguay Round (McGivern, 2006).
6. Howse and Esserman (2006) observed that the TRIPS and Public Health campaign and the Kimberley Agreement barring trade in conflict diamonds (diamonds used to finance rebellions against internationally recognized governments) suggest that the WTO's rulemaking bodies can function effectively when members muster the necessary political will.

REFERENCES

ACWL (2007), 'About Us, Staff' and 'Members', Geneva: Advisory Center for WTO Law (website accessed in January).

Appleton, A. (1999), 'Shrimp/turtle: untangling the nets', *Journal of International Economic Law*, **2**(3), 477–96.

Bacchus, J. (2004), 'The WTO must open up its trade dispute proceedings', *European Affairs*, **5**(2), 88–92.

Barfield, C. (2001), 'Free trade, sovereignty, democracy: the future of the World Trade Organization', *Chicago Journal of International Law*, **2**(2), 403–15.

Bartels, L. (2004), 'The separation of powers in the WTO: how to avoid judicial activism', *The International and Comparative Law Quarterly*, **53**(4), 861–95.

Bates, J. (1999), 'Civil society and the World Trade Organization', Progressive Policy Institute, *Backgrounder*, 1 November.

Bourgeois, J. (2003), 'Comment on a WTO permanent panel body', *Journal of International Economic Law*, **6**(1), 211–14.

Bown, C. (2004), 'On the economic success of GATT/WTO dispute settlement', *The Review of Economics and Statistics*, **86**(3), 811–23.

Bown, C. and B. Hoekman (2005), 'WTO dispute settlement and the missing developing country cases: engaging the private sector', *Journal of International Economic Law*, **8**(4), 861–90.

Caduff, L. (2002), 'Growth hormones and beyond', Center for International Studies, Zurich, Working Paper 8-2002.

Carruth, R. and B. Goldstein (2004), 'The asbestos case: a comment on the appointment and use of nonpartisan experts in World Trade Organization dispute resolution involving health risk', *Risk Analysis*, **24**(2), 471–81.

Cartland, M. (2003), 'Comment on a WTO permanent panel body', *Journal of International Economic Law*, **6**(1), 214–18.

Chang, S. (2003), 'Comment on a WTO permanent panel body', *Journal of International Economic Law*, **6**(1), 219–24.

Charnovitz, S. (2004), 'The WTO and cosmopolitics', *Journal of International Economic Law*, **7**(3), 675–82.

Cottier, Thomas (2001), 'Risk management experience in WTO dispute settlement', in David Robertson and Aynsley Kellow (eds), *Globalization and the Environment, Risk Assessment and the WTO*, Cheltenham, UK and Northampton, MA, USA: Edward Elgar, pp. 41–62.

Davey, W. (2005), 'The WTO dispute settlement system: the first ten years', *Journal of International Economic Law*, **8**(1), 17–50.

De La Fayette, L. (2002), 'WTO–GATT–trade and environment–import restrictions–endangered species', *The American Journal of International Law*, **96**(3), 685–92.

Ehlermann, C.-D, (2003), 'Experiences from the WTO Appellate Body', *Texas International Law Journal*, **38**(3), 469–88.

Esserman, S. and R. Howse (2003), 'The WTO on trial', *Foreign Affairs*, **82**(1), 130–41.

Fukunaga, Y. (2006), 'Securing compliance through the WTO dispute system: implementation of DSB recommendations', *Journal of International Economic Law*, **9**(2), 383–426.

Gleason, C. and P. Walther (2000), 'The WTO dispute settlement implementation procedures: a system in need of reform', *Law & Policy in International Business*, **31**(3), 709–36.

Guzman, A. (2004), 'Food fears: health & safety at the WTO', *Virginia Journal of International Law Association*, **45**(1), 1–39.

Guzman A. and B. Simmons (2005), 'Power plays and capacity constraints: the selection of defendants in World Trade Organization disputes', *The Journal of Legal Studies*, **34**(2), 557–98.

Harlow, S. (2004), 'Science-based trade disputes: a new challenge in harmonizing evidentiary systems of law and science', *Risk Analysis*, **24**(2), 443–7.

Henson, S. and R. Loader (2001), 'Barriers to agricultural exports from developing countries: the role of sanitary and phytosanitary requirements', *World Development*, **29**(1), 85–102.

Howse, R. (2000), 'Democracy, science and free trade: risk regulation on trial at the World Trade Organization', *Michigan Law Review*, **98**(7), 2329–57.

Howse, R. and S. Esserman (2006), 'The Appellate Body, the WTO dispute settlement system, and the politics of multilateralism', in Georgio Sacerdoti, Alan Yanovich and Jan Bohanes (eds), *The WTO at Ten, The Contribution of the Dispute Settlement System*, Cambridge: Cambridge University Press, pp. 61–80.

ICTSD (International Centre for Trade and Sustainable Development) (2006), 'With negotiations frozen, potential disputes looming', *Bridges Weekly Trade News Digest*, **10**(28), 2 August, 5.

Iida, K. (2004), 'Is WTO dispute settlement effective?', *Global Governance*, **10**(2), 207–25.

IOSEA (Indian Ocean–South-East Asian Marine Turtle Memorandum of

Understanding Secretariat) (2007), 'Official texts', and 'Membership', Bangkok, Thailand (website accessed during January).

Jara, A. (2006), 'WTO dispute settlement: a brief reality check', in Georgio Sacerdoti, Alan Yanovich and Jan Bohanes (eds), *The WTO at Ten, The Contribution of the Dispute Settlement System*, Cambridge: Cambridge University Press, pp. 81–5.

Lawrence, Robert Z. (2003), *Crimes and Punishments? Retaliation Under the WTO*, Washington, DC: Institute for International Economics.

Leitner, K. and S. Lester (2006), 'WTO dispute settlement from 1995 to 2005 – a statistical analysis', *Journal of International Economic Law*, **9**(1), 219–31.

Lowenfeld, A. (1994), 'Remedies along with rights: institutional reform in the new GATT', *American Journal of International Law*, **68**(3), 477–88.

McGivern, B. (2006), 'WTO dispute settlement after Doha: a "risk of imbalance"', *Bridges Monthly Review*, **10**(5), August, 10–11.

McRae, D. (2004), 'What is the future of WTO dispute settlement?', *Journal of International Economic Law*, **7**(1), 3–21.

Mosoti, V. (2006), 'Africa in the first decade of WTO dispute settlement', *Journal of International Economic Law*, **9**(2), 427–53.

National Marine Fisheries Service (2006), '2005 Product data, shrimp', Silver Springs, MD, Fisheries Statistics and Economics Division (website accessed during May).

Pauwelyn, J. (2000), 'Enforcement and countermeasures in the WTO: rules are rules – toward a more collective approach', *The American Journal of International Law*, **94**(2), 335–47.

Pauwelyn, J. (2002), 'The use of experts in WTO dispute settlement', *The International and Comparative Law Quarterly*, **51**(2), 325–64.

Ragosta, J. (2000), 'Unmasking the WTO – access to the DSB system: can the WTO DSB live up to its moniker "World Trade Court"?', *Law & Policy in International Business*, **3**(3), 739–68.

Scott, J. (2004), 'International trade and environmental governance: relating rules and standards in the EU and WTO', *European Journal of International Law*, **15**(2), 307–54.

Shaffer, G. (2001), 'The WTO under challenge: democracy and the law and politics of the WTO's treatment of trade and environment matters', *Harvard Environmental Law Review*, **25**(1), 1–93.

Shaffer, G. (2004), 'Recognizing public goods in WTO dispute settlement: who participates? who decides?', *Journal of International Economic Law*, **7**(2), 459–82.

Shaffer, G. (2005), 'Can WTO technical assistance and capacity-building serve developing countries?', *Wisconsin International Law Journal*, **23**(4), 643–86.

Stewart, T. and M. Burr (1998), 'The WTO panel process: an evaluation of the first three years', *The International Lawyer*, **32**(3), 709–35.

Stewart, T. and A. Karpel (2000), 'Review of the dispute settlement understanding: operations of panels', *Law & Policy in International Business*, **31**(3), 593–655.

Stoler, A. (2004), 'The WTO dispute settlement process: did the negotiators get what they wanted?' *World Trade Review*, **3**(1), 99–118.

US Department of State (2001, 2003, 2005), 'Shrimp turtle conservation and shrimp imports', *Media Note*, Washington, DC: Office of the Spokesperson, May.

Van den Bossche, P. (2006), 'From afterthought to centerpiece: the WTO Appellate Body and its rise to prominence in the world trading system', in Georgio Sacerdoti, Alan Yanovich and Jan Bohanes (eds), *The WTO at Ten, The Contribution of the Dispute Settlement System*, Cambridge: Cambridge University Press, pp. 289–325.

Wolfe, A. (2001), 'Problems with WTO dispute settlement', *Chicago Journal of International Law*, **2**(2), 417–26.

WTO (1994), *Understanding on Rules and Procedures Governing the Settlement of Disputes* (DSU), Geneva: WTO.

WTO (1996a), *US – Standards for Reformulated and Conventional Gasoline, Report of the Panel* (WT/DS2/R), Geneva: WTO, 29 January.

WTO (1996b), *US – Standards for Reformulated and Conventional Gasoline, Report of the Appellate Body* (WT/DS2/AB/R), Geneva: WTO, 29 April.

WTO (1997), *EC – Measures Concerning Meat and Meat Products (Hormones), Complaint by the US, Report of the Panel* (WT/DS26/R/USA), Geneva: WTO, 18 August.

WTO (1998a), *EC – Measures Concerning Meat and Meat Products (Hormones), Report of the Appellate Body* (WT/DS26/AB/R and WT/DS48/AB/R), Geneva: WTO, 16 January.

WTO (1998b), *US – Import Prohibition of Certain Shrimp and Shrimp Products, Report of the Panel* (WT/DS58/R), Geneva: WTO, 15 May.

WTO (1998c), *EC – Measures Concerning Meat and Meat Products (Hormones), Arbitration Under Article 21.3 of the DSU, Award of the Arbitrator* (WT/DS26/15 and WT/DS48/13), Geneva: WTO, 29 May.

WTO (1998d), *US – Import Prohibition of Certain Shrimp and Shrimp Products, Report of the Appellate Body* (WT/DS58/AB/R), Geneva: WTO, 12 October.

WTO (1998e), *Australia – Measures Affecting the Importation of Salmon, Report of the Appellate Body* (WT/DS18/AB/R), Geneva: WTO, 20 October.

WTO (1999), *Japan – Measures Affecting Agricultural Products, Report of the Appellate Body* (WT/DS76/AB/R), Geneva: WTO, 22 February.

WTO (2000), *Canada – Patent Protection of Pharmaceutical Products, Report of the Panel* (WT/DS114/R), Geneva: WTO, 17 March.

WTO (2001a), *EC – Measures Affecting Asbestos and Products Containing Asbestos, Report of the Appellate Body* (WT/DS135/AB/R), Geneva: WTO, 12 March.

WTO (2001b), *US – Import Prohibition of Certain Shrimp and Shrimp Products, Recourse to Article 21.5 by Malaysia, Report of the Appellate Body* (WT/DS58/AB/RW), Geneva: WTO, 22 October.

WTO (2001c), *Doha Declaration on the TRIPS Agreement and Public Health* (WT/MIN(01)/DEC/2), Geneva: WTO, 20 November.

WTO (2002), *Non-Governmental Organizations (NGOS): Derestriction Procedure, WTO Moves Toward a More Open Organization*, Geneva: WTO, 14 May.

WTO (2003a), *Implementation of Paragraph 6 of the Doha Declaration on the TRIPS Agreement and Public Health, Decision of 30 August 2003* (WT/L/540), Geneva: WTO, 2 September.

WTO (2003b), *Japan – Measures Affecting the Importation of Apples, Report of the Appellate Body* (WT/DS245/AB/R), Geneva: WTO, 26 November.

WTO (2005a), *The Future of the WTO, Addressing Institutional Challenges in the New Millennium, Report by the Consultative Board to the Director General Supachai Panitchpakdi*, Geneva: WTO.

WTO (2005b), *US – Subsidies on Upland Cotton, Recourse to Article 7.9 of the SCM Agreement, and Article 22.2 of the DSU by Brazil* (WT/DS267/26), Geneva: WTO, 7 October.

WTO (2005c), *Members OK Amendment to Make Health Flexibility Permanent* (WTO: 2005 Press Releases (Press 426)), Geneva: WTO, 6 December.

WTO (2006a), *TRIPS Council, Minutes of Meeting, 25–26 and 28 October, 29 November and 6 December 2005* (IP/C/M/49), Geneva: WTO, 31 January.

WTO (2006b) *Documents* and *Trade Topics*, Geneva: WTO (website accessed during August).

WTO (2006c), *US – Subsidies on Upland Cotton, Recourse to Article 21.5 of the DSU by Brazil, Request for the Establishment of a Panel* (WT/DS267/30), Geneva: WTO, 21 August.

WTO (2006d), *WTO Training Courses*, Geneva: WTO (website accessed during August).

WTO (2006e), *EC – Measures Affecting the Approval and Marketing of Biotech Products, Report of the Panel* (WT/DS291/R, WT/DS292/R, WT/DS293/R), Geneva: WTO, 29 September.

WTO (2007), *The Disputes*, Geneva: WTO (website accessed during January).

Index